THE WAR AGAINST ROMMEL'S SUPPLY LINES, 1942–43

The Stackpole Military History Series

THE AMERICAN CIVIL WAR

Cavalry Raids of the Civil War
Ghost, Thunderbolt, and Wizard
Pickett's Charge
Witness to Gettysburg

WORLD WAR II

Armor Battles of the Waffen-SS, 1943–45
Army of the West
Australian Commandos
The B-24 in China
Backwater War
The Battle of Sicily
Beyond the Beachhead
The Brandenburger Commandos
The Brigade
Bringing the Thunder
Coast Watching in World War II
Colossal Cracks
D-Day to Berlin
Dive Bomber!
Eagles of the Third Reich
Exit Rommel
Fist from the Sky
Flying American Combat Aircraft
of World War II
Forging the Thunderbolt
Fortress France
The German Defeat in the East, 1944–45
German Order of Battle, Vol. 1
German Order of Battle, Vol. 2
German Order of Battle, Vol. 3
Germany's Panzer Arm in World War II
GI Ingenuity
Grenadiers
Infantry Aces
Iron Arm
Iron Knights
Kampfgruppe Peiper at the Battle of the
Bulge
Luftwaffe Aces
Massacre at Tobruk
Messerschmitts over Sicily

Michael Wittmann, Vol. 1
Michael Wittmann, Vol. 2
Mountain Warriors
The Nazi Rocketeers
On the Canal
Packs On!
Panzer Aces
Panzer Aces II
The Panzer Legions
Panzers in Winter
The Path to Blitzkrieg
Retreat to the Reich
Rommel's Desert War
The Savage Sky
A Soldier in the Cockpit
Soviet Blitzkrieg
Stalin's Keys to Victory
Surviving Bataan and Beyond
T-34 in Action
Tigers in the Mud
The 12th SS, Vol. 1
The 12th SS, Vol. 2
The War against Rommel's Supply Lines

THE COLD WAR / VIETNAM

Flying American Combat Aircraft:
The Cold War
Here There Are Tigers
Land with No Sun
Street without Joy

WARS OF THE MIDDLE EAST

Never-Ending Conflict

GENERAL MILITARY HISTORY

Carriers in Combat
Desert Battles

THE WAR AGAINST ROMMEL'S SUPPLY LINES, 1942–43

Alan J. Levine

STACKPOLE
BOOKS

Published in paperback in 2008 by
STACKPOLE BOOKS
5067 Ritter Road
Mechanicsburg, PA 17055
www.stackpolebooks.com

THE WAR AGAINST ROMMEL'S SUPPLY LINES, 1942–1943, by Alan J. Levine, was originally published in hard cover by Praeger, an imprint of Greenwood Publishing Group, Inc., Westport, CT. Copyright © 1999 by Alan J. Levine. Paperback edition by arrangement with Greenwood Publishing Group, Inc. All rights reserved.

Cover design by Tracy Patterson
All photos courtesy of Philip Francis

Printed in the United States of America

10 9 8 7 6 5 4 3 2 1

Library of Congress Cataloging-in-Publication Data

Levine, Alan J.
  [War against Rommel's supply lines, 1942–1943]
  The war against Rommel's supply lines, 1942–43 / Alan J. Levine.
      p. cm. — (Stackpole military history series)
  Originally published: Westport, CT : Praeger, 1999.
  Includes bibliographical references and index.
  ISBN-13: 978-0-8117-3458-5
  ISBN-10: 0-8117-3458-7
  1. World War, 1939–1945—Campaigns—Mediterranean Sea. 2. World War, 1939–1945—Aerial operations. 3. World War, 1939–1945—Naval operations. 4. Germany. Heer. Panzerarmeekorps Afrika. I. Title.

D766.L48 2008
940.54'23—dc22
                                                    2007037102

Table of Contents

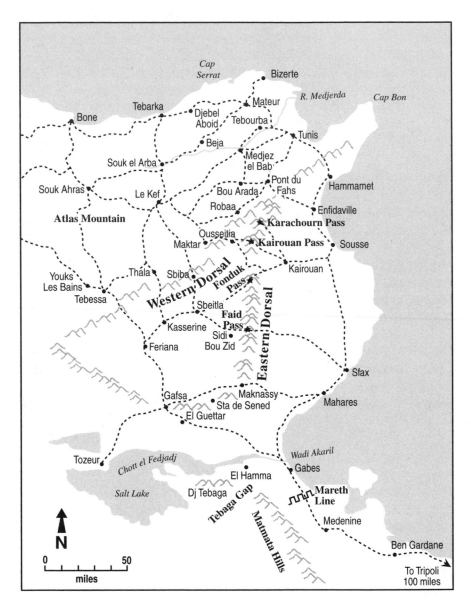

Tunisia

SOURCE: W. G. F. JACKSON, *THE BATTLE FOR NORTH AFRICA* (NEW YORK: MASON CHARTER, 1975).

Introduction

This book is an account of a major yet relatively neglected campaign of World War II, the efforts of Allied air and naval forces in the Mediterranean to cut off the supplies of the Axis forces in Northwest Africa during 1942 and 1943. Its success led to a relatively cheap triumph over a large enemy force on land, with a major impact on the subsequent campaigns in Europe. Its naval phase was one of only two successful submarine campaigns ever fought. Its aerial aspects included the first major success of the American air force over the European enemy and involved several of the great air commanders of World War II, notably Carl Spaatz, James Doolittle, and Sir Arthur Tedder. To win the Allies had to overcome major difficulties. In Northwest Africa, the U.S. Army Air Force (AAF) got past its growing pains. Although it was a "tactical" air campaign aimed at "interdicting" supplies to an enemy field army, it had more affinities than most "tactical" air campaigns with strategic bombing—among other things, the AAF's heavy bombers played an important role in the battle. As an interdiction campaign, it was one of the most spectacularly successful in history, involving many attacks on ships at sea, comparable to those in the Pacific theater. Thus it is of considerable interest, from the point of view of those seeking comparisons, to those interested in the bombing of Germany on the one hand and to those interested in the Pacific campaigns on the other. As we shall see, contrary to what is often supposed, this campaign was a difficult one, not a walkover by immensely superior forces, and it involved concerting several different arms and forms of attack. The weather and other difficulties made it difficult for the Allies to apply their superior strength. The distance between the enemy-held shores of the Mediterranean was wide enough to expose the enemy's supply lines to attack but short enough to make it hard for World War II–era planes and submarines to catch enemy ships, especially in bad weather and on short winter days, and it made it possible to protect those supply lines with air cover and minefields. An examination of it also suggests a partial reevaluation of the role of the Italian forces in World War II. At least in this phase of the struggle, they were not the incompetent clowns nor the cowards often depicted.

The campaign against Rommel's supply lines was important, and in many ways exceptionally interesting, yet it has attracted relatively little attention from historians of World War II, especially in the United States. It is a rare example of an important campaign waged by the Western Allies that has been largely ignored by subsequent writers. Comparatively little has been written about it, save by the official historians who worked in the two decades after the war, and even some of them neglected it. (The excellent British official history, *The Mediterranean and Middle East*, Vol. IV, by I. S. O. Playfair, is an outstanding exception.) Even the official AAF history paid little attention to air operations aimed against enemy supply lines during the Northwest African struggle, possibly because the writers were diverted by the need to recount the bitter disputes over supplying direct support to the Allied ground forces that marked the Tunisian campaign and justify AAF doctrines. Sinking Axis ships and smashing ports and airfields, however important, involved less controversy. The fighting during late 1942 and 1943 also may have been neglected because it was the last phase of an ongoing effort. The attack on Axis shipping during the Northwest African campaign was, in some ways, a continuation of a struggle against the enemy supply lines to Libya that had already gone on for over two years—a continuation that had not been wanted or expected. Like the whole Tunisian campaign, it was a consequence of the failure of the Allies to seize all of French Northwest Africa in one blow, as had been hoped. A certain distaste for a battle that, had Allied plans come off, should never have been fought, may have infected later writers. The fact that it was a campaign fought to a great extent against the Italians, and the contempt for them, also may be a factor. As a largely maritime or air-sea campaign, but one lacking really big and spectacular sea battles, it perhaps seemed like the Pacific fighting, and somehow out of place in accounts of the European portion of World War II.

I would like to thank those who have helped me in researching this work, especially Eduard Mark, Doris Kinkaid, Stanley Akers, Esther Oyster, Joseph Madrano, William Baird, and Israel Levine. I would particularly like to thank my sister, Robin Levine, for her help with translations from Italian. All responsibility for errors is mine.

CHAPTER 1

The War in the Mediterranean, 1940–42

With the fall of France in June 1940, Britain was the last active enemy of Nazi Germany, and Britain was threatened by blockade and invasion. The British forces in the Mediterranean and the Middle East seemed to face an unpromising future. Italy's entry into the war had opened a whole new front there when Britain seemed hardly able to defend herself, much less support a distant overseas theater.

The Middle East and the Mediterranean, although not absolutely vital, were extremely important. The Middle East's oil was not vital for the Allied world as a whole—during the war, Britain got most of her fuel from the Americas—but if the Axis got hold of it, the enemy's fuel resources would be enormously increased, and Allied activity around the Indian Ocean would be paralyzed. A single refinery, at Abadan in Iran, was the only source of 100-octane aviation gasoline in the vast area between Egypt and Indonesia. In the long run, the Mediterranean and the Middle East would let the Allies reach "behind" their enemies in Europe. It offered opportunities to bring France back into the war through French North Africa, open a land front in southern Europe, and bomb critical targets, notably the Axis's main source of natural oil at Ploesti in Romania, targets otherwise hard or impossible to reach from Britain.

But in 1940, even if the British homeland survived, the Middle East was in desperate straits. The small British forces, facing attack from Libya and East Africa by overwhelming numbers of Italians, were isolated by the fall of France, now a partly occupied semi-satellite of Germany, while the Italians dominated the central Mediterranean and closed it to normal traffic. Only an occasional long-range plane, and ships that had to sail 12,000 miles around the Cape of Good Hope, kept the British in touch with home. General Archibald Wavell, the British commander in the Middle East, had done wonders in building a base able to support major forces in an under-developed region, but at first he had little to fight with and was amid a sea of enemies. Vichy French-held Syria and Iran were, at best, unfriendly. Most of

1

the Arabs were restive, if not bitterly hostile to Britain, many foolishly imag-ining that an Axis victory meant "liberation." In the hope of placating the Arabs, the British refrained from making much use of the only local pro-Allied force, the Jewish settlements in Palestine. The British did have one card whose value was not yet apparent, but which enabled them, in the last resort, to dominate the Arab Near East. A British officer, John Bagot Glubb ("Glubb Pasha"), had built the "Arab Legion," the small army of the Emirate of Transjordan, into the only effective military force in the Arab world. Unlike the armies of Egypt and Iraq, on which the British had lavished far more aid, it proved efficient and willing to fight alongside Britain rather than against her.

The British had only about 80,000 troops and 200 obsolete planes against half a million Italians already in Libya and East Africa, and an Italian air force of over 1,500 operational planes. Malta, the British base in the cen-ter of the Mediterranean, was only weakly defended. Its small garrison had only a few ancient biplane fighters and antiaircraft guns, and stocks of food and other supplies were low. The Italian fleet appeared to have a consider-able superiority in modernized battleships and a still greater one in cruisers, destroyers, and submarines. Italian surface ships were well designed, fast, and well armed, although they lacked radar, and few ships had sonar. It looked as though Italian conquest of the whole Mediterranean and the Middle East was imminent.

But the British acted boldly and intelligently. In the face of apparently hopeless odds, they went from victory to victory over the Italians, until their very success forced Hitler to intervene. Saving and reinforcing Malta, they inflicted severe defeats on the Italian navy, threw back an attempted invasion of Egypt and overran half of Libya, conquered Italian East Africa, and helped the Greeks repel Italian conquest. They showed that the power of Fascist Italy had been wildly exaggerated, and they exposed Benito Mussolini as a blustering incompetent. The Italian armed forces were not ready to fight a major enemy. Their showing during the period 1940–41 was so bad that those who had once feared Italy jumped to the opposite extreme. They underrated her later contributions to the Axis war effort and treated the Ital-ian forces as a joke, which they were not.

Beneath the numbers and the show that Mussolini had put up lay vital weaknesses. Italy's industry was of high quality, but its capacity, especially in shipbuilding, aircraft, and electronics production, was limited. Operations at sea were increasingly hampered by a shortage of fuel oil.

The Italian fleet's commanders often were reluctant to force a major surface battle, even when the odds were in their favor; on several occasions, this would save the British from disaster.

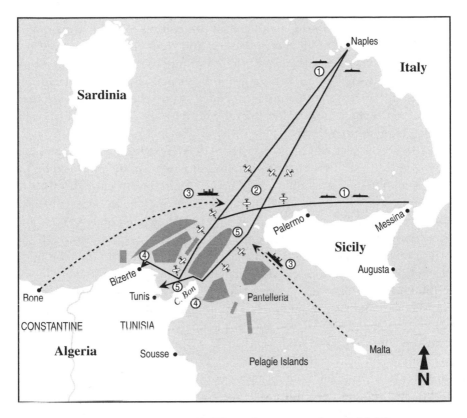

The "Death Route" (First four months of 1943)

Convoys for Tunisia had to take routes between minefields and in some stretches through narrow channels. This greatly increased the enemy's chances of success and added to the operational hazards of (1) submarines near the ports of departure and along the first part of the routes; (2) night torpedo aircraft north of the Sicilian Channel; (3) night actions by radar-equipped cruisers west of Sicily; (4) night attacks by motor torpedo boats around Cape Bon and north of Bizerte; and, above all, (5) large formations of aircraft on constant patrol above the restricted routes and the focal zones of the Channel crossing. SOURCE: MARC ANTONIO BRAGADIN, THE ITALIAN NAVY IN WORLD WAR II (ANNAPOLIS, MD.: UNITED STATES NAVAL INSTITUTE PRESS, 1957), 246. COPYRIGHT 1957. REPRINTED WITH PERMISSION.

The Italian navy—which had been oriented toward fighting France rather than Britain—had neglected preparation and training for night action and antisubmarine warfare. Its fine battleships proved far less useful than the Italian admirals, like most of their counterparts in the rest of the world had imagined. Italian submarines were poorly designed; noisy, clumsy, and slow, their silhouettes were too large (they were later cut down somewhat), their periscopes too short, and they dived slowly. These were fatal faults in the Mediterranean, a particularly difficult sea for submarine opera-tions. But its escort ships had commanders and crews who were capable and determined and made the most of their equipment despite its limitations. And the navy's smallest units, notably motor torpedo boats and certain spe-cial weapons such as the "manned torpedoes," were very effective. The latter, ridden by frogmen, penetrated British-held harbors and planted delayed-action charges under ships.

The Italian navy had no aircraft carriers. That in itself was not fatal in a narrow inland sea where there were many air bases, but the navy had no air arm at all; nor had Mussolini made his air force devote enough effort to cooperation with the navy. When Italy entered the war, the Regia Aeronautica was only just getting its first torpedo bombers. It depended on level bombing from fairly high altitudes to hit ships as well as land targets. Although the British rated the Italians' high-level attacks as being more accurate than those of the Germans', and thought some Italian units more determined than any in the Luftwaffe, they were not very effective against fast-moving ships.[1]

While the Italians had many well-trained pilots, they had few good lead-ers above the squadron level. Italian planes were obsolete (although the British planes they faced in the early days of the war were often even more so). Italian bombers were perhaps adequate, but Italian fighters were two to three years behind their counterparts in other air forces. The CR 32 and CR 42 biplane fighters were still widely used in first-line squadrons, while the Fiat G 50 and Macchi 200 monoplanes, despite excellent airframes, were underpowered and inferior to their German and British contemporaries. The best Italian fighters, the Fiat G 55, Reggiane 2001, and Macchi 202, the latter using German Daimler-Benz engines, did not appear in any numbers until 1942. Allied pilots found captured Macchi 202s highly maneuverable and a pleasure to fly but, like all Italian planes, the Mc 202 was lightly armed, with just two 12.7 mm machine guns, inferior equivalents of the American Browning .50, and two lighter rifle-caliber weapons. Its perform-ance was just about equal to the Spitfire I, which the British had begun replacing during the Battle of Britain.[2]

The Italian army was in even worse shape. Its generals, with few excep-tions, were of poor quality, and the Germans did not think much of the jun-ior officers and noncommissioned officers (NCOs) either. Relations between officers and the rank and file were bad; enlisted men were given poor food. The army was not well equipped. Although the Allies admitted that the Ital-ian artillery always fought well, most Italian guns were short-ranged. Italian tanks were too light and unreliable. Most, in fact, were tiny machine-gun car-riers that other armies derided as "tankettes." The otherwise useless British antitank rifles easily penetrated their armor. Even the few modern Italian tanks (which lacked radios) were no match for British tanks; the Germans described them as "self-propelled coffins." Italian radios were unsuited to modern warfare. Apart from the artillery, some old cavalry regiments and other units fought well, even during the 1940–41 period. The Italians put up an impressive defense by any standards at Keren in Eritrea; at Sidi Barrani in Egypt, some attacked the British tanks with just machine guns and hand grenades. And later, the Italian army would show some improvement. In general, however, it was no match for the British.[3]

Italy's armed forces, although by no means totally incompetent, performed unevenly. They were generally ineffective in offensive warfare when not closely supported by the Germans. But even many Germans later conceded that the Italians often understood "overseas warfare" and the strategic position in the Mediterranean better than the German leaders. Mussolini, for all his mismanagement of his own country's affairs, sometimes had better insight than Hitler into the right course for the Axis. And as we shall see in this book, the Italians would often fight fiercely and skillfully to defend their supply lines and to save ships and seamen.

THE LIBYAN SUPPLY ROUTE

The Allies' attacks on the enemy's overseas supply lines would play a crucial role in the struggle for Libya and Egypt, and later, Tunisia; many of the features of the war against the Axis supply lines to Tunisia can already be seen in the earlier fight to cut the route to Libya, which lasted from June 1940 to January 1943.

Supplying the Axis forces in North Africa would have been hard in any case; the Italians made it worse by their misjudgments. The capacity of the Libyan ports to unload cargo and to refuel ships was limited. Tripoli, the largest port, and often the only one open to the Axis, could handle only 45,000 tons a month and was far from the front. Benghazi (maximum capacity 2,700 tons a month) and Tobruk (2,000 tons a month) often were unavailable or their capacity was reduced by Allied attacks. Getting material overland to the front burned up much fuel. Although the Italians tried to improve the North African ports, they did so only after wasting much effort on rebuilding harbors in Albania. The small capacity of the African ports limited the size of convoys. Instead of running a relatively few large convoys (the most efficient method in terms of convoy defense), the Italians had to send many small ones, which was wasteful of the escorts and fuel. The Italians initially used truly massive escort forces, including cruisers, but a looming fuel shortage forced them to drop this, except when the threat of British surface attack made them utterly indispensable. (Later, cruisers were sometimes used to haul critical supplies to Africa, a practice that proved horribly costly.) The convoys did have a high proportion of escorts. At first they averaged four merchant ships apiece, with about as many destroyers, or the less effective torpedo boats; at least one plane patrolled ahead of the convoy in daylight. Air cover for the convoys was later greatly increased and became a major commitment for the Italian air force. The short range of its fighters made it necessary to use many planes to give a convoy even a weak air umbrella. Later, the Italian convoys shrank, averaging only two ships; and the ships themselves became smaller, as the British gradually wiped out the larger ones.

The Italian torpedo boats, which played a critical role in the convoy battles right to the end of the struggle for Tunisia, had no counterpart in the British or U.S. navies. They should not be confused with the familiar motor torpedo ("PT") boats, whose Italian counterparts were called "MAS." The torpedo boats were small, turbine-powered ships armed with 100 mm guns; they were somewhat like scaled-down destroyers. (Some English-language works describe them as "destroyer escorts," but they were designed for purposes quite different from that U.S. navy type.)

Routing and scheduling convoys for Libya (they usually originated at Naples) often was complex. Initially the Italians tried to sail on moonless nights. Later, the threat of attack at night was far greater than during the day. Running in daylight became preferable. The Italians were forced to take costly diversions to stay as far away as possible from Malta, either by sailing to the west along the Tunisian coast or far to the east, often sailing via the Balkans. Such diversions sometimes doubled the trip across the Mediterranean and were expensive in time, fuel, and wear and tear on ships. During 1941, the Italians resorted to complex and costly ruses; they sometimes sent out two convoys at once, the less important passing closer to Malta to draw British attacks so the more important convoy could go unscathed. And Libya was not the Italians' only maritime supply commitment. They also had to protect convoys to their armies in the Balkans and the Aegean, military and commercial traffic to Sardinia and Sicily, and the tankers carrying oil from the head of the Adriatic to Italy. Although these routes were under less pressure than the Libyan convoys, they were a significant drain on Italian resources.[4]

MALTA

The critical fight for Malta quickly revealed the weakness of the Italian forces.

Malta, in the middle of the Mediterranean, was a vital strategic position. It lay near the direct route between Italy and Libya and would serve as a base for air, submarine, and sometimes surface ship attacks on the Axis supply lines to Libya, and later to Tunisia, and finally as a useful advanced base to support the invasion of Sicily. But the part it would play in World War II had not been anticipated. In the 1930s, proposals to build a bombproof submarine base on Malta had been turned down, and little was done to prepare the island for war. Surrounded by enemy bases, it had been written off as untenable. In mid-1940, the small garrison had few antiaircraft guns. A few old biplane fighters, in crates, had been left on Malta by mistake. Stocks of food and other supplies were low. Malta's coast was so rocky that a landing, even against a small defending force, would be difficult, but it was generally expected that a determined invasion would succeed. It was widely believed, however, that Malta would simply be starved out—and it very nearly was.

Ignoring prewar plans, Winston Churchill insisted on holding Malta. That decision strongly affected the whole course of the war, for Malta's fate was closely interwoven with that of the North African fighting. While the British were sometimes able to put up an effective defense in the desert, even when the Axis supply line was secure (as in July 1942), the Germans and Italians could not launch an offensive unless Malta's threat to their supply lines was at least temporarily suppressed—as it sometimes was. For long periods, Malta was only of potential value. Early in the war there were simply no important forces available to use it. Later, intense German air attacks sometimes "neutralized" Malta as an effective base, as in early 1941 and the first seven months of 1942. But when those attacks ended, Malta sprang back to life, and the Germans could not maintain a major air effort against Malta and provide air support for a land offensive in Africa at the same time. The interplay between Malta and the desert fighting was complex; indeed, most British offensives in the desert had, as at least a secondary aim, the capture of forward airfields to support convoys to Malta. And although Malta was mainly a base for air and undersea forces, and showed to what extent they rather than surface ships now dominated the war at sea, for brief periods in April–May and November–December 1941 it was possible to base destroyers or even cruisers on Malta. The surface striking forces, when they could operate at all, were disproportionately effective. They could wipe out a whole convoy and its escorts in one blow, in a way that planes and submarines usually could not.

The Maltese played a big part in Malta's effectiveness as a British base. Theirs was a tranquil, aristocratic society of a very unusual sort. Devout and conservative, the Maltese were not wealthy but enjoyed a relatively high standard of living for the Mediterranean, with little of the horrible poverty common around them. They had good relations with the British and deferred to their authority, as they did to the small Maltese upper and middle classes. Easygoing, peaceful, and unusually well behaved, the Maltese showed powers of endurance that more modern and violent societies might envy.[5]

In July 1940, the British fleet began escorting cargo ships to Malta. Despite strong attacks by Italian high-level bombers, the British did not suffer great losses. (The Italians' few torpedo bomber units were still in training.) It became clear that even well-conducted attacks of this sort rarely hit warships that were able to move and maneuver; the flight time of the Italian bombs was so long that the British could spot them and take evasive action. Until the German air force arrived, the British fleet, covered by just a few carrier-based fighters, could stay in the central Mediterranean without too much trouble, as long as its antiaircraft ammunition held out; and the first clashes of the war showed that it did not have to worry much about the Italian surface fleet. But the British fleet could not stay in the area indefinitely or block the route to Libya. The Italians, for all of their ineptitude, still dominated the central Mediterranean and closed it to regular British traffic. And while Malta could be supplied, a major fleet operation would always be needed to do so. Such operations would become progressively more difficult as the Italians acquired torpedo bombers and the Luftwaffe appeared. Even in 1940, air power was a dominating factor at sea, even when available in small quantity or in unsuitable form. The great battleships of the British and Italian navies, although not valueless, had less and less effect on the course of events. When British torpedo bombers crippled the Italian battleships at Taranto in November 1940 (the model for the Pearl Harbor attack) and Italian "manned torpedoes" disabled two British battleships at Alexandria in December 1941, these feats had surprisingly little influence on the strategic situation in the middle sea.[6]

For planes to actually sink ships remained a tricky and dangerous business, requiring specialized equipment and techniques. Conventional high-level bombing of the sort employed by the Italian air force, and also by the British and U.S. army air forces, was not an effective way to attack warships at sea. A certain contempt for this form of attack developed in many navies. (As we shall see later, however, with the right equipment and methods, high-altitude bombing could be effective against merchant ships.) Really effective attacks against ships required getting in close, one way or another, and aiming the plane itself right at the target. Dive-bombing, which proved the most effective form of attack for the Luftwaffe, and for the U.S. navy in the Pacific, was used relatively little by the Allies in the Mediterranean. Although Royal Navy Skuas (dive-bombers) had sunk the German cruiser *Koenigsberg*, the first warship ever destroyed by dive-bombing, during the Norwegian campaign, the Fleet Air Arm, the Royal Air Force (RAF), and the U.S. Army Air Force had little interest in the specialized dive-bomber.

If dive-bombing was ruled out, it was necessary to come in low. Low-altitude "masthead" attacks, at 50–100 feet, could be carried out by ordinary bombers, sometimes even by four-engine heavy bombers. One variant of this was "skip-bombing." Instead of trying to strike the target directly, a skip-bomber dropped its bombs at a speed, height, and distance precisely calculated so that the bombs skipped along the surface of the water like stones into the side of a ship. Even if the bombs did not actually hit the ship, they would explode close enough to cause serious damage. Low-level attacks were dangerous. They exposed the bombers to the fire of automatic weapons at close range, and the chance of hitting the sea, or colliding with the target, was ever present. A bomber badly hit at low level might not be able to climb high enough for the crew to bail out.

Another very different sort of low-level attack was the deadliest of all against ships, but it was the most dangerous and required very specialized equipment and training. Especially in the Mediterranean, torpedo bombers were more effective than any other type at sinking ships. Delivering large warheads below the waterline, torpedoes were deadlier than bombs; for most of the war they were almost the only dependable way to sink heavily armored ships. But torpedo attacks were even more dangerous than mast-head bombing because of the rigid format they required. For most of the war torpedoes could not be dropped at great speeds or from any height; the bomber had to fly a long, straight, and not-too-fast approach. It was particularly desirable for torpedo bombers to go in en masse, combined with other forms of attack and preceded by "flak-busting" planes, strafing and, later in the war, firing rockets at escort craft to keep down the antiaircraft fire. In Northwest Europe in 1944–45, the British would perfect "strike wing" tactics by thirty or more planes, with heavily armed rocket firing fighters going in just ahead of converging forces of torpedo bombers, whose attacks the target ships could not hope to evade. In the Pacific, U.S. carrier strikes would typically consist of fighters strafing and rocketing, followed by dive-bombers, with the torpedo bombers going in last. But the numbers and equipment involved were only a distant dream in the early years of World War II.

ENIGMA AND ULTRA

The efforts of the relatively small striking forces the British were able to send against the Axis supply lines to Africa were greatly helped by one of the great secrets of the war, an enterprise known to very few and which would remain unknown for long after the war—the reading of German and Italian messages. This was the result of a long-standing effort that dated back many years, to an era before the Nazis took power, when the Second World War was only a distant nightmare.

Since the 1920s, the German armed forces had used various models of the "Enigma" electromechanical cipher machine to guard their communications. The Enigma was a battery-powered, portable device that looked like an electric typewriter, with a screen or a lampboard mounted above it. When a key was depressed by an operator, an electric current went through a set of several different movable rotors or wheels, and a letter on the screen, which was the *encode* of the letter being typed, lit up. The lighted letters were written down by a second man for transmission by ordinary Morse code. Both the rotors, their order, and position were varied. By World War II, the operator inserted three of five different types of rotors at a time; eventually the German navy used five of seven rotors. The way in which the rotors were set up was the critical element, the "key" to the system. Keys were used for only twenty-four hours, changing every midnight. (They were issued beforehand in batches for each month.) To some extent, the Allied cryptographers had to start afresh each day. Learning to read the Enigma ciphers was a difficult task. It would have been impossible if the Germans had used the machine correctly. Fortunately their procedures always proved defective in some way, or the operators made mistakes that offered the Allies vital clues.

The Polish mathematicians, Marian Rejewski, Jerzy Rozycki, and Henryk Zygalski, aided by documents obtained by French intelligence, broke the Enigma ciphers in 1932. The Poles read German messages until 1938, when the Germans improved the Enigma device and changed some of their procedures. Shortly before they were invaded, the Poles shared their achievements with the British. During the early months of the war the Western powers slowly began to pry open the improved German system. In May 1940 they began reading the Luftwaffe's general-purpose cipher, which the British called "Red." It carried much information on the army as well. It was read almost every day, with little delay, for the rest of the war. The breakthrough was too late to save the French, but thereafter Enigma traffic was a major source of information. After the fall of France, cryptographical work was centered in Britain at the "Government Code and Cypher School" at Bletchley Park. It expanded the earlier "break" to read other German ciphers. The Luftwaffe signals service was the most careless on the German side and proved the easiest to deal with. During 1941, the British cracked important German and Italian naval ciphers and army ciphers used in the North African campaign. The British built electromechanical "bombes" based on earlier Polish designs, but vastly improved by the mathematicians Alan Turing and Gordon Welchman. These devices duplicated the Enigma machine's scrambler units, so apparent "cribs" or clues to the traffic could be quickly tested. Developments along these lines led to a major technological breakthrough. Deciphering became more difficult in early 1943, when the Germans made some changes in the Enigma machine and in their methods. To speed up the work and to deal with the more elaborate Siemens "Geheimschreiber" device, which the Germans already used for some high-level messages and which the British feared would replace Enigma, the British built the world's first electronic computer, "Colossus," which began operating in December 1943.[7]

Distributing intelligence that was derived from Enigma traffic and keeping it secret was a major problem. The British called this type of information "Ultra." They eventually distributed it through a system of elaborately camouflaged "Special Liaison Units" (SLUs) attached to field headquarters around the world; the SLUs passed on messages deciphered at Bletchley Park and enforced the elaborate system of rules designed to protect the "Ultra" secret.

An SLU reached the Middle East in the summer of 1941, replacing an earlier, more informal system of communications that had already aided the Middle East command at crucial moments. It guided the war against the Axis supply lines by passing on information derived from deciphered Luftwaffe and Italian naval and air force messages. The Italians used a commercial version of the Enigma machine (which originally had been designed to guard business secrets) with special rotors, and later, the Hagelin device, which was similar to the Enigma. The Italians often were careless and gave the cryptographers many openings. Except for a few short intervals, the British were unable to read the main Italian naval cipher after July 1940—it was rarely used on radio—but they read other codes. In late June 1941, they broke c38m, the Hagelin machine cipher used to transmit convoy information. It disclosed the composition of shipping and escorts, ports of origin and destinations, and often cargoes. They broke the July setting for c38m on July 10 and read it, with progressively shorter gaps as monthly key changes took place, for the rest of the war. They read Italian air force ciphers fairly steadily from September 1940, although the Italians used it mostly on landlines. The Luftwaffe, however, used radio freely, revealing plans to provide air cover for convoys. The two sets of information were married at Bletchley Park and sent to the Middle East. From the summer of 1941 until the end of the war in North Africa, news of enemy sailings was available almost every day. Major Enoch Powell became the leading expert on Axis supply at Middle East Headquarters. He and other members of an interservice committee advised the Middle East command on the state of the enemy supply system and the best way to strike at it.

Ultra, however, was not always reliable or usable. For one thing, the enemy often changed convoy plans; indeed, Allied action often forced him to do so. So air reconnaissance was needed to both check and "cover" Ultra. Rules, normally rigidly enforced, forbade direct action on Ultra information that might reveal to the enemy that his messages were being read. In the Mediterranean, this meant that a plane on a seemingly routine patrol must sight enemy ships before an attack was launched; the necessary preliminary reconnaissance was ordered to cover a certain sea area rather than look for specified ships. On one or two occasions in 1942, in the most critical days before El Alamein, the British commanders "cheated" and sent out air strikes against enemy ships without preliminary sightings. But the rules generally held good.[8]

Ultra was a fragile achievement. The Germans and Italians could have foiled the Allied effort if they had been more careful. Only weaknesses in the Germans' procedures and their failure to monitor their own communications allowed the Allies to succeed. Gordon Welchman later wrote that Enigma "would have been impregnable if it had been used properly" and "at any time during the war, enforcement of a few minor security measures could have defeated us completely," while some simple changes in the Enigma machine would have baffled the Allies despite the Germans' mistakes. He concluded his retrospective analysis with the comment, "We were lucky."[9] The Allies were lucky in other ways. Some of the French and Poles who had worked in the earlier efforts against Enigma remained in France; five of the Poles were actually captured by the Gestapo. Had any of those men revealed any of their work, as might easily have happened, the Germans could not have failed to shake up their communications security. As it was, while some junior German officers suspected the truth, those in charge remained complacent to the end. It should be noted that the British forces' own communications in the Mediterranean were by no means always secure. The Italians broke some low-level British ciphers, especially those used by aircraft crews. The German army's signals intelligence unit in Africa, up to the summer of 1942, broke British army codes and knew at least as much about the British army as the British knew about the Germans.[10]

UNDER THE SEA

The war against the Axis supply lines to Africa started slowly and contributed relatively little to the first British victories over the Italians. Apart from the fact that good intelligence began flowing only in 1941, the British had little with which to strike at enemy shipping. There were too few planes in the Mediterranean to spare many aircraft for such operations, and fewer still were suited for them. Until late 1940, Malta could barely defend itself against an air attack. The submarine base at Malta was evacuated in July 1940 and was used little until the year's end.

The initial burden of the attack on shipping was left to the one weapon that could operate, to some extent, even in areas where the enemy controlled the air and sea—the submarine. Although, like the aircraft, the submarines were most effective when Malta was available as a base, the submarine effort fluctuated less drastically. Even in the darkest days of 1941 and 1942, the submarines chipped away at the Italian merchant fleet.

The British submarine effort in the Mediterranean has attracted strangely little attention, despite the fact that, along with the American campaign in the Pacific, it was one of the only two successful submarine campaigns in history. Notwithstanding the reputation of the mostly Italian opposition, it was anything but a pushover. The British lost forty-five submarines in the Mediterranean, almost as many as the Americans lost to the Japanese. The peculiar difficulties of the Mediterranean theater forced the British submarines to operate somewhat more like modern submarines than most of their contemporaries. The World War II–era submarine was really a "submersible," and in the Atlantic and the Pacific, it spent most of its time on the surface, where it was most effective as a weapon. Unlike the German and American submarines, the British submarines in the Mediterranean operated mainly submerged.

Like the American submarines in the Pacific, although for somewhat different reasons, the British submarines were slow to become effective. Prewar submarine doctrines and training were not too realistic, nor were most of the submarines very good. The British had envisaged primarily attacking warships, firing only a single torpedo at a time, and almost no serious training took place at night. The older "O," "P," and "R" class submarines dating from the 1920s had serious defects in engines and hulls. The earlier submarines in these classes had leaky fuel tanks that revealed their positions. The later models fortunately cured this, but were still too big for operations in the Mediterranean. British analysts later concluded that in the Mediterranean size was the biggest factor in submarine losses; the larger they were, the more likely they were to be sunk. The "O," "P," and "R" classes had large silhouettes, presented large sonar targets, and dived very slowly. They were near the end of their operational lifetimes, and their crews were already tired after long tours in Asia. Nine were lost by the end of 1940, while doing little harm to the Italians.

Fortunately the British had better craft. The "T" class submarines, designed to replace the "O," "P," and "R" boats, had the heaviest torpedo armament—ten bow tubes—of any submarines in the world, and although rather large for the Mediterranean, some operated effectively from Gibraltar and in the eastern Mediterranean. More suitable for the inland sea were the medium "S" class and the small "U" class. They were at least reliable, although not really good designs. Ben Bryant, the very successful skipper of an "S" class sub, later wrote that he almost wept after seeing a captured German U-boat, for it was better than its British counterpart in almost every way.

British fire control remained primitive, and their radios were unsuited for submarines.

The "U" class submarines, designed to make 12 knots, were "cripplingly" slow at their actual maximum of 10.5 knots. Carrying only four torpedo tubes and eight torpedoes, they were well suited for operations from Malta, and a flotilla of ten began working from the inland in February 1941. The base there lacked torpedoes and spare parts, but it was only sixty miles from the main route between Italy and Libya, and the "U "class submarines could operate in the shallow waters off the Tunisian coast. Malta-based submarines sank over twice the tonnage of those based at Gibraltar and in the eastern Mediterranean. There were never less than four Malta-based boats at sea. The British were short of torpedoes until well into 1942; they had to convert old destroyer torpedoes for submarine use, for which they were not too suited, to keep going. Although experience showed that it was necessary to fire entire salvoes to score, orders were issued to never fire more than three except at a major warship, and to never shoot at a northbound ship at all!

The British submariners settled on tactics that served them for the rest of the war. They had to operate cautiously. Often working close inshore, they faced heavily escorted convoys with air cover. Although Italian escort ships rarely had sonar early in the war and were not too efficient until the end of 1941, the Italians were lavish in laying minefields. Mines sank twenty-two British submarines, nearly half of those lost in the Mediterranean. They also were unstinting with depth charges, dropping one every twenty minutes or so en route to Africa. British submariners, however, thought that this practice merely guided them to convoys they might otherwise have missed. The Mediterranean waters were very clear; planes could see submerged submarines as deep as sixty feet under the surface, and conditions favored sound detection most of the year. Strangely, planes apparently never actually sank a British submarine in the Mediterranean, and a few men, like Ben Bryant, treated them with contempt, but most submariners considered prudence the best course in dealing with aircraft. The British normally stayed submerged throughout the day. They patrolled deep, "porpoising" for a brief look through the periscope every ten minutes or so, and they used radio only when absolutely necessary. Normally they attacked by day. (All of this was the exact opposite of German practice in the Atlantic.)

Lacking the computers and more elaborate fire control of the Germans and Americans, British skippers found managing attacks a complicated business, and the long range of their torpedoes (much greater than those of the other powers) not all that useful. (British torpedoes, however, had one real advantage over the American torpedoes until late 1943: they worked!) The British preferred to get within 2,000 yards (and if possible, closer than 1,500 yards) of a target before firing. Six hundred yards on the beam of a target was considered the ideal position; much less than that and a torpedo would not work properly. To get really close it was usually necessary to pass right through the surface escort screen, which was usually 1,500 to 3,000 yards from the ships being guarded. The captain and his attack team had to judge the enemy's course and speed by eye, sometimes helped by a sonar operator's counting of the revolutions of the enemy propellers, and close in with as little use of periscope and high motor power as possible. With the enemy zigzagging, the captain had to constantly adjust his plans and aim as he worked into firing position. His chance to do so was limited because convoys were normally faster than submerged submarines. After the torpedoes were launched, enemy escorts would steam along the torpedo tracks, so the submarine would then turn away from the tracks, running away at its best submerged speed for a few minutes, then slowing to "silent speed" to evade the inevitable counterattack. The achievements of British submariners were all the more impressive given their miserable living conditions. Although perhaps not as bad as those in German Uboats, which made much longer patrols, they were far worse off than U.S. submariners. It was often impossible to shave or even change clothing for weeks. Sickness was surprisingly rare, but some men got tuberculosis, a disease that was still quite difficult to treat in the early 1940s.[11]

THE DESERT SEESAW BEGINS

In December 1940, Sir Richard O'Connor's Western Desert Force attacked the Italian advance force at Sidi Barrani, in what was then envisaged as just a raid. The cleverly planned blow took the enemy by surprise, and the British found their heavy "I" tanks nearly immune to almost all Italian weapons except for some heavy antiaircraft guns. The raid turned into a major offensive. By mid-February 1941, the British had overrun eastern Libya, virtually destroying the Italian Tenth Army, capturing 130,000 prisoners, 1,290 guns, 400 tanks, and a unique Italian contribution to the art of war, a mobile whorehouse. The British could probably have resumed the offensive in a short time and taken Tripoli, eliminating the Axis foothold in Africa, but they switched their efforts to dispatching a small expeditionary force to Greece and finishing the conquest of Italian East Africa.

Their success had forced Hitler, who had been excessively patient with the Italians, to come to Mussolini's aid. In January 1941, German air units arrived in Sicily and launched an air offensive against Malta. The Germans crippled and came within an ace of sinking the aircraft carrier *Illustrious*; losses on the ground forced the British to temporarily withdraw the Wellington bombers based on Malta. The air assault allowed General Erwin

Rommel's Afrika Korps of German panzer and motorized units to reach
Libya with small losses. Rommel, originally a light infantry officer, had ably
commanded one of the most successful panzer divisions in the French campaign. Hitler liked Rommel, a middleclass South German with no affinities
with the General Staff and Prussian Junkers Hitler disliked.

The British command was not very worried by this, expecting, like
Berlin, that supply problems would prevent a German offensive in the desert
until May, and concentrated on the campaign in Greece. The latter was a
total disaster. In April 1941, the Germans overran Yugoslavia with fantastic
speed and invaded Greece. Faced with overwhelming enemy forces, the
Royal Navy evacuated most of the British force; but of 58,000 men, 12,000
were lost, with almost all of the heavy equipment landed in Greece. In late
May, the Germans followed up the conquest of the Greek mainland with an
airborne invasion of Crete. The lightly armed airborne troops narrowly succeeded at overcoming the motley, poorly equipped defenders, but Crete was
something of a pyrrhic victory for the Germans. Their comparatively small
airborne forces suffered such tremendous casualties that they were never
again used in a major airborne operation, and Crete was not the best target
the Germans could have chosen. The capture of Malta would have done the
British far more damage. But they had again inflicted heavy losses on the
British. Less than half of the defenders were evacuated, and the Royal Navy
lost many ships.

Even before Greece was lost, Rommel had unexpectedly attacked in the
desert. General O'Connor's force had been broken up and many units sent
back to Egypt to refit. The result was the only battle in the desert war where
the Germans seriously outnumbered the Allies. But, as in other desert battles,
numbers were not the most important factor. The poorly equipped and inexperienced troops, whose supply and communications systems broke down,
were quickly overrun; O'Connor, hastily sent back to take command, was captured amid the rout. The Germans retook all of Libya except for Tobruk,
where the 9th Australian Division took over the well-built Italian defenses and
repelled repeated attacks. Tobruk remained a thorn in Rommel's side for the
rest of 1941; he could not prudently advance farther east without dealing
with it.

Nevertheless, the Axis powers could now have overrun the whole Middle
East via Turkey and Libya; the British were saved from total defeat in the
region by the Nazis' preference for attacking the Soviet Union.

Churchill had forced the Royal Navy to rush a convoy of tanks and other
vital equipment directly through the Mediterranean to Egypt instead of
around the Cape. This daring move succeeded, due to bad weather and the
fact that the Luftwaffe was engaged elsewhere, and enabled the British to

launch a hastily prepared offensive to relieve Tobruk as early as June. But the attack failed. The British tank crews had not had time to get used to their new vehicles and ran into well-placed German antitank guns. Conceiving of the battle as a clash of tank versus tank, the British did not realize that the Germans' successes were based on teamwork between all arms—tanks, antitank guns, infantry, and artillery. The Germans' favorite way to counter tank attacks, at this time, was with antitank guns and the fine 88 mm antiaircraft gun, which proved even more effective against tanks than weapons designed for that purpose. The Germans often used their own tanks to lure the British armor onto their antitank screens. But the British did not learn much from the defeat; they ascribed their tank losses to the fire of enemy tank guns, which they could see, and not the carefully hidden and dug-in antitank weapons. They also grumbled, not without reason, about the quality of some of their tanks. Their cruiser or medium tanks were unreliable and often broke down, and the Germans did have a limited qualitative superiority in guns and armor in some battles. Moreover, the heaviest German tank, the Mark IV, unlike its British counterparts, could fire high-explosive shells, not just solid shots, and it was more dangerous to infantry and "soft targets" than anything the British had in 1941. But the quality and quantity of the opposing tanks was not necessarily decisive in the desert fighting. In 1941 and 1942, even when the British generals mustered a considerably superior force, as they usually did at the start of a battle, they showed an amazing ability to disperse it into ineffectiveness or ram it headlong into enemy defenses, or else they failed to commit important elements until it was too late. It should be noted that the Italians were by no means a negligible factor in 1941 and 1942; under Rommel, their performance improved. Italian armored, motorized, and paratroop divisions, and some other units, fought well, especially in defense. Italian tanks, although no match for British ones, were a serious danger to British infantry.

STRIKING AT THE ENEMY SUPPLY LINE

The Allies in Africa would have been in far worse shape if British air and sea forces had not begun to cut heavily into the enemy supply effort. In the latter part of 1940, Malta began to receive more aircraft. A single Hurricane fighter squadron of sixteen planes defended the island. A Fleet Air Arm squadron of a dozen Fairey Swordfish torpedo bombers and sixteen RAF Vickers Wellington bombers (which attacked land targets at night) provided a striking force, while a few Short Sunderland flying boats and American-built Martin Maryland photo-reconnaissance planes flew scouting missions.

Initially they did not accomplish much; arguably the ability of these units to function at all was amazing. The Sunderland, a big, clumsy, albeit heavily armed plane, would have been a sitting duck in any other theater, while the Maryland—which was never used by U.S. forces—was guardedly described as "temperamental."

The Swordfish was a remarkable plane to be flying in the Second World War. A three-seat, open-cockpit biplane with a fixed landing gear, it looked like something from the Western Front in 1918. Yet it served with amazing effectiveness throughout the war. Very maneuverable and almost foolproof, it hauled amazing loads. It attacked at just ninety knots, dropping torpedoes at a height of exactly sixty feet, no more and no less. In daylight, it attacked after pulling out of a steep dive, which tended to throw off enemy gunners; at night, it came in on a gentle glide. From July 1941, they were fitted with radar and became the most effective type of strike plane based on Malta.[12]

In the spring of 1941, Malta-based subs and planes were beginning to seriously interfere with enemy shipping. After sinking only ten enemy ships in the first quarter of 1941, they sank twenty-six in April and May. After the Luftwaffe shifted its attentions to the Balkans and the desert, Malta was less hampered by bombing. For a brief time, in April and May, a force of four destroyers was able to operate from Malta. In one spectacular operation, on April 16, it destroyed a whole convoy of five transports and two escorts for one British destroyer lost. The Wellingtons, briefly withdrawn, returned to the island. In late April, a half dozen Bristol Blenheims, light twin-engine bombers, flew in from Britain. They carried out masthead attacks like those Blenheims mounted against German shipping in Western Europe, without escort. But Malta's facilities were still limited, so there was not enough space for both Blenheims and Wellingtons; the latter had to leave for Egypt again. The Blenheims were dreadfully vulnerable. Lightly built and poorly armed, they had a high accident rate and carried a very small bombload, smaller than that of the Swordfish. Their experience in the Mediterranean paralleled that of the Blenheim operations from Britain. The Italians put more antiaircraft guns on their ships, and losses shot up; some felt their attacks were near-suicidal. Radar made the Swordfish, when striking at night, more effective. The radar-equipped planes found enemy ships and dropped flares to light them up for the torpedo carriers; flares and torpedoes expended, the Swordfish would hasten home to avoid the fighter patrols that lurked near Malta at dawn. Later on, a slightly newer Fleet Air Arm torpedo bomber, the Fairey Albacore, arrived. It looked like something Charles Lindbergh might have flown before he became famous. Amazingly, for a plane introduced in 1940, it was a fixed-gear biplane, although it did enjoy an enclosed cabin and a more powerful engine than the Swordfish, which it was supposed to replace but did not.

The air bases on Malta were improved. In August 1941, the Wellingtons were able to return. By the end of the month, seven Marylands, twelve Swordfish, fifteen Wellingtons, and thirty-two Blenheims were based on the island, aside from the vital fighters. Some of the Hurricanes were modified to carry light bombs, and they struck enemy airfields and railroads on Sicily. The Marylands continued day reconnaissance, occasionally carrying bombs when they surveyed Tripoli. The Wellingtons carried out night reconnaissances and attacked enemy ports, aiming to destroy permanent installations; the Italians ruefully attested to their effectiveness. They sometimes damaged, but did not actually sink, ships in harbor. In late 1941, they introduced the use of 4,000-pound "block-busters" against their prime targets, Naples and Tripoli.

Submarines achieved spectacular successes, sinking three of Italy's largest troop transports, the ocean liners *Esperia*, *Neptunia*, and *Oceania*, in August and September 1941. From mid-October 1941, the Italians began carrying troops almost exclusively in destroyers, an expensive practice that at least ensured that they actually reached Libya. The Italians were beginning to devote more effort to antisubmarine warfare, and the forces were becoming more efficient. The British noted that their opponents were becoming more skillful. They also were installing sonar more widely, particularly in torpedo boats, and getting better depth charges. Submarines remained the chief killer of enemy shipping during 1941, causing 44 percent of enemy losses, but the planes were rapidly catching up. In late October 1941, surface ships returned to Malta; this "Force K" included cruisers as well as destroyers, guided by Ultra. For a time Force K was spectacularly effective, sinking eleven ships in two months. During November 8–9, Force K wiped out a whole convoy of seven ships in a single night. In December, however, Force K ran afoul of an Italian minefield, and several ships were lost or badly damaged. It finally withdrew as Malta became untenable.

Italian shipping losses had shot up in July; through October they had lost forty ships, and an average of 16 percent of cargo intended for Africa was lost. After that, their losses shot up even farther; 62 percent of all cargoes was lost. The only gasoline that reached Libya was carried in Italian navy combat ships. Had losses gone on at this rate, the Axis would have been forced out of Libya in early 1942. As it was, the attack on enemy supplies contributed to a severe thrashing.[13]

Wavell was replaced by General Claude Auchinleck. Auchinleck was personally able, but a poor judge of men, and perhaps because he was an Indian army officer, he had great difficulty getting the British and Dominion officers under him to do what he wanted. When Auchinleck took personal command in the desert, he ran things well. But the men he appointed to lead the new Eighth Army did not.

The Eighth Army, under General Alan Cunningham, attacked on November 18 with considerable superiority in numbers. The British were well informed about the enemy's situation, due to Ultra intelligence. While the XIII Corps, a mostly infantry force, attacked the fortified coastal sector on the Egyptian frontier, XXX Corps, with most of the armor, swung around to the south. The British wished to force a decisive tank battle on Rommel, relieve Tobruk, and then smash the remainder of his army. But instead of going straight for Tobruk, which probably would have provoked the fight they wanted, they halted at Gabr Saleh, waiting for the enemy to react. Rommel's attention had been focused on his own plans for Tobruk. At first he did not realize that the British had launched a major attack—by some accounts he learned the truth by listening to the British Broadcasting Corporation (BBC)! While he absorbed this shock, the British fumbled, letting their armored force get too spread out—one armored brigade stayed at Gabr Saleh, another drove for Tobruk, and a third attacked an Italian armored division. A complex, hard-fought battle resulted as Rommel struck the dispersed British. Both sides suffered heavy losses.

By November 24, Rommel had inflicted a sharp reverse on the British; he exploited it by driving far to the east to disrupt their supply lines and relieve the garrisons in the frontier area. He expected that that would panic the British into retreating, and it nearly did. But General Auchinleck knew from reading the enemy's messages that Rommel was weaker than he seemed, and the eastern drive could not be maintained for long. He replaced Cunningham with Neil Ritchie and continued the offensive. Rommel had to retreat, leaving the frontier garrisons to ultimate capture. The thrust east proved a mistake. Had Rommel kept his forces near Tobruk, he might well have defeated the British. Recovering their poise, the British forced the Axis out of Cyrenaica. The Axis had suffered a major defeat in the desert—the losses of both sides in the month-long battle were higher than those at El Alamein a year later.

But the situation at sea had changed to the advantage of the Axis. In the fall of 1941, the Germans began transferring a large number of U-boats to the Mediterranean. The U-boats, and an Italian "manned torpedo" attack on the British fleet at Alexandria, inflicted serious losses. The war with Japan forced the British to divert reinforcements from the Middle East and transfer some forces from the area to the Far East. And, with the onset of winter in Russia, Marshal Albert Kesselring's Luftflotte 2 was transferred, although not with all of its planes, from the eastern front to the Mediterranean. Kesselring became commander-in-chief of the German forces in the region.

Luftflotte 2 began attacking Malta, which reduced the loss of Axis supply ships. New panzer units and replacement tanks reached Rommel, enabling him to launch a dramatic attack.

The British in Cyrenaica were at the end of a long supply line. Their armored force, the 1st Armored Division, was new to the desert. Rommel's staff calculated that the Axis would enjoy a degree of numerical superiority in the forward area until the British straightened out their supply problems. Rommel decided to launch a counterattack. Suspecting that the enemy was "reading his mail," although wrongly attributing this to treachery among the Italians, he did not tell his superiors of his plans and took the British by surprise.

On January 21, Rommel struck. The British proved badly trained and could not deal with the Germans' offensive use of antitank screens. A series of lightning moves forced the British back to the "Gazala Line" in eastern Cyrenaica.

THE MALTA BLITZ

The role of the German forces in the Mediterranean changed in 1942. Hitler resolved to take the offensive there; it was the only place, other than the U-boat war in the Atlantic, where he could strike at the Western powers. Malta would be starved out or captured, and Rommel would take Egypt. His force, now entitled "Panzer Army Afrika," would form one arm of a pincers movement into the Middle East. The main thrust would come from the north once the Caucasus was taken from the Soviets.

From January 1942 onward, Malta endured one of the great ordeals of the war. Over 400 Axis planes based on Sicily attacked day after day. In January, when the British could still base some supporting planes in Libya, it was relatively easy to supply Malta. After Rommel's counterattack, it became far harder. The obsolescent Hurricanes defending Malta found it hard to get past the superior Me-109s escorting the enemy bombers, which did great damage to the airfields and everything else on Malta. Clever tactical combinations of fighter sweeps and bombing raids caught many British planes while landing, and Malta's bomber force was eliminated. Offensive air operations from Malta practically collapsed; the submarines found it harder and harder to work. The Italians no longer bothered to sail more than fifty miles from the island.

In March 1942, the British fought a supply convoy through to Malta, although the Italian surface fleet tried to intervene. Admiral Vian's force of light cruisers and destroyers practically bluffed a far stronger Italian force, including a battleship, and got the convoy through—but the cargo ships were sunk by bombs before they could be fully unloaded. The shift of attacks from airfields to the dockyard gave the RAF precious breathing space. But Malta desperately needed more fighters. In April 1942, the U.S. carrier *Wasp* brought in a large force of Spitfires, but the Germans were better prepared to receive them than Malta. Before the arriving Spitfires could refuel, they were caught on the ground by a carefully timed attack. Over the next two days, most of the fighter force was wiped out. The submarine base was paralyzed; three British submarines and one Greek submarine were sunk, and the surviving boats had stay on the harbor bottom during the day. Axis motor torpedo boats laid mines around Malta; the bombing stopped minesweeping, which finally rendered the base untenable. In late April and early May, the submarines left for the east; two more were lost escaping from Malta. It was a long trip for the submarines from the eastern end of the sea to the Libyan route, and the worst was to come. As Rommel advanced into Egypt, the naval base at Alexandria was evacuated. On June 30, a U-boat sank the submarine depot ship *Medway*, the sole support of the submarines based in the eastern Mediterranean. Much of the remaining strength had to be concentrated off enemy naval bases to support the Malta convoys. Still, the submarines were almost the last force left that could hurt Rommel's supply line.

Wasp returned to the Mediterranean on May 9 and flew off a new load of Spitfires. Quickly serviced and refueled at Malta, they took off in time to catch the German bombers that had been sent to destroy them. The reinforcements, and the transfer of a large number of German planes from Sicily to Russia, transformed the situation at Malta. The Axis offensive came to an end.

Malta, still desperately short of supplies, was harder than ever to reach. In June 1942, the British tried to run two convoys to Malta, one from the eastern Mediterranean and one from Gibraltar. The main Italian fleet came out to attack the eastern convoy, forcing it to reverse its course. Attacked by British planes, the Italians finally turned back to avoid a night surface battle for which they felt unready. But the convoy had exhausted its antiaircraft ammunition fighting off Axis planes. It had to turn back too.

The western convoy ran a gauntlet of intense air and submarine attacks, while Italian cruisers and destroyers attacked it in the Sicilian Narrows. The convoy escort, although outgunned, was well handled and staved off a superior force while suffering heavy losses. But just two of the convoy's six cargo ships reached Malta. The island, for the moment, was saved.[14] In the desert, however, the British faced disaster.

In April, Hitler and Mussolini had agreed that Malta must be captured outright by a combined airborne and amphibious attack. But Hitler never liked this "Operation Hercules." The airborne phase reminded him painfully of Crete, and he feared that the Italians would fumble the naval aspects. He may have hoped—and this was not an unreasonable hope—that Malta would be starved out. In any case, preparations for the landing would take three months. It was agreed to take Cyrenaica in May and June, and to invade Malta in July.

Malta had been sufficiently suppressed so that the Axis forces in Libya were now well supplied. During the entire first half of 1942, only 6 percent of the supplies dispatched were lost en route to Libya; the Italians judged the supply problem in April and May to be easier than at any other time during the war.

Despite this, the Axis forces were not in a good position; 560 Axis tanks faced 850 British tanks, including many American-made "General Grant" tanks, which were better than most German tanks. The British expected an attack and had laid out a series of "boxes"—positions designed for all-around defense, surrounded by deep minefields, held by infantry units and some supporting tanks. Strong armored forces were well back in reserve. The effort put into static defenses that could be easily outflanked was perhaps unwise, but the British were basically well prepared. As British historians have bitterly noted, the subsequent battle was one they could and should have won.

On the night of May 26–27, the Axis forces struck. The largely immobile Italian infantry launched a holding attack on the Gazala Line, while the armored forces swung around the end of the line to hit it from the rear.

The British as usual did not properly concentrate their armor; the Germans were able to tackle and defeat the 7th and 1st Armored Divisions separately. But the British were too strong and recovered. The appearance of the Grant tanks was a shock, and forces from the Bir Hacheim box raided Rommel's supply convoys. Rommel's forces retreated into a defensive position with its back on the Gazala Line. Their situation was truly desperate; they lacked supplies and even water. A prompt, well-planned British attack would have crushed the Axis forces in Africa then and there. But General Ritchie never got a grip on the situation. The British left Rommel alone, and he was able to attack the Sidi Muftah box and open a short supply route to the west. He overcame the British brigade holding the box on June 1. The Eighth Army finally attacked only on June 5—with only half of the available troops. Rommel's forces stopped the badly planned attack and then took Bir Hacheim, overcoming a heroic defense by the Free French and Jewish garrison. With their rear free, the Germans advanced east on Tobruk. In a series of tank battles, they finally routed the British, who had shown amazing persistence, if not skill. But Ritchie began pulling back farther than expected. Under pressure from Churchill, Auchinleck left a force built around a

South African division in Tobruk. This proved a terrible blunder. Tobruk's defenses were in disrepair; most of its minefields had been lifted. Rommel launched the attack planned for late 1941 with his whole army, against a far weaker defense. On June 21, 33,000 men, with huge supply dumps, fell into German hands.

Rommel, now promoted to field marshal, urged exploiting the victory by driving on instead of halting on the Egyptian frontier and awaiting the capture of Malta. Kesselring and the Italians opposed him, rightly arguing that, despite the losses inflicted on the British and the mountain of supplies taken at Tobruk, supply difficulties would halt Rommel's advance. But Hitler and Mussolini welcomed Rommel's views as an excuse to avoid the attack on Malta; Hitler may have decided not to go through with the Malta operation should Tobruk be taken as early as May 21. He ruled in favor of Rommel.

Rommel won yet another victory over the British when they made a half-hearted, confused attempt to stand at Mersa Matruh.

Auchinleck finally relieved General Ritchie. Taking command of the Eighth Army himself, he elected to fight at the Alamein position, sixty miles west of Alexandria, where a series of boxes like those at Gazala had been laid out. At this point, the Qattara Depression, a vast, dead lake bed whose bottom was a salt marsh, narrowed the possible fighting front to forty miles. (Supposedly impassable, it was crossed by tracks usable by light vehicles.) Alamein was apparently the only place in the desert which could not be outflanked by a move through the interior. But in fact Auchinleck no longer had the forces to hold a continuous front, and his main line of resistance had a "refused" left flank along ridges running from east to west. (Ironically, the narrowing of the front forced by the Qattara Depression ultimately benefited the Axis more than the British.) Auchinleck did not plan a last stand at Alamein. Should the Eighth Army be beaten again, he planned to retreat up the Nile, using Port Sudan as a base. He would prevent Rommel from crossing the Suez Canal by threatening his flank. But it is questionable whether the British forces in the Middle East could have withstood the loss of the immobile bases on the lower Nile. Whether Auchinleck wanted it or not, the coming battle would be decisive. He decreed important changes of tactics and reorganized the Eighth Army's artillery under his direct, centralized control.

The Eighth Army had been whittled down but so had Rommel's Panzer Army, which was very tired. He arrived before Alamein with just 55 German tanks, 30 Italian tanks, 1,500 German infantry, and 5,000 Italian infantry; only his artillery remained strong. Rommel planned to drive between the Alamein box on the coast and the next British position to the south at Deir el Abayad. Then he would turn north to get in the British rear, cutting the coast road behind the Alamein box. But the Germans' picture of the British position was confused. There was no box at Abayad, but there was one at Deir el Shein to the east, held by an Indian brigade. The panzers found it by running right into it on July 1. The Germans saw that an attempt to outflank Deir el Shein would simply hit another strong position on Ruweisat Ridge and chose to attack it directly. The Indians were overcome only after a day-long, heroic defense in which eighteen precious panzers were destroyed. Meanwhile, farther north, a German motorized infantry division tried to bypass the Alamein box. But due to a navigational error, it blundered into the box instead and was stopped by the South African defenders and intense artillery fire. Rommel had been stopped; as his staff officer, F. W. von Mellenthin, wrote later, "Our prospects of victory were hopelessly prejudiced on 1 July." An attack on the Ruweisat Ridge failed on July 2, as did another attempt to outflank the Alamein box the following day. The Eighth Army took the offensive. Fighting raged on until July 27, as reinforcements were fed in by both sides. Several times Auchinleck came close to a decisive success, and he inflicted heavy losses on the Axis forces. But the first battle of Alamein ended with both sides in their original positions. Nevertheless, it was the decisive battle of the war in the desert. Rommel had been stopped, and that was what really counted.

SAVING MALTA

Rommel's prospects were dim even if Malta was neutralized. Only 6 percent of the Axis supplies had been lost en route to Africa in July, but what arrived was still not enough to keep Rommel properly supplied. A renewed air offensive against the island in July failed; the British submarines returned to their base. However, Malta remained short of fuel, spare parts, and ammunition, and the Maltese were on a diet that spelled slow starvation. For months they had lived on 1,200–1,500 calories a day; now rations were cut again. The last dogs and cats had long ago been eaten. Medical supplies were scarce, and sickness of all sorts was common; there was no electric power. The Maltese walked through the ruins of their towns like ghosts. The fate of the island was still finely balanced; the British had to send a new convoy in August. Unless it got through, Malta must surrender by the end of the first week of September.

There was now no possibility of a convoy from the east; everything depended on one convoy fighting its way through from the west against everything the Axis could throw against it; 784 Axis planes faced 256 British planes based on Malta and the three available British carriers. The convoy entered the Straits of Gibraltar on August 10; one of the great air-sea battles of the war began. For the next four days, the British ran a gauntlet of furious attacks by German and Italian submarines, motor torpedo boats, level-, dive-, and torpedo-bombers, and a primitive guided missile—a radio-controlled drone plane. It carried a huge load of explosives, but fortunately went out of control. Italian fighter-bombers camouflaged to look like British planes sneaked into the landing patterns over the British carriers to drop special bombs on the planes parked on their decks. An attack by Italian cruisers and destroyers might have finished off the convoy, but the Axis air commanders would not promise fighter cover for the ships. As it was, the British escorts suffered terrible losses. Out of fourteen merchant ships, only five, all damaged, reached Malta. The only tanker in the convoy, *Ohio*, was hit by both bombs and torpedoes. Carrying a cargo of fuel worth far more than its weight in gold, she barely staggered into Malta at the end of a tow rope, with two crashed German bombers strewn on its decks, which were barely above water.[15] Malta was saved.

Even while Malta's survival had been doubtful, it had begun striking back at Rommel's supply line. The submarine base was reoccupied in late July; the flotilla in the eastern Mediterranean, working out of a French submarine base at Beirut, now functioned more smoothly.

The British now had better planes as well as a centrally located base, although, as before, the effective striking force was remarkably small. The RAF's Bristol Beaufort, a fast, twin-engine torpedo bomber, could attack during the day, unlike the Navy's Swordfish and Albacores. The Beaufort was tricky to fly and lacked a good torpedo sight, but it had fought effectively in Western Europe since 1940. It had a crucial role in the Mediterranean campaign although, as important World War II aircraft types go, it has remained relatively little known. That may well be related to the fact that flying torpedo bombers was the most dangerous job in the RAF. Beaufort attacks saved thousands of Allied lives, but few who flew in them survived the war. A trickle of Beauforts began to reach the Middle East in late 1941, but when Malta was untenable, they could not hit the enemy's main supply route from Egyptian bases. Some "torpedo Wellingtons," able to carry as many as two torpedoes, also became available. Too big and too slow to attack in daylight, they worked well at night, using moonlight or guided by flares dropped by radar-equipped Wellingtons. Beauforts formed the main striking force, although there were rarely more than twenty Beauforts and crews on Malta, and fuel shortages still limited strikes.

The Beauforts began operating there in support of the June Malta convoy and flew irregularly thereafter, often suffering terrible losses. The first significant success when enemy losses of any sort were rare was the sinking of the German ship *Reichenfels* on June 21, which cost three Beauforts out of nine attacking planes. Similar losses out of striking forces of no more than a dozen Beauforts were all too common in June and July. One shot-down Beaufort crew got back in one of the war's most dramatic escapes. Captured off Greece on July 28, the men were being taken to Italy on a seaplane. They overpowered the Italian crew and flew home to Malta. British tactics improved and losses dropped. As before, Ultra led reconnaissance planes to convoys; the scouts disclosed the real location and the actual cruising disposition of the convoy. Occasionally, close to Malta, the attackers got Spitfire escort, but usually they were protected by no more than a dozen Beaufighters. The latter were slow and heavy, but heavily armed, two-seat fighters developed from the Beaufort. They usually could cope with whatever air umbrella—rarely more than a half dozen planes, often of varying types and often bombers rather than fighters—covered the Axis convoys. The strike forces, normally accompanied by a Martin Baltimore photoreconnaissance plane, flew out from Malta on a deception course at just fifty feet to evade or at least confuse enemy surveillance. Once away from the island, they turned to intercept the target convoy's course, but well ahead of the point the convoy had actually reached. They then turned up the convoy's line of advance. Some Beaufighters went in ahead of the torpedo bombers to strafe the escort ships and suppress flak; they often caused heavy losses to the warship crews. When possible, some Beaufighters carried bombs; they dive-bombed the target ships as the Beauforts made converging attacks.

Later in the campaign, as the enemy routed convoys to Tobruk, out of range of Malta-based Beauforts, some long-range strikes were mounted from Egypt. There the Beauforts and Beaufighters enjoyed the support of a half dozen South African Bisleys (a fancy name for the Blenheim V, the last model of that unfortunate plane). The Bisleys made a diversionary low-level attack with bombs ahead of the Beauforts. But they flew into a hornet's nest of enemy interceptors based in Africa.[16]

Allied bombing of Libyan ports also was increasingly effective, nullifying much of the advantages the Axis had gained from taking Tobruk. Twenty to thirty Wellingtons and ten American B-24s bombed Benghazi and Tobruk each night. The RAF destroyed the fuel storage depot at Tobruk in July; on August 6, a particularly effective attack reduced the capacity of Tobruk from 2,000 tons to 600; it never again handled more than 1,000 tons of cargo. On the night of September 22–23, having learned of the arrival of *Apuania* at Benghazi with ten tanks and a big load of ammunition, the Allies mounted a particularly effective attack. B-24s destroyed the ship and the main unloading jetty in a spectacular blast that seriously damaged other port installations and ships.[17]

At sea, the British had sunk only a dozen ships from late June through July, all on coastal runs in African waters. In the first half of August, they only sank three ships (all due to submarines.) In the latter half of the month, they really began to bite, just as Rommel was planning one last throw for the end of August, before the British got too strong.

The submarine *Porpoise* sank the next large ship, *Lerici*, on August 15. On August 17, Malta-based Beauforts got the freighter *Rosalino Pilo* with an important cargo, despite unusually heavy German air cover. She was finished off by the submarine *United*, which was seriously damaged when *Pilo* blew up. On August 21, Beauforts hit the unusually well-escorted big tanker *Pozarica*, carrying fuel for the Italian army, and forced her to beach on Corfu, but it took two attacks and cost three Beauforts and as many Beaufighters to get her. On August 26, Ultra disclosed an ambitious program to sail no less than twenty ships between August 25 and September 5 to support the planned offensive. The RAF promptly bombed the Corinth Canal to disrupt ship movements. No less than sixteen of these ships were either tankers or carried at least some fuel in barrels; only seven—some carrying very small amounts of fuel—reached Africa. Later, the British learned of a new "emergency program" to get eight fuel carriers to Africa between August 28 and September 2. Even as they read this, on August 27, Beauforts sank one of these ships, *Dielpi*, and Wellingtons got another, *Istria*, while submarines got another ship, *Manfredo Camperio*, not part of the fuel program.

On August 29, Rommel, short of fuel, glumly limited his attack to a "local offensive." On August 30, a big tanker, *San Andrea*, which was not part of the emergency program (it had been scheduled to sail earlier but had been delayed), was sunk by Beauforts. Two more fuel ships ran afoul of the RAF on September 2; they were already too late to be of use to Rommel. The tanker *Picci Fassio*, heading for Tobruk, was sunk by Beauforts; *Abruzzi* was badly damaged, although it was towed into port and its cargo was finally salvaged.

In August, a third of all Rommel's supplies and 41 percent of his fuel had been lost en route to Africa. Nevertheless, he had decided against the advice of his staff to gamble on an attack. He planned to strike in the southern sector, breaking through the lightly held area north of the Qattara Depression, and then wheel northeast to the coast, cutting off the British forces.

The British were ready for him; they were well-informed about his plan, which their staff had predicted even before Ultra picked it up. Auchinleck had been replaced by General Harold Alexander. General Bernard Montgomery had taken command of the Eighth Army. If not the second coming of the Duke of Wellington, as he and many other British liked to imagine, Montgomery was a highly competent, though very cautious, professional. His forte was the "set-piece" battle that could be planned in advance.

Rommel had about 510 tanks, including twenty-seven Mark IV Specials superior to any of the Allied tanks, but other supplies, as well as fuel, were short. He faced 700 tanks, including 164 Grants, and the British controlled the air. He told his doctor, "The decision to attack today is the hardest I have ever taken. Either the army in Russia succeeds in getting through to Grozny and we in Africa manage to reach the Suez Canal, or . . ." and made a gesture of defeat. His only remote chance was that the British would make some gross blunder and give him an opening. But Montgomery was the last man likely to do that.

On the night of August 30, the attack began. The British fought a skillful delaying action and threw the Axis off schedule. The Panzer Army advanced very slowly. On the evening of August 31, it finally attacked the Alam Halfa ridge, the core of the British defense, which in British hands, threatened the flank of any Axis move east or north. The German attack failed, as did a renewed effort the next day. A lack of gasoline and constant air attack made it hard for Rommel to even retreat. The Panzer Army finally fell back on September 2. A strong, prompt attack south might have trapped most of Rommel's army and ended the war in the desert quickly, but Montgomery's cautious and belated attempt to do this failed. As it was, Rommel's losses were not particularly great, but the last chance for an Axis victory in the Mediterranean was gone.

During September and October, the British and Americans continued to chip away at the Axis supply effort. The desperate Germans diverted much of their bomber force in the Mediterranean to providing convoy cover. The Italian air force was already largely disposed to protect shipping and ports; it mounted only seventy-five sorties a day near the front in Africa, which did little good. No fuel reached Libya in the first week of October because of an air-submarine victory off Greece. The submarine *Umbra* sank the cargo-carrier *Francesco Barbaro* en route to Benghazi via Greece. *Unione*, carrying fuel in the same convoy, was torpedoed the same night by a Beaufort. She was salvaged by heroic seamanship, but her cargo never reached Africa. Another ship, *Nino Bixio*, which was carrying fuel, was sunk by a torpedo bomber four days later.

As the Allied offensive at El Alamein began, Ultra showed the enemy's desperate need for fuel. The British learned that the tanker *Proserpina* was due to reach Tobruk from Taranto on October 25 with 4,500 tons of fuel. Her sailing was delayed. Finally she headed for Tobruk with the small German freighter *Dora* and the big cargo ship *Tergestea*, carrying a major load of ammunition and fuel and escorted by four torpedo boats with a fairly heavy air cover. Attacks by torpedo- and bomb-carrying Wellingtons and American B-24s failed to hit anything. On October 26, a difficult long-range strike of

Beauforts, Bisleys, and Beaufighters from Egyptian bases destroyed *Proser-pina*, at the cost of a Beaufighter, two of the eight attacking Beauforts, and half of the six Bisleys engaged. Tergestea blew up with her whole crew after a Wellington torpedoed her at dusk; one Wellington was lost. *Luisiano*, a smaller tanker hauling army fuel, the last shipment likely to reach Rommel while he was still at El Alamein, was sunk by a Wellington's torpedo off of Navarino in Greece late on October 28. Rommel found her loss shattering. He had lost only 20 percent of his supplies on the route to Africa in September, but no less than 44 percent in October. As he retreated through Libya, losses remained high.[18]

THE U.S. ARMY AIR FORCE IN THE MIDDLE EAST

Since June 1942, the Royal Air Force in the Mediterranean and the Middle East had been joined by American units. Contrary to what is widely supposed, the first American air operations against the European Axis were not carried out by the Eighth Air Force from England but in the Mediterranean theater. In that area, the Army Air Force with the help of the RAF, gained valuable experience, some of a sort quite different from anything it could have picked up in Britain. In the Middle East, the AAF learned much about tactical air support and keeping up with the ground forces in a rapid war of movement.

The nucleus of a U.S. air force arrived in the Middle East almost by accident, as a by-product of an attempt to repeat the Doolittle raid on Japan. A detachment of twenty-three B-24Ds, commanded by Colonel Harry Halverson, was organized to bomb Japan from bases in China. It was to get to China by flying east from America across the Atlantic, Africa, the Middle East, and India. Halverson's "HALPRO" force carrying their own minimum ground crews successfully flew the recently developed "southern ferry route," which was critical for reinforcing the Mediterranean theater and even Britain for the rest of the war. Planes taking the ferry route left any of several South Florida bases. Refueling at either Borinquen, Puerto Rico, or Trinidad, they flew on to Atkinson airfield, in what was then British Guiana (now Guyana), then to Belem and Natal in Brazil. Natal was the departure point for the hop across the Atlantic Narrows to Africa. Four-engined planes like the B-24s could fly all the way from Natal to Accra on the Gold Coast (now Ghana), where it joined with the older Takoradi route across Africa, established by the British in 1940. Twin-engined planes stopped at Hastings Field, Sierra Leone, or Roberts Field, Liberia. In July 1942, another stop was provided at Ascension Island in the middle of the South Atlantic. In 1942, long-range flights by large numbers of planes were still new, long, and difficult. By today's standards, even the biggest planes were short ranged, engine failures were frequent, and air navigation was both more difficult and less reliable. Planes had to fly through bad weather that modern aircraft simply fly over. It was a source of satisfaction and a good omen for the thousands of planes that followed that HALPRO, unlike earlier efforts to fly bombers east to stop the Japanese, negotiated the Atlantic and Takoradi routes without accidents or serious delays.

Halverson's planes were at Khartoum when he was diverted, "temporarily," to carry out a mission that Washington had been pondering for some time, in which President Roosevelt had had a personal interest—a one-shot attack on the oil refineries in Romania that supplied a quarter of Germany's oil. The B-24s were the only bombers that could, just barely, reach Ploesti from existing bases. On June 11, thirteen B-24s took off on the first mission against the European enemy. They failed to hit any refineries, and the returning bombers landed at bases all over the eastern Mediterranean—four were interned in Turkey. It was an inauspicious start for the AAF. At the request of the British, Halverson's unit carried out another mission in support of the June Malta convoy, attacking the Italian fleet. In an unusual success for high-level bombing, it actually hit the Italian battleship *Littorio*, although it did little real harm. As the extent of the British defeat in the desert became clear, Halverson was ordered to stay in the Middle East, still just "temporarily." His planes began attacking Benghazi and Tobruk. On June 23, Washington ordered General Louis Brereton, the American air commander in the China-Burma-India theater, to take all available bombers west to support the British. Brereton reached the Middle East with just nine weary B-17s of the 7th Heavy Bomb Group. (It is a comment on the desperate and scattered state of the AAF in the early months of the war that the other half of the 7th Bomb Group ended up in Australia.) Brereton took command of the new "U.S. Army Air Forces in the Middle East." The bombers were based at Lydda in Palestine. At about the same time, Washington decided to establish a full-scale air force in the region and send Brereton the 98th Heavy Bomb Group, equipped with B-24s, the 12th Medium Bomb Group, equipped with B-25 medium bombers, and the 57th Fighter Group, equipped with P-40s. In July, the bombers already present were consolidated into the 1st Provisional Group (redesignated the 376th Heavy Bomb Group in November). They continued pounding away at the Libyan ports, occasionally flying north to hit targets in Greece and Crete.

The ground echelons of the three new groups sailed from New York on July 16 on the long trip around the Cape to Egypt. During July and early August, the aircrews flew the bombers along the southern ferry route, while the aircraft carrier *Ranger* took the 57th's P-40s across the Atlantic; they flew off the carrier to land at Takoradi. The new units went into action early in

August. They depended heavily on British help and training, but soon performed well enough so that the RAF attached its 112 Fighter Squadron to
the 57th Group. The Americans picked up the organization and tricks that
the RAF had painfully learned over the last two years that enabled units to
fly and fight even while moving from one inadequate desert base to another.
The American heavy bombers continued attacking ports, airfields, and
ships. Unlike the Eighth Air Force, they hit "tactical" targets, but deep in the
enemy rear, while the fighters and medium bombers joined in the British
effort to maintain air superiority and support the ground forces in the forward area. Brereton's command, redesignated the Ninth Air Force on
November 12, would continue this pattern as part of the British advance
west, finally joining in the similar efforts of the Twelfth Air Force, coming
from the other end of Africa.[19]

CHAPTER 2

Planning the Invasion of North Africa and the Twelfth Air Force

The German-Italian Panzer Army had had its supply line strangled by planes and submarines when the British began their offensive on October 23. Although it took longer and cost more lives than expected, the greatly superior British forces broke the last Axis defense line. On November 2, Rommel ordered a retreat. Hitler countermanded this the next day, but contrary to widespread belief, that folly had little effect. The British pressure was too great; the Axis units kept falling back, despite orders from above. The British took 30,000 prisoners; Rommel lost nearly all of his tanks and most of his artillery. But the pursuit failed; Rommel evaded Montgomery's badly planned attempts to cut him off. The Eighth Army moved fast, but Rommel kept ahead of it all the way. Although he never had more than fifty-four tanks against at least 200 in the Allied vanguard, he saved his army from destruction and got it to Tunisia.

There the small desert campaign merged into a larger struggle that was the Western powers' first major offensive success of the war, a success that opened a drive across the Mediterranean. That drive, whose way was at least greatly eased by the magnitude of the victory in Tunisia, knocked Italy out of the war. It forced the Germans to invest an enormous effort in replacing the Italian occupation forces in the Balkans and southern France and holding a front in Italy itself. By D-Day in 1944, over fifty German divisions were tied down in Italy and the Balkans, a force almost as great as that defending Western Europe. That diversion of enemy forces greatly assisted the Soviet advance and the invasion of Normandy. In the course of the operations in the Mediterranean, the Luftwaffe suffered defeat and heavy losses when it was still holding its own in Northern Europe, and the Allies gained bases that greatly aided the strategic bombing offensive.

ORIGINS OF THE NORTH AFRICAN INVASION
Since December 1941, the Western powers had sought a way to take the initiative in Europe at an early date. Even before the Americans had entered

the war, they and the British had agreed that in a war against both Germany and Japan, defeating Germany must have priority. After Pearl Harbor, this was not a popular course, but it was the rational course and President Roosevelt stuck by it. The Allies implicitly accepted that they must defeat the Germans in a land campaign in Europe. The Allied leaders were willing to invest great resources in the strategic bombing offensive, but whatever the airmen's hopes, they never depended on it to bring victory by itself. It was a way to prepare and support a land invasion.

Already, in December 1941, at the suggestion of Churchill, who was then visiting Washington, the Allies had tried to plan an invasion of French North Africa. It was hoped that the Vichy French authorities there would cooperate with an Anglo-American landing. Conquest of the area would forestall any German move there, place the Axis forces in Africa in a hopeless position, and provide a base for operations against southern Europe. American military leaders did not like this very much, but they had no viable alternative. So an invasion of North Africa was actually agreed upon. But soon afterward, it became clear that the French were unlikely to cooperate, and the need to stop the Japanese advance and the worldwide shipping shortage forced cancellation of the plan.

The U.S. army favored different strategic ideas. It held that the best, if not the only, way to beat Germany was by an offensive through Western Europe. That offered the shortest route to the heart of Germany's industrial power; it had the best land communications of any war theater, and the sea routes to it were shorter than to any other. The sea lanes to Britain must be guarded in any event, and Britain had plenty of air bases. Only an offensive based there could employ most of Britain's strength; and even before an invasion could take place, a buildup there would threaten the Germans and prevent their concentrating completely against the Soviets.

Conversely, the U.S. army rejected an attack through the Mediterranean. Defeating Italy would not decisively hurt Germany, and the Alps would prevent attacking Germany from the south. A Mediterranean campaign would need a separate and longer supply line and would encounter poorer communications and worse terrain. An offensive there might start earlier than one in Western Europe, but would merely waste time and tie up forces needed for the decisive blow in the west.

By April 1942, General Dwight Eisenhower, then head of the U.S. army's war plans division, had planned a buildup in Britain and an invasion of France ("Operation Roundup") by forty-eight Allied divisions in April 1943. No other action against the European Axis would be taken before then. The plan assumed that the Japanese would be held in the Pacific and that the Red army would engage most of the German army. Eisenhower also drew up an alternative emergency plan, "Sledgehammer," for a small landing in France in 1942 to divert German forces if the Soviets seemed to be on the verge of defeat, or to exploit the less likely event of a German collapse. Omar Bradley observed that this operation might better have been called "Tackhammer."

The British quickly agreed to the plan. Churchill wanted to land in France in 1943 too; and he did not want to do anything that might make the Americans lose their resolve to beat Germany first. But General Alan Brooke, the Chief of the Imperial General Staff, did not really believe in the possibility of an invasion in 1943. Other British leaders were not so pessimistic on this point, but none had any use for "Sledgehammer." They rightly deemed it a suicidal operation that would not aid the Soviets. At bottom, also, they were more favorable than the Americans to an offensive in the Mediterranean, not as a substitute for a landing in France—for they agreed with the American arguments there—but as a preliminary and subsidiary operation that would pave the way for it.

The Soviets demanded a "second front" in Western Europe in 1942. And by May 1942, both Roosevelt and Churchill felt that they could not wait until 1943 to launch an operation against the European Axis. In June, the British made it clear that they opposed "Sledgehammer." Churchill began trying to resell the Americans a North African invasion. He was sure it need not prevent a landing in France in 1943, and Roosevelt agreed. At first, Churchill had trouble getting his own military in line. They wanted to postpone a final decision on North Africa, for it would tie up vital naval forces and divert reinforcements from the Middle East. The U.S. Army and Secretary of War Henry Stimson strongly opposed the North African plan, and Churchill could not obtain a direct American agreement to it at a conference in Washington. Roosevelt may well have privately decided in his favor as early as June, but he wished to avoid a quarrel with Stimson and the army. In July, the president sent the military leaders to London with orders to agree on some operation against the European enemy in 1942. This forced the American military leaders to advocate "Sledgehammer," which they did not really believe in themselves, in the hope that they could maintain the strategic emphasis on Western Europe. (Eisenhower himself estimated "Sledgehammer's" chance of success as just "one in five.") The British flatly rejected "Sledgehammer." The Americans finally, reluctantly, agreed to invade North Africa, since they deemed it better than the only remaining alternatives—invading northern Norway or directly reinforcing the Middle East.[1]

In this strange, roundabout way, the Western powers made their greatest strategic decision of the war. The North African invasion resulted in a continuing offensive in the Mediterranean area and postponed an attempt to invade Western Europe from 1943 to 1944. A successful invasion of France in 1943 probably would have meant a much earlier defeat of Germany, for once the Allied armies were established ashore, France was a far better place to fight in than southern Europe. Therefore, some have questioned the wisdom of the decision.[2] But, as Eisenhower had begun to fear by the summer of 1942, there was an excellent chance that "Roundup" would not have been launched in 1943, whether or not the Allies invaded North Africa. The plan, he realized, had been premised on the British being stronger than they really were. The U-boat menace, not fully mastered until May 1943, probably would have prevented an adequate buildup in Britain. Enough landing craft—the numbers needed were underestimated in 1942—could not have been built until well into 1943. Training their crews would have taken still more time. Unfortunately, landing craft production could not have been easily speeded up, for it was directly competitive with that of vitally needed antisubmarine vessels. Worst of all, perhaps, carrying out the "Roundup" plan would have meant launching American troops on the toughest of all operations, a landing on a defended coast, without any combat experience against the German army. As we shall see, the history of the North African campaign does not inspire much confidence in the outcome of such an encounter. The U.S. army was not a well-functioning machine in 1942–43. The invasion of Normandy in June 1944 occurred when the Allied superiority of strength was far greater and the German position far weaker than in 1943. The Mediterranean campaigns were to contribute greatly to that weakening.[3]

THE NORTH AFRICAN PLAN

Planning "Torch," as the invasion of North Africa was code-named, proved as contentious as the decision to launch it. The Americans thought that their troops, under their command, would be better received by the French than the British, who had fought Vichy forces at Oran, Dakar, Syria, and Madagascar. The British doubted that but agreed to an American commander. Eisenhower, originally "Torch's" bitter opponent, got the post.

Taking North Africa with minimal French resistance, running it after it was captured, and turning it into an effective base all prevented complex problems. The region was a huge, underdeveloped area with poor communications. The distance from the Atlantic Coast to Tunisia was about that between London and Moscow, traversed by a single rickety railroad line which, in some places, had narrow-gauge offshoots. Only four airfields had hard-surface runways in Morocco and Algeria—Port Lyautey in Morocco, and Tafaraoui, Maison Blanche, and Bone in Algeria. Most of the area was barren desert and semi-desert; most of the population inhabited a comparatively narrow strip squeezed between the Atlas range and the sea.

Politically, Morocco (conquered by France only in the early twentieth century) and Tunisia were "protectorates" rather than colonies in the strict sense. The Sultan of Morocco, unlike the native rulers in most protectorates, retained some real power, and relations between the Moroccans and the French were delicate. Algeria, in theory, was legally part of France, and not a colony, and it had a large minority of French settlers. Relations between the French, Moslems, and Jews were venomous. Sorting out these issues would take two bloody decades after World War II, and the British and Americans did not intend to try to do so. They aimed to bring North Africa under the control of friendly Frenchmen—but which French proved to be a problem. The United States had maintained relations with Vichy, and its consular officials ran an intelligence network which contacted pro-Allied officers (none higher than divisional commanders) and underground groups in North Africa. The officers, at least, while eager for an Allied landing, were hostile to General de Gaulle's Free French. So the Americans, who rather disliked de Gaulle anyway, insisted on excluding the Free French from a role in the invasion. Since they and the British feared that there was a spy or leak somewhere in de Gaulle's organization, he was not told of the plan. (He learned of it anyway.) As a substitute, the Americans decided to bring in Henri Giraud, a staunchly anti-German general who had escaped from a prisoner-of-war camp. They expected the French to readily shift their allegiance to Giraud once the Allies appeared in force. That idea proved a bit overoptimistic.

WHERE TO LAND

Nevertheless, military planning for the invasion had to assume a worst case in which the French might strongly resist. Planning was difficult. Not only was there a dearth of experience and, even more, encouraging experience in large-scale amphibious landings, but the operation had to be planned and mounted hastily. Worsening weather would make it impossible after November, and it was uncertain what forces would be available. Where to land was a major controversy, and the decisions made about this determined the nature of the resulting campaign. The Allies wanted to take all of North Africa quickly and not have it be a prolonged campaign. As we shall see, it was fortunate in many ways that their plans misfired, but it is instructive to see why.

According to the directive the Combined Chiefs of Staff belatedly gave Eisenhower on August 14, the aim of Torch was to gain control of all of French North Africa. Its ultimate objective was to attack the rear of the Axis forces in the Western Desert and the "intensification of air and sea forces against the Axis on the European continent." Success hinged on quickly taking major ports and the airfields near them, and the Allies would have to land near, if not in, those ports. And it was desirable, at least, to promptly secure Tunisia, which Axis forces could easily enter from Italy and Libya.

The Allies expected the Germans to rush forces to Tunisia, although intelligence underestimated the strength and speed of their buildup. The most optimistic faction, the Joint Intelligence Subcommittee of the British Chiefs of Staff, even thought it unlikely that any Italian forces would be sent to Tunisia, or that the Germans would react to an invasion of North Africa by occupying Vichy France. They also thought (again wrongly) that the Germans would not base any planes other than fighters in Tunisia. Others, however, believed that the enemy would react strongly. Even the most pessimistic estimates held that no more than 14,000 lightly armed enemy troops could reach Tunisia by air by the end of the second week, and seaborne troops would only start arriving by then. A full panzer division could not be ready to fight before four weeks had passed. In fact, the Germans and Italians considerably exceeded all of these estimates. Italian air and ground forces arrived promptly, seaborne troops coming within four days of the Allied landings. The Germans quickly based bombers as well as fighters in Tunisia, and while only 10,000 German troops were flown in in the first two weeks, they brought in heavy equipment as well. A full panzer division was ready within three weeks.[4]

Because the major Tunisian ports, Tunis and Bizerta, were near Axis bases, and the Allied invasion force would have only limited carrier-based air support, landing in Tunisia would be very dangerous. Admiral Andrew Cunningham, now the naval commander for Torch, argued that the enemy would mistake an invasion force heading for Bizerta for a Malta convoy—but what had happened to many Malta convoys made that argument for an attack on Bizerta a two-edged sword. Bizerta was heavily protected by coastal defenses which, later events showed, probably would have been manned with great determination—against the Allies. Admiral Lumley Lyster, who commanded the British aircraft carriers in Torch, was a strong proponent of doing everything possible to beat the Axis into Tunisia. He suggested readying a force of 5,000 troops on Malta and rushing them into Tunis in stripped-down bombers at the first possible moment after the Allies got ashore in Algeria. But his farsighted idea was not pursued.[5] In fact, as planning proceeded, the final objective in Tunisia tended to recede from view.

Timing remained a major issue. The British wanted a target date of October 7. But the U.S. navy insisted on November 7; it needed more time to gather shipping—which required conversions to some ships—and complete training, while the army also wanted more time for armored units still in the United States to absorb the new Sherman tanks.

With a landing in Tunisia ruled out, four possible targets remained. The small port of Bone, in eastern Algeria, had a valuable airfield and would be a useful starting point for a march on Tunis, but it was not suited for a major landing. Algiers, the capital of Algeria, was the center of French power in North Africa and a logical point of attack. Oran, farther west, had to be taken so short-ranged planes could be staged from Gibraltar to fields farther east.

While more fearful of Spain than the British, the Americans were more optimistic about French reactions. The British, in turn, seem to have been more conscious of the desirability of an early move on Tunisia, hence a landing at Bone. Washington, more than the British (or Eisenhower), wanted a major landing in Morocco. The Americans, more than the British, feared the Franco regime would agree to German demands to close the Straits of Gibraltar and let German forces cross Spain, trapping the Allied forces in the Mediterranean. (That, in fact, would have been the logical Axis counterstroke to Torch had the Germans had the strength for such a move.)

The Americans held that a landing in Morocco would deter the Spanish from joining the Axis; if they did so anyway, Casablanca and the railroad running east to and along the Mediterranean coast would be a lifeline for the forces in Algeria. The U.S. navy also wanted Casablanca as a base for antisubmarine operations at an early date. A Moroccan landing would be carried out by a force commanded by Eisenhower's old friend, the irascible but very able George Patton; it would sail directly from the United States, while the attacks inside the Mediterranean would be mounted from Britain.

Eisenhower and many of the British were not too enthusiastic about the Moroccan operation. Although essentially designed as a safety measure, it was actually the riskiest part of the whole invasion. Casablanca was far too strongly defended to be directly attacked, while a long ocean swell and a terrific surf prevented a landing on the open coast four days out of five. The weather problem alone would have made Eisenhower dislike the Moroccan operation, while on strategic grounds he and most of the British preferred to concentrate all available forces within the Mediterranean, where the weather could be depended on. They counted on overwhelming the French and making possible an early advance east. If the French in Morocco held out, a force would be sent back down the railroad from Oran to take Casablanca. But the first draft plan for Torch, submitted in early August, followed Washington's wishes. It set a date of November 5 for simultaneous landings at Casablanca, Oran, Algiers, and Bone. Only a single regimental combat team, or the British equivalent, would land at Bone. But the Combined Chiefs of Staff concluded that the plan spread Eisenhower's forces too thin; the Allies just were not strong enough. The planners then produced a Mediterranean-only plan, submitted on August 21. Patton's U.S.-based force would land at Oran on October 15, freeing British-based forces for landings at Algiers and Bone. But Washington insisted on a Moroccan landing, even at the cost of dropping all landings east of Oran. That would have entailed a major, almost certainly disastrous, delay in clearing North Africa and subsequent Mediterranean offensives.

The British were not united on the issue; Admiral Cunningham and General Brooke believed that the Moroccan landing was a necessary precaution. With vital time being lost, a compromise was hastily arranged. Eisenhower and the British dropped hopes for an early invasion and a landing at Bone and accepted the Moroccan move, while the U.S. navy agreed to supply additional forces for Torch. On September 5, the final plan—actually a cut-down version of the first plan—was accepted. In early November, mixed British and U.S. forces, with the Americans in the lead to placate the French, would land at Oran and Algiers. Patton's all-American force, the largest single contingent, would, weather permitting, land simultaneously at three points on the Moroccan coast, then advance overland to Casablanca. Should the surf be too high, Patton's force would wait at sea for better conditions. If that did not seem promising, it would enter the Mediterranean and instead land on the Mediterranean coast of Morocco, then move southwest on Casablanca.

In a late addition to the plan, the Oran landing would be supported by a small but daring paratroop drop. The U.S. 509th Parachute Infantry Battalion would fly all the way from Britain to seize airfields at Oran. Air Marshal Welsh, the British air commander for Torch, disliked this plan. He wanted to send all of the Allied airborne units by sea to conserve them for later operations against Bone and Tunisia. In other respects, too, the planners concentrated on getting ashore, not the ultimate objective of getting Tunisia. The need to ensure the first wave against a tough fight with the French, and the dispersal of the available forces, meant that the really mobile forces needed for an advance on Tunisia would not get ashore until some days had passed and the second reinforcement convoys had arrived.[6]

It was still officially estimated that the Allies might overrun northern Tunisia by mid-December, the rest of Tunisia by mid-January 1943, and western Libya by mid-March, although it was foreseen that the Eighth Army might easily take the last area first. But the race to Tunis would be run on a very narrow margin. Eisenhower's objective was finally revised in recognition of this; the last draft of the Torch plan limited the objective to securing Morocco and Algeria "with a view to the earliest possible occupation of Tunisia" and forming a striking force in French Morocco to take control of the Straits if that became necessary. Eisenhower, more aware than most of the importance of reaching Tunis quickly, did not really expect to win the race. At one point, he even wrote that "all calculations were against capturing Tunisia either initially or eventually."[7]

The limited time available for planning Torch, much of it used to settle on basic strategy, and the overriding focus on the problems of overcoming the French and guarding the rear against an Axis attack via Spain, had distracted the planners from the problem of getting to Tunis—and still more of what to do if the Allies did *not* take Tunis quickly. Thus there were several gaps and inadequacies in the Torch plan, especially in air and naval matters. Although the North African invasion was the first operation disclosed in advance to Bletchley Park, which duly made an effort to rebreak the key used by the Luftwaffe force based on Sicily, signal intelligence arrangements were poor. No air units were assigned to naval reconnaissance or strike tasks, which would be needed to intercept Axis reinforcements heading for Tunisia. The Malta-based forces were not integrated into the Torch plan. Naval plans called for reforming a surface ship force at Malta, but nothing was actually done to follow through on this. The plan envisaged establishing a "strategic bombing force" in Africa to attack Spain, or other targets in Europe, not to attack enemy efforts to reinforce or supply a bridgehead in Tunisia.[8] There was not even a unified air command for the North African invasion.

PLANS AND PREPARATIONS FOR THE NORTHWEST AFRICAN AIR WAR

The air plan for Torch was finished on September 20. It was both peculiar and unworkable. The Allies tried to maintain two separate national air commands, with different tasks and operating in separate areas; there would be no overall air commander under Eisenhower. The RAF would supply the Eastern Air Command under Air Marshal Welsh, which was to support the Eastern Task Force, assaulting Algiers and the movement east. Welsh also was to arrange any cooperation necessary with Malta-based air forces. The Western Air Command, also known as the U.S. Twelfth Air Force, commanded by General James Doolittle, was to support the Oran and Moroccan operations. (The boundary between the two commands ran 100 miles west of Algiers.) Doolittle's command would then guard the Allied rear against attack from Spain, depending on heavy bombers to be based at the Oran airfields. The plans vaguely envisaged moving the B-17s east for operations against Italy after Tunisia was cleared. Within seven weeks of the landings in North Africa, the Western Air Command was to complete a buildup to a strength of 1,244 planes (282 in reserve).

The Eastern Air Command (EAC) was belatedly formed from the RAF's 333 Group on November 1—just a week before the invasion. Its staff was hastily assembled, and it had a hodgepodge of units not fully trained. (Neither were Doolittle's.) The EAC consisted overwhelmingly of short-ranged fighters, with forty-three reconnaissance planes and less than one hundred bombers. Most of its aircraft were already obsolescent; it was assigned seven squadrons of Spitfire Vs, three squadrons of Hurricane II fighter-bombers, four squadrons of Bisley light bombers, two Beaufighter night-fighter squadrons, and one photo-reconnaissance Spitfire squadron.

The Spitfire, in general, was the best short-range interceptor of World War II. Its basic design was better than that of the German fighters, especially the Messerschmitt 109. It was easier to fly and had better cockpit visibility; its broader landing gear made it less susceptible to bad landings than the Me-109, and the placement of its fuel tanks was safer for the pilot in the event of a crash. It also was much easier to arm, and the basic airframe had more "stretch." The ultimate models of the Spitfire outperformed the last versions of the Me-109. But in 1941–42, the Germans had temporarily overtaken the British in the race to improve fighter performance. The Spitfire V was inferior to both current German fighters, the Focke-Wulf 190A and the Messerschmitt 109G, in almost all characteristics except turning radius. By the summer of 1942, the British were replacing the Spitfire V with the newer Mark IX, but the latter were still reserved for home defense.[9]

The EAC would concentrate mainly on winning air superiority over the battlefield and directly supporting the ground forces. It would have relatively little to do with the struggle to cut the enemy's supply lines to Tunisia, unlike the Twelfth Air Force.

AN AMERICAN AIR FORCE FOR TORCH

The Army Air Force's Chief of Staff, Henry H. Arnold, had decided by August 6 that a separate air force would be formed for Torch under the command of General Doolittle. General Marshall concurred. Eisenhower was not too happy with the choice; he would have preferred General Ira Eaker, who commanded the VIIIth Bomber Command, or General Walter Frank. At first he thought Doolittle lacked command experience (indeed Doolittle thought so too) and seems to have regarded Doolittle, who had been a famous air racer, as just a daring stunt flyer, hastily promoted after leading the famous raid on Japan in April 1942. But Eisenhower soon learned that he was wrong. Doolittle became one of his most trusted subordinates, and Eisenhower insisted on taking Doolittle with him when he returned to Britain to take command of the invasion of France. Far from being a reckless barnstormer, Doolittle was a coolly calculating engineer. He had been interested in air racing only as a way to advance aviation, a cause to which he contributed enormously. Doolittle had a major role in the development of instrument flying (critical to the development of commercial airlines and the ability to fly the Atlantic) and had promoted the development of 100-octane gasoline (a major, although often ignored, contribution to Allied air superiority over the Axis, who never achieved high-octane fuels). Unlike many in high commands, Doolittle was securely in control of his ego. It was characteristic of the man that he had expected to be court-martialed after the "Doolittle raid," since, through no fault of his own, none of his planes had reached bases in China and he was dumbfounded to learn that it had made him a national hero.

On August 13, Eisenhower decided that the American air force for Torch had to be formed around a nucleus drawn from the Eighth Air Force, which was conducting the strategic bombing campaign against Germany.[10] The formation of the new Twelfth Air Force had a big impact on the Eighth. The Twelfth was initially allotted two heavy bomber groups, four fighter groups, one transport ("troop carrier") group, three medium bomber groups, one light group of light bombers, and an additional light bomber squadron. All but the light and medium bomb groups would come from the Eighth. The Eighth would lose its 97th and 301st Heavy Bomb Groups, flying Boeing B-17 Flying Fortresses, a substantial part of its still small heavy bomber force. All four of its existing fighter groups—the 1st and 14th Fighter Groups (the latter had left a squadron behind in Iceland), which flew Lockheed P-38 Lightnings, and the 31st and 52nd Fighter Groups, flying "reverse lend lease" Spitfire Vs—would go to the Twelfth. Only the transfer of three "Eagle Squadrons," Royal Air Force and Royal Canadian Air Force units composed of American volunteers, to the Eighth Air Force, where they would become the 4th Fighter Group, ensured that it would have some fighters. The Eighth would also lose the 15th Bomb Squadron (Light) flying Douglas DB-7 Bostons (an export version of the A-20 light bomber), which it had been planning to convert to a night-fighter unit.

THE EIGHTH AIR FORCE

The Eighth Air Force itself had originally been formed in January to provide the air element for the invasion of North Africa that was then being planned. After the first North African plan was dropped, the Eighth was reassigned to waging the strategic bombing offensive from Britain. The Eighth had problems that seriously affected the units it contributed to the Twelfth, problems that affected the newer units that joined the Twelfth Air Force later even more seriously.

Just getting the Eighth to Britain had involved serious risks and costs. Advance parties from a few units had sailed as early as April and May 1942. The main body of the Eighth's ground echelon had crossed the Atlantic aboard the *Queen Elizabeth* in June; it was one of the "monster" converted liners packed with troops that sailed without escort, depending on speed to escape the U-boats. The chance of a U-boat being in the right position at the right time to hit a "monster" was small, but a bit of bad luck would have killed thousands of men, set back the strategic air war by a year, and would at least have seriously harmed the North African operation. The Eighth's air echelon—which included a few mechanics which the bombers carried in addition to the regular aircrews—began moving in late June. Some units had been delayed by a temporary diversion to the West Coast, while the outcome of the battle of Midway was still undecided.

Flying the North Atlantic with the equipment and personnel available in 1942 was no joke; few had done it since Lindbergh. Commercial airline service, by huge flying boats that crossed well to the south, with a refueling stop at the Azores, had started only in 1939. Since 1940, the British, using well-trained crews flying in small numbers at a time had ferried long-range planes from American factories over a northern route from Montreal via Gander Lake in Newfoundland to Scotland. The Eighth pioneered mass movements, including P-38 fighters, and most of its pilots and navigators had never been out of sight of land. It made the first large-scale use of a newer ferry route, with more stops, which ran farther north. Departing from Presque Isle in Maine, the Eighth's planes refueled at Goose Bay, Labrador, a new installation with better weather than Gander, and closer to the direct line of flight to the west coast of Greenland. There the Americans stopped at one of two new airfields, "Bluie West One" (Narsassuak) or "Bluie West Eight" (Sondre Stromfjord). They then flew on to Iceland, and from there to Prestwick in Scotland. The route could be slow, tricky, and dangerous; even in 1944, bombers sometimes took up to three weeks to finish the trip. The Eighth lost five B-17s and seven P-38s of the first 180 planes to make the flight; six of the fighters and two Fortresses were forced down on the Greenland icecap. All of the men were saved, but the authorities seem to have thought that the fighter pilots were badly shaken; they were sent back to the States instead of rejoining their units in Britain. The losses were actually less than had been anticipated, but it was fortunate that the AAF dropped plans to fly the single-engined P-39s to Britain. Wisely, it shipped them by sea.

The Eighth's units, like most AAF units sent overseas, until the latter half of 1943, were inadequately trained. The men of the 97th Bomb Group recalled their training as being haphazard and poorly directed. There were just not enough instructors, or B-17s, or firing ranges, or .50- caliber machine guns. When the Eighth's bombers reached Britain, its pilots had little experience in flying on oxygen or formation flying; bombardiere, gunners, and radio operators were poorly trained. Many gunners had hardly fired their weapons, much less practiced against moving targets. The British helped with gunnery training, but the Eighth still suffered from lack of flying time and equipment, and even ammunition.

The British also helped to train intelligence officers and photographic interpreters. The Eighth had fortunately established a close, friendly relationship with the RAF, despite differences, which were not small, between the two air forces' concepts of how to wage the war. The Eighth depended heavily on the British for essential maintenance facilities, equipment, and supplies until well into 1943. The British readily supplied the 31st and 52nd Fighter Groups with Spitfire Vs, replacing their P-39s, a type useless in Western European conditions. The British provided radar, and most of the Eighth's radios. The British replaced the inferior American high-frequency radios with VHF gear and supplied ammunition, bombs, lubricating oils, vehicles, tools, spare parts, and flying clothing.[11]

FORMING THE TWELFTH AIR FORCE

Even as the British helped the Eighth Air Force find its feet, the Eighth had a major commitment—forming the Twelfth. In addition to losing complete units, the Eighth would transfer nearly 30,000 men and give up half of its supplies to the Twelfth. Half of the Eighth's maintenance work, up to early 1943, was for Twelfth Air Force units. The headquarters of the new XII Bomber Command was formed using personnel from the VIII Bomber Command.

Other headquarters units—XII Fighter Command and XII Air Service Command—were formed from units that had been in training for the Ninth Air Force in the Middle East. The critical signals and signals engineering units were scraped together partly by diverting units from the Pacific, and partly by using only semi-trained men.

The Twelfth was assigned several units still in the States: the 47th Light Bomb Group, flying A-20s, the 310th Medium Bomb Group, flying North American B-25 Mitchells, and the 17th and 319th Medium Bomb Groups, flying Martin B-26 Marauders. Yet more units—another B-26 group, the 320th, two more troop carrier groups, the 3rd Photoreconnaissance Group, the 82nd Fighter Group (flying P-38s), the 81st Fighter Group, flying Bell P-39 Airacobras, the 68th Observation Group, flying a mixture of A-20s and P-39s—were soon promised to the Twelfth. These units, or parts of them, would go to Britain and then to Africa. The 33rd Fighter Group, with Curtiss P-40F Kittyhawks, originally intended for the Middle East, was assigned to the Moroccan operation; its planes would be launched from an escort carrier once Port Lyautey was in American hands. On October 1, the Eighth activated a completely new fighter group, the 350th, equipped with P-39s taken from lend-lease shipments to the Soviets. That sparked a diplomatic incident. Getting the Airacobras ready and forming the new group was a big burden on the hard-pressed Eighth. Apart from the 350th Fighter Group, many of these units were even greener than those being transferred from the Eighth; the readiness of the light and medium bomber units, in particular, had been overestimated. In January 1943, after it had gone into action, the 47th Bomb Group was bluntly rated as untrained and ineffective. The 17th Bomb Group, which had broken in the B-25 for the AAF and provided the crews for the Doolittle raid, had, in a rather perplexing decision, been converted to B-26s. It had spun off cadres for the 319th and 320th Groups, which were only formed in late June 1942. Flying to Britain was increasingly tough in the worsening fall weather. The 310th, 47th, and 319th Groups flew the northern ferry route, but the last two groups had an especially bad time. The 47th Group lost one of its fifty-eight A-20s; the 319th lost three B-26s (one plane, after leaving Iceland, strayed off course and crash-landed in the enemy-occupied Netherlands), while seventeen others fell out en route, stuck at intermediate bases. The perilous northern route was closed to all but four-engined planes on December 11, and to them a week later, which proved a bit late for one B-26 crew. On December 10, Lieutenant Grover Hodge of the 319th Group, after being held up at Bluie West 1 for weeks, tried to return to North America. His plane crashed in the Labrador wilderness. On December 23, three men tried to get out in a rubber boat. They were never seen again. Eskimos found the bodies of the other four in March 1943; they had apparently starved to death the month before. The difficulties led the AAF to ship the 82nd Fighter Group's P-38s to Britain by sea and hold back the B-26s of the 17th and 320th Groups until North African bases were available; then they would go by the southern ferry route.

The ground echelons of several groups went to Britain by ship in September and October. Not all of the perils were in the air. The men of several groups witnessed a horrible accident when their ship, *Queen Mary*, ran down the British cruiser *Curacao* off Ireland. The cruiser sank, with most of her crew.

Doolittle's air force, despite superhuman efforts, was far from ready when Torch started on November 8. The bomber units it inherited from the Eighth had had a fair amount of combat experience, and the 1st, 14th, and 31st Fighter Groups a bit less, but in general it was an inexperienced force. As late as December 21, Doolittle estimated that at least three-fourths of his men were untrained or only partly trained. And for weeks, even months, elements of some of his groups, some of which were badly understrength, were scattered on three different continents.[12]

These things, lack of transport, the poor bases available in North Africa, a poorly designed command structure, and the attempt to maintain inappropriate, geographically separate national forces, meant that the Twelfth Air Force, like the Eastern Air Command, would reach its assigned strength slowly, and that strength would be brought to bear even more slowly. And the Twelfth's equipment suffered from some serious limitations. Some of its aircraft were excellent, some just plain bad. Some were suited for air defense or for securing air superiority over the battle area, but not much else.

AIRCRAFT OF THE TWELFTH AIR FORCE

"Airplanes alone do not an air force make," but it is obvious that the men of the Twelfth Air Force depended on the planes they flew.

The most important offensive weapon of the Twelfth, and of the AAF as a whole, was the B-17F Flying Fortress, which equipped the 97th and 301st Bomb Groups, and the 99th and 2nd Bomb Groups, which joined the Twelfth in 1943. The B-17F could haul 4,000 to 6,000 pounds of bombs to targets 600–700 miles away, usually operating at heights of 20,000 to 28,000 feet. The B-17F was merely the latest development of an aircraft that had first flown in 1935, and it had introduced many new features to aviation— electrical operation of landing gear, flaps and bomb-bay doors, "control tabs" that used the air flow to help move the plane's control surfaces, and heating and insulation.

The original versions of the Fortress lacked powered gun turrets or tail guns (although the streamlined blisters that served as gun positions were a major advance in the 1930s), and the British attempt to use or misuse them in combat in 1941 did not prove very encouraging. But that experience contributed to a complete redesign of the Fortress, the B-17E, with a larger tail, tail guns, powered top and belly turrets, improved fields of fire for other gun positions, and self-sealing fuel tanks. The new version of the Fortress— really a new plane—was an engineering feat. It was just as fast, on the same engines, despite being heavier and less streamlined, as the older models, and it was more stable.

The B-17F, used in the North African campaign, in production from April 1942, looked much like the E externally but incorporated hundreds of major changes. The most important were broader, "paddle-blade" propellers, self-sealing oil tanks, and additional wing fuel tanks ("Tokyo tanks"), as well as additional electrical power sources, stronger landing gear, better gun mounts, and improved oxygen and communications systems. The Tokyo tanks, however, proved the B-17s most vulnerable point; gasoline fumes gathered there and could explode if the tanks were hit. A satisfactory venting system for the Tokyo tanks, to reduce the danger of explosions, was developed only late in the war.

The B-17F's other major weakness was its lack of firepower in the nose— the first Fs to come off of the production line were even worse in that respect than the B-17E, whose inadequacy the Germans and Japanese had soon discovered. Some later variants of the F added "cheek positions" for .50-caliber guns on either side of the nose; field modifications in England and Africa usually added at least a pair of .50s, and sometimes up to four or five guns (in bombers lacking "cheek" guns) that fired through mounts in the Plexiglas nose itself, manned by the bombardier and navigator who normally rode there. This was still not enough; fortunately, head-on attacks, although the most effective, were also difficult, and many enemy pilots were reluctant to engage in them.

The rest of the plane sported pairs of .50s mounted in the top and belly turrets, another pair in the tail. A "flexible" single .50 in the radio compartment fired upward with a limited field of fire to supplement the protection the top turret gave against attacks from above. Two more single guns fired from open hatches in the waist. B-17 crews normally consisted of ten men: pilot, co-pilot, bombardier, navigator, flight engineer (who doubled as top turret gunner), who manned the forward section, separated by the bomb bay and a catwalk from the aft section, which contained the radio operator, and four full-time gunners, who manned the waist, tail, and belly positions. The belly turret gunner was quite uncomfortable; he had to squat for hours in an awkward position without his parachute. The tail gunner worked on his knees. Although the Flying Fortress was not the "self-defending bomber" the AAF sought, it was nevertheless formidable, especially when flown in the right formation. German and Japanese pilots regarded attacking B-17s as an extremely dangerous endeavor, quite unlike the way fighter pilots normally viewed attacking bombers. And the B-17 was rugged; the Germans and Japanese calculated that an average of twenty to twenty-five hits by 20 mm shells was necessary to down a Fortress. Many B-17s survived much worse than that.

The B-17, like other American planes of World War II, owed much of its success to two other items. One was the excellent Norden bombsight; the other was the Browning .50-caliber machine gun, a reliable weapon with a high rate of fire, much better than the large-caliber machine guns of other powers. Although the .50-caliber bullet lacked the destructive impact of the bigger 20 mm cannon shells favored by most other air forces, the .50 outranged the cannon and was more reliable.

Some Eighth Air Force units, like the Ninth Air Force, used the AAF's other, newer, heavy bomber, the Consolidated B-24 Liberator, an ugly, slab-sided, twin-tailed aircraft. It was at least nominally faster than the B-17 and could reach farther with a ton more bombs. With tricycle landing gear, it was a bit easier to land, and it was more comfortable for the crew at lower heights; it usually flew at lower altitudes than the B-17. The earlier models of the B-24, used in Africa, were less well-armed than the B-17, lacking in particular, protection against attacks from below. The B-24 was less stable, harder to fly in formation, or on one engine, and more likely to catch fire when hit than the B-17. It used hydraulic systems for many functions carried out electrically on the B-17; that and its high "Davis" wing made it more vulnerable to damage. For these reasons, the B-17, in Europe, was generally given the hottest targets; and men who flew both the B-17 and the B-24 usually preferred the B-17.[13]

At the other end of the scale, the Twelfth Air Force made some use of the twin-engined Douglas A-20 light bomber, which equipped the 47th Bomb Group and the independent 15th Bomb Squadron. Light bombers were not very important in the AAF's scheme of things, and Arnold and his staff did not have a high opinion of the A-20; it was more popular, however, with the British and Soviets, and with General Kenney's Fifth Air Force in the Pacific. In Africa it served mostly as a short-range battlefield support weapon, and it had only a small role in the struggle for air superiority. It barely figured in the war against the enemy's supply lines.

The AAF's fine medium bombers, the North American B-25 Mitchell and the Martin B-26 Marauder, played a bigger role in that struggle. Medium bombers were primarily used against enemy airfields, dumps, railroad yards, troop concentrations, and ships. The B-25, built in greater numbers, became the most famous of the AAF mediums, because of the Doolittle raid. It equipped the Twelfth Air Force's 310th and 321st Bomb Groups and the Ninth's 12th and 340th Groups. Carrying a five- or six-man crew, it was a blunt-nosed, twin-tailed midwing plane. More austere, slower, noisier, and less rugged than the Marauder, it had a smaller maximum bombload. But it was easier to fly and more reliable than the B-26 and more suited for operations from short, rugged airfields. It was also better for low-level attacks; thus it was a better "ship-buster" than the Marauder.

The main defect of the early model B-25s, including the early B-25Cs used in Africa, was their poor armament. They had no tail gun, depending for rearward defense on top and belly power turrets placed far back on the fuselage. The turrets were poorly positioned and unreliable. Doolittle, preparing for the raid on Japan in early 1942, noted the B-25's defects. He thought that the lower turret was so badly designed that it would take a genius to operate it. He had two broomsticks fixed to the tails of his planes so the Japanese would think they had tail guns, and discarded the belly turret. His immediate reason for that was to save weight and space for an additional fuel tank for the long flight to China, but the Fifth Air Force, which did not face that problem, followed his example. B-25 crews in North Africa flew with the belly turret but would have preferred free guns in its place. They wanted powered guns in the tail, and found the nose gun not flexible enough; they also wanted more armor for the top turret gunner and co-pilot. Late in the campaign, the 321st Group got some late-model B-25Cs with no belly turret, but with tail and waist guns. (Later models of the B-25 moved the top turret well forward, to a position just behind the pilot.) It should be noted that the B-25Cs used in North Africa were all "glass-(actually Plexiglas) noses."

In late 1942, the Fifth Air Force, helped by North American representatives in Australia, had modified some B-25Cs, removing the bombardier and his sight and replacing the Plexiglas nose with a metal one packed with .50-caliber guns to produce a "strafer" or "solid-nose," which was very effective at low-level attacks, especially against ships. Later on, "solid-noses" were factory-built and standard kits were issued so that "glass-noses" could be converted into strafers in forward areas. But to the disappointment of the men flying missions against enemy convoys to Tunisia, strafers were not available during the North African campaign.

The B-26, which equipped the Twelfth Air Force's 17th, 319th, and 320th Bomb Groups, was a slightly larger and far more innovative plane. Carrying a six-man crew, sleek and streamlined, it looked like a jet bomber of the 1950s, somehow mistakenly given propellers, and it seemed "futuristic" in the early 1940s. Indeed, some veterans thought that it was a mistake to junk the Marauder in 1945 and believed they could easily have been modified to take jet engines. The B-26 introduced almost as many firsts as the original B-17: four-bladed propellers, power turrets, self-sealing fuel tanks, "weapon pods" of "packaged" .50-caliber guns attached to the outside of the fuselage to increase forward firepower, an all-electrical bomb release mechanism, and the large-scale use of plastics. It was strong, fast, responsive to controls, and well armed with functioning turrets and tail guns, and far better defended than the early B-25s; it also carried a heavier bombload and had a far better autopilot.

Yet the B-26 became one of the most controversial planes of the war; it was criticized by Senator Truman's committee, and its production was nearly cancelled twice. It was widely damned as a result of many crashes. An amazing collection of epithets collected around the B-26: "Martin Murderer," "Flying Coffin," "Widowmaker," "Wingless Wonder," "The Incredible Prostitute" ("its wings are so short it has no visible means of support") and the "Baltimore Whore." (Martin's home factory was in Baltimore.) Several factors gave the B-26 a bad reputation. It was, in fact, an "unforgiving" plane, harder to fly than most of its contemporaries, and it had a much higher takeoff and landing speed than anything most pilots had encountered. The AAF lacked a suitable plane to provide a transition between slow trainers and the "hot" B-26.

The early B-26s suffered several problems. Bomb-release mechanisms often failed, and its pose landing gear strut was too weak. More seriously, the engines and propellers suffered malfunctions, some due to use of poor materials; the engine problems were exacerbated by poor maintenance. The mechanics were simply not properly trained to service them—some units, in 1942, could not even obtain the proper manual—and pilots were not taught the proper procedure to handle an engine failure. The placement of critical generator switches at the entry hatch instead of the cockpit also caused some pilots to forget to set them—so they drained the batteries during take-off. That caused the electrically operated variable-pitch propellers to go flat, suddenly cutting the plane's speed. All of this led to a high accident rate; and new pilots were terrified of a plane combat veterans swore by.

Doolittle, investigating the B-26 for Arnold right after Pearl Harbor, laid all of the blame on bad training, but pressure to cancel the plane mounted. General Spaatz's investigating board in March 1942 largely concurred with Doolittle, but suggested that future models of the B-26 should get bigger wings. Pressured by the Truman Committee, Arnold again considered stopping B-26 production in October 1942; but the Fifth Air Force, the only command then using it on a large scale in combat, praised the plane and caused Arnold to drop the idea. Improvements in training and combat experience finally quieted fears about the B-26. (Its final version did get a bigger wing, with a higher "incidence"—angle to airflow—to make takeoff and landing easier.) While the B-26's ruggedness, armament, and speed saved many lives, it did have characteristics that would hamper operations in Africa. It used a lot of runway and "mushed" excessively, being slow to recover from even a shallow dive. Thus it was not well suited to low-level attacks.[14]

AMERICAN FIGHTERS

In contrast to the general excellence of U.S. bombers, American fighter planes in 1941–43 were, at best, a mixed bag. More than half of the AAF's fighters, until July 1943, were P-39s and P-40s, which the AAF's official history, probably optimistically, conceded were "approaching" obsolescence by

Pearl Harbor. P-39s equipped the Twelfth Air Force's 81st and 350th Fighter Groups and two squadrons of the 68th Observation Group; the Twelfth's 33rd and 325th Fighter Groups, and the 57th and 79th Fighter Groups of the Ninth Air Force used P-40s during the North African campaign. Both types were underpowered by General Motors Allison engines with poor high altitude performance. (Some later models of the P-40 were given Packard-built copies of the British Merlin engine, which powered the Spitfire.) Neither the P-39 nor P-40 had much range.

The Bell P-39 Airacobra was a small, sleek plane; it was an exception to the old saw that a good-looking plane flew well. It was an unusual design. The pilot entered by a door in the side, instead of opening the cockpit canopy. The engine was mounted behind the pilot and drove the propeller by a long shaft running under the cockpit, allowing a big 37 mm cannon to be mounted in the propeller hub. The P-39 was thus designed around its armament, instead of vice versa, as was customary at the time. But the slow-firing cannon proved of little use in air combat; it usually jammed after one or two shots anyway. That quirk was solved by Twelfth Air Force technicians during the North African campaign, but it made little difference to the plane's reputation. Unmaneuverable, it had a low rate of climb and a low ceiling, and its flying characteristics were downright unsafe. It was prone to go into uncontrollable tumbles and flat spins. Last, it was impossible for the pilot to get out if he had to ditch at sea. Fortunately, by late 1942, its limitations were well understood. The P-39 was not rated as a fighter plane in Africa, although it was sometimes used to cover convoys outside of enemy fighter range. It was primarily employed to attack ground targets, always with Spitfire or P-40 escort, and its high speed and heavy armament led some to praise it in this role. But it contributed nothing to the struggle for air superiority or the ability to strike the enemy's deep rear.

The Curtiss P-40 (its later models were variously named "Kittyhawks" or "Warhawks") was a more orthodox and reliable, although not an outstanding, aircraft; some who flew it in the Pacific actually liked it. A development of the older, radial-engined P-36, it was years behind the latest European fighters. Such repute as it had resulted from combat in the Pacific. Although the Zero could outclimb and outmaneuver it, the P-40 could outdive the Zero and outrun it, at least at some heights. That, its armor, self-sealing tanks, and good armament—the six .50s typical of most U.S. fighters—enabled it to deal with the Japanese, at least in defensive fighting, with the right tactics. But it was far inferior to the Me-109 and the FW-190. British pilots flying early model P-40 Tomahawks in the Western Desert learned to avoid combat with enemy fighters except when they had both superior numbers and a height advantage.

An attempt was made to give the P-40F better performance by replacing the Allison with the more powerful Merlin, but the improvement was only modest. A later Merlin-powered version, the P-40L, was drastically lightened, its armament reduced to just four guns, but that did not help much either. The AAF official history estimated that the Kittyhawk could handle the Me-109 below 12,000 feet, but that may have been overenthusiastic. The commander of the 325th Fighter Group bluntly declared that the P-40 was sixty miles an hour too slow and that its rate of climb should be doubled. Some officers bluntly described the P-40 with obscenities. In early 1943, A. J. Liebling described watching air fighting from the ground in Tunisia: "It is nearly impossible to tell Messerschmitts from P-40s when they are maneuvering in a fight, except when one plane breaks off action and leaves its opponent hopelessly behind. Then you know that the one which is distanced is a P-40."[15]

Fortunately, the AAF did have a fighter in 1942 and early 1943 capable of taking on the German fighters, at least in the conditions of the Mediterranean theater, the Lockheed P-38 Lightning, which equipped the Twelfth's 1st, 14th, and 82nd Fighter Groups. The Lightning was another unusual design. Instead of having a conventional fuselage, it housed the pilot and guns in a nacelle mounted in the wing, between twin engines housed in long booms. It used a modified version of the Allison V-1710 engines used in P-39s and most P-40s, but with turbo superchargers that gave it a reasonable performance. The Lightning was heavily armed with four .50-caliber machine guns and a 20 mm cannon mounted directly in front of the pilot. The concentration of powerful armament in the nose was more effective than the wing guns of most Allied fighters and greatly simplified gunnery for the P-38 pilots, which was a good thing since many U.S. pilots did not get much gunnery training early in the war.

The P-38's long range made it the first real escort fighter the Allies had. Unfortunately it was hard to manufacture, and production was delayed because the Army had foolishly tried to set a speed record in 1939 with the only prototype. It crashed, setting back the P-38's development by nearly two years. Until well into 1943, the Lightning was available only in small numbers. As we shall see, it was difficult to keep all of the groups equipped with P-38s going at the same time.

The P-38's long range made it vital to the North African invasion; it was the only fighter able to fly from England to Oran and escort heavy and medium bombers deep into enemy territory. Conditions in North Africa were relatively favorable to the Lightning. Most fighting took place below 20,000 feet where, surprisingly, the big twin-engined P-38 was more maneuverable than the smaller German single-engined fighters. The Germans, however, found that they could dive away from the Lightning. The P-38 suffered from compressibility in a fast dive; American pilots knew that the P-38 could become uncontrollable and might tear apart, and they were rightly afraid to follow the Germans. Dive-brakes, a partial solution to the problem, were fitted only late in the war. The compressibility problem, inadequate cockpit heating, and the faults of the Allison engine, which did not work well at 30,000 feet or more in cold, damp Northern European winters, as well as other flaws, made the P-38 unsatisfactory as a long-range escort when it was used there in 1943–44. But in the Mediterranean, it served well.[16]

CHAPTER 3

The Invasion of North Africa and the Race for Tunis

The invasion forces finally set out for Africa in October; they were to land on November 8. Eisenhower moved to a temporary headquarters at Gibraltar, where he was hampered by bad communications, and he anxiously awaited their arrival. Although Ultra indicated that the enemy was lulled, he knew, as some later historians did not, that success was hardly inevitable. His forces were not well trained, and preparations had been rushed; much depended on maintaining secrecy. The vital base at Gibraltar was jammed with 350 planes parked wingtip to wingtip, and with enormous quantities of gasoline. Although far from enemy bases, it would have been vulnerable to even a small, well-conducted preemptive air strike. French and Spanish reaction remained imponderable, as did the weather. Eisenhower later wrote that at no time during the war did he have a greater sense of relief than when he heard that the Moroccan landing had come off. While it is unlikely that Torch could have failed completely, it might easily have gone much worse than it did.

The Allied convoys reached their destinations without interference.

In the fall of 1942, the Germans thought that an attack on Dakar in West Africa was possible, while the Italians rated a Moroccan landing more likely, but both Axis powers believed that an Allied landing in the Mediterranean area was unlikely before 1943. If there was such an attack, the Germans thought it probably would take the form of a direct descent on Rommel's rear in Libya, or even an invasion of southern Europe, rather than a landing in French North Africa. The Italians held some forces and small transports originally slated for the invasion of Malta at home for a move into Tunisia if that proved necessary, but basically they too underrated the danger.

By November 4, the Axis had detected naval movements around Gibraltar, but the Germans believed them to be the preliminaries for another Malta convoy. The Italian naval high command, however, began to suspect that a landing in Algeria, or even Tunisia, was imminent. Although Admiral Weichold, the German liaison officer at "Supermarina," concurred, neither they nor Mussolini, who came to agree with them on November 7, could convince Berlin. By November 6, the Germans had come to think that an invasion would take place. But stubbornly holding to their preconceptions, they expected a landing in Libya or on the European side of the middle sea—right up to the minute the Allies came ashore in French territory.

Some aspects of Vichy French behavior remain perplexing to this day. Marshal Petain and Admiral Jean-Francois Darlan, the Commander in Chief of the Vichy armed forces, seem to have had some advance indication of the invasion of Algeria. Darlan was in Algiers, purportedly to be at the bedside of a son stricken with polio. In October he had extended a feeler of sorts to the Americans (who did not respond). But if he was thinking of joining the Allies, he proved strangely reluctant to take the plunge. Neither he nor Petain alerted the North African commands. The latter, like the Axis, spotted the convoys passing the Strait, but all were oblivious to the Western Task Force off of Morocco.[1] The enemy was thus confused to the last possible moment.

THE INVASION

When it became clear that the French in Morocco would resist, one U.S. sailor joked, "Let's pretend they're Japs!"[2] The Americans discovered that their French friends were unable to prevent resistance. The Americans had been right to think that de Gaulle had no following in North Africa; unfortunately, Giraud had none either. The French ignored him, and he made a nuisance of himself at Eisenhower's headquarters. The Americans had underestimated the stupidity of the French leaders, their loyalty to Petain, and their attachment to a twisted, pseudo-legalistic concept of authority. Their peculiar concept of honor enabled them to shoot Americans, as well the British, with a good conscience. The toughest resistance of all took place in Morocco against Patton's all-American force. Nevertheless, resistance on the whole was not very determined.

An attempt to storm Algiers' harbor with troops carried in small warships failed disastrously, but the main landings on nearby beaches, despite some confusion, went well.

A direct attack on the port also failed at Oran, and the Americans met with more resistance on the beaches. The supporting paratroop drop was a fiasco. A combination of bad weather, the failure of navigational aids, and inexperienced aircrews led to many planes being forced down in neutral or French-held areas and scattered drops. Nevertheless, the French surrendered on November 10.

In Morocco the Americans suffered heavy losses of landing craft and much confusion in the high surf. The supporting carrier force lost many planes, although most of the crews were saved. A French naval force sortied; in the resulting battle, the French fleet was largely wrecked. The Americans took their first objectives, but they still faced a major battle for Casablanca.

The fighting for Morocco was ended by an agreement with Darlan in Algiers. Giraud's failure to rally the French forced them to deal with Darlan, a disreputable arch-collaborationist, something the Allies had hoped to avoid. Pressed by General Juin, the Vichy commander in North Africa, Darlan had allowed the local cease-fire in Algiers. In difficult negotiations, Eisenhower's deputy, General Mark Clark, and Juin finally got the evasive Darlan to reluctantly agree to a general cease-fire in North Africa on November 11. At this point the North African French were "neutral." They had not yet agreed to actually join the Allies. Vichy had submitted to German demands for airfields in Tunisia and eastern Algeria to "help" the French defend North Africa, and the French command in Tunisia let German forces land there. Once more, however, Vichy found that crawling was not enough. Hitler ordered his forces to seize the unoccupied zone of France.

On November 13, Darlan finally agreed to cooperate with the Allies, who accepted him as "High Commissioner" in North Africa. The Allied leaders viewed this move as a distasteful, temporary expedient to enable them to turn their efforts on the real enemy. But the "Darlan deal" caused an explosion of rage in the democracies. To many it seemed a betrayal of what the Allies were fighting for, a sellout to a creature of the Axis. Actually Darlan's adherence to the Allied cause was the produce of relentless pressure from the Allies and the genuinely patriotic Juin, while Eisenhower had little choice if he was to move against the Axis. But the agreement involved an insult to de Gaulle, a true French hero who had every claim to Allied sympathy. Eisenhower, disgusted with Darlan and the French in general, accurately described what was going on as "making the best of a rather bad bargain." He observed that the Allies were in the odd position of invading a country to gain a friend, not to fight an enemy. The arrangement with Darlan was a continuing embarrassment; until March 1943, the Allies had to tolerate the continuation of some Vichy policies in Africa. After Darlan was murdered by a supporter of de Gaulle in December 1942, Giraud replaced him as the French leader in North Africa. It took slow and painful negotiations to unite de Gaulle's and Giraud's forces. After an unedifying struggle, de Gaulle won control of the French in exile. The Americans, whose policy up to Darlan's death had been reasonable, if not wise, unfortunately involved themselves in trying to help Giraud. That blunder further poisoned their relations with de Gaulle, relations that remained poor throughout the war. Dealing with all of this consumed much of Eisenhower's time and energy.[3]

THE AXIS INTERVENE

When they finally saw that the Allies were landing in North Africa, the Germans reacted promptly and decisively—in fact, too much so for their own good, in the long run. In the short run, however, they did foil the Allies' plans.

Belated submarine and air attacks on the invasion force did not threaten the success of Torch, but they sank the British escort carrier Avenger with almost all hands, and several transports and supply ships, seriously hampering the buildup ashore.

The Germans had considerably reinforced their air forces in the Mediterranean since September, transferring units from Norway and Russia. They and the Italians had launched another small-scale "blitz" against Malta in October. By November 8, the Germans had 940 combat planes in the Mediterranean theater (375 in the Western Desert). Some 400 of these, with about 515 Italian planes, were based on Sicily and Sardinia. In the next month, the Germans raised their total combat strength in the Mediterranean to 1,220 planes, supported by a transport fleet that was increased from 205 to 673 planes.[4] This was a heavy drain on the Luftwaffe's strength, and another heavy commitment was about to be imposed by the airlift to Stalingrad, where the German Sixth Army was surrounded in late November.

The Axis leaders automatically assumed that they must secure a bridgehead in Tunisia, if only to give Rommel's hard-pressed forces a place to retreat to, and the Vichy French gave them what they wanted.

On November 8, Vichy had readily accepted German air support, as long as the Germans flew from Italian bases. The Axis leaders hoped for an active alliance with Vichy, including the cooperation of the strong fleet based at Toulon. (The hope that Darlan could bring that fleet over to the Allies was a major factor in Allied willingness to deal with him.) The French evaded agreeing to all-out collaboration, but on November 9 they agreed to let the Germans, but not the Italians, use airfields in Tunisia and eastern Algeria. The Germans promised that they would not let in the Italians, who had long coveted Tunisia—a pledge they broke the next day. Early on November 10, Italian fighters joined the German planes and paratroops already at Tunis, and the Germans agreed to let the Italians occupy Corsica. At Munich, later that day, Hitler and the Italian Foreign Minister met Vichy Prime Minister Pierre Laval, a man who made Darlan look like Joan of Arc. Hitler made it clear that both Axis powers would send troops to Tunisia, and he insisted on a definite answer about all-out cooperation against the Allies. Laval could not give one. Petain still hoped to slide through the war as a sort of quasi-neutral and would not yet order Frenchmen to fight alongside Germans. (Even Laval must have wondered if such an order would be obeyed.) Hitler therefore ordered the occupation of Vichy France, but kept the Vichy regime in existence and maintained the fiction that the Germans were in Tunisia to protect the French from the evil Allies.

Admiral Jean-Pierre Esteva, the French Resident-General or viceroy in Tunisia, Admiral Edmond-Louis Derrien, who commanded the naval forces in Tunisia (and all forces at Bizerta), and General Georges Barre, who commanded the army's Tunis Division, obeyed Vichy's orders to let the Germans in but to resist the Allies. Later, confused by rival orders from Darlan in Algiers, they remained passive as the Axis forces poured in, to the amazement of the German troops. Gradually, a division appeared between the admirals and Barre. The general did not actively fight the Germans but gradually withdrew with most of his division toward Beja, deploying it as though he expected to fight the Axis. Vichy now pushed him to actively resist the Allies, as Esteva and, more reluctantly, Derrien agreed to do. Finally, Barre rejected a German ultimatum and formally joined the Allies. It may be doubted whether he "astutely played for time," as British official historians later wrote. They were too generous. If Barre had behaved the way he should have, he could easily have stopped the Germans from landing at all. Still, he shone, compared to men like Esteva and Derrien.[5]

On November 9, German planes had flown into Tunis' El Aouina airfield; twenty-seven Me-109s of Jagdgeschwader 53's II Gruppe and twenty-four Stuka divebombers of II Gruppe, Stukageschwader 3, took up station there as transports shuttled back and forth from Italy, delivering Luftwaffe troops, ground equipment and supplies, and light flak guns. Transport planes had been diverted from supplying Rommel to the Tunisian airlift. British reconnaissance planes flying over El Aouina on November 10 photographed no less than ninety-seven German combat planes, transports, and gliders on the ground, along with twenty Italian fighters, and spotted light tanks being unloaded from transport planes. (The huge six-engine Messerschmitt 323s, then the biggest transport planes in the world, could even carry a Mark IV medium tank.)

Colonel Harlinghausen ("Fliegerfuhrer Tunisia") commanded the bridgehead until Colonel Lederer of the army arrived. Operations in Tunisia were to be taken over by the army's XC Corps, under the energetic and able General Walter Nehring, who had led the Afrika Korps under Rommel until he was wounded. Between November 14 and 17, Berlin decided that Nehring would be given the 10th Panzer Division, the Herman Goering Panzer Division, the 334th Infantry Division, and a corps of two Italian divisions. The troop-carrier planes flew in an average of 750 men a day. Lederer took over on November 11, but Nehring soon dismissed him for wanting to hold only Bizerta. Nehring planned to hold two bridgeheads, one at Tunis and the other at Bizerta, linking them up later.[6] A small German force landed at Bizerta's Sidi Ahmed airfield. Dissident French had sunk ships in the approaches to Tunis and Bizerta, but Bizerta was cleared on November 12 as the Italians opened a sea supply route to Tunisia with a heavily escorted convoy that had left Naples. *Citta di Napoli* and *Caterina Costa*, escorted by four destroyers and a torpedo boat, anchored in Bizerta harbor, unloading 1,000 men and a cargo including tanks and 1,800 tons of supplies. The destroyers quickly left and dashed to Palermo to pick up 480 men of the 10th Bersaglieri Regiment and 165 tons of fuel, rushing them to Bizerta on November 14. Meanwhile, on November 13, two unescorted merchant ships reached Tunis.[7] These first trips were unhampered by Allied interference. Eisenhower, as yet, had little to stop them with, while the British on Malta still focused on the route to Tripoli, although Ultra and photoreconnaissance had disclosed the enemy's shift of priority to Tunisia and the extent of the buildup there.

That buildup continued. By November 15, there were eighty-one German fighters and twenty-eight Stukas based in Tunisia. By November 25, there were five fighter groups (one Italian) and a Stuka group, and a unit of short-range reconnaissance planes based at El Aouina, Sidi Ahmed, and Djedeida, near Tunis, and 15,575 German and 9,000 Italian troops were in the country. The Italians belonged to three infantry regiments, two assault gun battalions, and two antitank battalions, mostly part of the Superga Division. More Italian troops were crossing the southern frontier from Libya. The Germans had two airborne infantry regiments, a battalion of airborne engineers, three army field or "Marsch" battalions, replacement units originally destined for Rommel's forces and now renamed "Tunis field battalions," a Luftwaffe guard battalion, two reconnaissance companies (one with heavy armored cars mounting 75 mm guns), a motorcycle company, a motorized antitank company, one artillery battalion and two and a half antiaircraft battalions with twenty of the excellent 88 mm guns, extremely effective against ground targets as well as planes, and one full tank battalion and part of another. The headquarters of the 10th Panzer Division, and a detachment of the 501st Heavy Panzer Battalion, with the huge new Tiger tanks, armed with 88 mm guns, had arrived on November 23. By the end of November, the whole of the 10th Panzer Division had arrived.[8] Under Nehring's capable leadership, this motley force was able to stop the Allies and force a prolonged campaign for Tunisia.

THE RACE FOR TUNIS BEGINS

Although comparatively small forces were involved, the race for Tunis would have a powerful effect on the course of the war; it also was the first battle in which American ground forces engaged the European Axis. It is thus a battle of double interest, although strangely it has received relatively little attention from historians.

On November 9, the Eastern Task Force became the British First Army. Until 1943, this was an army in name only, consisting of a jumble of units amounting to little more than the equivalent of a reinforced infantry division and an armored division. It was commanded by General Kenneth Anderson, a stereotypically dour Scot. A respected American general, Ernest Harmon, recalled him as a "disagreeable man disliked by practically everyone."[9] All of the Americans, except Eisenhower, and many or most of the British, had a low opinion of his abilities. Even the most favorable judges conceded that he was, at best, a "good plain cook," and he never held a combat command after the African campaign. But even a genius would have found it hard to win the race for Tunis. It was a race against two things: the Axis buildup and the rainy season. The Allies knew that they had only about a month before the winter rains turned the northern Tunisian countryside into a morass. Anderson faced formidable problems of terrain and communications. His nominal army was not well equipped; it was short of transport and antiaircraft protection. It suffered from mistaken equipment allocations that might have been avoidable even in the straitened circumstances of late 1942. It is hard to understand why his armored force, the only tank units based in Britain likely to fight the Germans in the near future, still had old Valentine and Crusader tanks with two-pounder (40 mm) guns, proven inadequate in the desert six months earlier.

Eisenhower and Anderson knew that success was unlikely, but they were determined to get as far east as possible, even if Tunis was out of reach. Now, while the situation was fluid, and the forces on each side were relatively small, it was possible to seize wide stretches of difficult terrain that might cost much blood to take in 1943. And the farther east they could establish air bases, the easier it would be to dominate the sky over Tunisia and the approaches to it. That was not a minor consideration. At this point, the Germans, not the Allies, controlled the air over the battlefield and were in a better position to bring their strength to bear. As Eisenhower commented to H. H. Arnold on November 21, "My biggest worry at this moment is that the Axis reinforcements, pouring into Tunisia from Sicily and Italy, are coming faster than I can kick troops up the line to the eastward."[10]

THE TUNISIAN THEATER

The capture of Tunis and Bizerta would end the North African campaign. The two ports were fairly close together on the northeast coast, separated by the lower Medjerda river. The terrain north of the Medjerda, in front of

Bizerta, was a mass of mountains, often well forested, running right down to the sea. It was nearly ideal defensive terrain and unsuited to tanks. The coast road ran east from Algiers to Bizerta through Bougie, Bone, Tabarka, Djebel Abiod, and Mateur, and it was a rare hard-surfaced route. But it passed through many gorges, passes, bridges, and tunnels, and it was easily blocked at many points. The Medjerda valley, which carried the main inland road and rail line from Algiers to Tunis via Le Kef, ran through several plains, but in some places it was confined to gorges. The plains would turn into seas of mud in the winter, where tanks could sink up to their turrets. For an important stretch, between the vital road centers of Medjez el Bab and Tebourba, the main road and the railroad were squeezed onto a narrow shelf between the hills and the north bank of the Medjerda. Nevertheless, it was the best approach to Tunis, and the road was usable in all weather. The main Medjerda valley road ran through Tebourba to Djedeida, which had an important airfield; the main route between Tunis and Bizerta, via Mateur, ran through the place. Thus the main road gave access to both ports. At Medjez el Bab, the main road forked, sending a southern branch through Massicault direct to Tunis. Between the Medjerda valley road and the coast road, a secondary unpaved road ran from Souk el Arba, through Beja and Sidi Nsir to Mateur. In the Tine river valley, this road forked to send a link via Chouigui to join the main road at Tebourba. Farther west, a lateral, north-south paved road ran from Djebel Abiod through Beja to Medjez el Bab, linking the coast road, the secondary road, and the Medjerda valley. Well south of the Medjerda sector and the Medjez-Massicault-Tunis road, there was yet another approach to Tunis, through El Aroussa, Bou Arada, Pont du Fahs, and Oudna. But the connections to it were roundabout and unpaved, and it was awkward for a force advancing from the northwest to get onto it. It played little role in the fighting of late 1942.

South of Tunis a long chain of mountains ran southwest from the Cape Bon peninsula. It soon split in two; one range, the Western Dorsale, continued southwest into Algeria. The other range, the Eastern or Grand Dorsale, ran approximately north and south. Control of the many gaps in the mountain walls and the area between the ranges would prove critical during 1942–1943. The area just west of the Western Dorsale and the plateau between the ranges provided good airfield sites, relatively usable even in the winter, and offensive operations remained possible there even while the rains imposed a stalemate in the south. Forces here would protect Eisenhower's right flank, valuable forward air bases and, eventually, the dumps that would supply British forces coming from Libya when the latter shifted their base from east to west. An Allied thrust here could drive a wedge between the forces in northern Tunisia and Rommel's army retreating from

Libya. A hard-surfaced road ran southeast from Constantine through Youks-les-Bains, Tebessa, and Gafsa to Gabes on the coast. Around Gabes the land flattened out and became semidesert or true desert, much unlike the pleas-antly green area of the north, which resembled Italy or even England. West of Gabes, a big salt lake, the Chott Djerid, left only a narrow, easily defended bottleneck between it and the sea. Strangely, the French, planning to stop an invasion from Libya, and later on the Axis, chose to stand on a much less formidable line farther south, the Mareth Line. Its western end was open, but it ran into very difficult hills and sand dunes.

ADVANCE TO CONTACT

On November 9, with a local peace with the French patched together at Algiers, General Anderson considered plans laid earlier for a daring leap eastward—simultaneous landings at the ports of Bougie and Bone on the night of November 10–11, followed by a series of airborne drops by the few British and U.S. paratroops available, at Bone on November 11, and Bizerta and Tunis on the following two days. But uncertainty about French reaction and the strength of the Luftwaffe's attacks led Anderson to choose a more conservative course, which proved hard enough to execute.

His first move was an amphibious hop 300 miles east to Bougie, using the British 36th Infantry Brigade Group (part of the 78th Division), which had been the floating reserve for the Algiers landing. One landing ship, *Awatea*, would land RAF groundcrews, equipment, and supplies at Djidjelli airfield, east of Bougie. A small mobile column, "Hartforce," drawn from the 5th Northamptonshires of the 78th Division's 11th Brigade, would drive overland from Algiers. The convoys left Algiers on November 10, arriving off the targets the next morning. Heavy surf at Djidjelli prevented *Awatea*'s unloading there, so she joined the main force off of Bougie. Uncertain of the French reaction, the navy refused to enter the harbor and insisted on a beach landing instead. The French did not resist, but the Axis air forces struck hard. Air cover over the Allied ships was thin. The Luftwaffe had dam-aged one escort carrier and forced the British to employ the other available flattop more cautiously; they depended on land-based aircraft flying from Algiers. *Awatea* and two other landing ships carrying valuable supplies and equipment were sunk, along with an antiaircraft ship; the monitor *Roberts* was damaged. Djidjelli airfield had to be reached overland from Bougie, and RAF fighters did not fly from it until November 13.

Meanwhile, Hartforce had left Algiers on November 11; it too had been delayed by fears of French reactions. On November 12, U.S. C-47 troop-carriers dropped two companies of the British 3rd Parachute Battalion at Bone, while commandos landed from two destroyers. Again, the French did not resist. The same day, the first British "followup" convoy had landed at Algiers, delivering men and equipment to bring the two brigades of the 78th Division, already present, up to "light scale" as well as most of a paratroop brigade and "Blade Force," a task force from the British 6th Armored Division. Blade Force included a regiment of obsolete tanks, an infantry company, and armored cars, guns, and engineers. The convoy also unloaded the First Army's Advanced Headquarters, the headquarters of the Eastern Air Command, and vital rear-area units.

The main body of the 78th Division and Blade Force quickly set out from Algiers to the east. On the same day, November 15, the U.S. 509th Parachute Battalion jumped at Youks-les-Bains, just west of the Tunisian frontier, to secure an important forward airfield. Raff's men pushed southeast to Gafsa. Joining with small French units, and later reinforced by a few U.S. tanks, they began a remarkable little campaign, sparring with the small German and Italian forces that had occupied the ports of Sfax, Sousse, and Gabes and were pushing west.

On November 16, after a delay imposed by the weather, the British 1st Parachute Battalion dropped on another airfield at Souk el Arba in advance of the main overland push. Hartforce, with the 36th Brigade Group following in its wake, advanced along the coast road toward Bizerta, while inland Blade Force, reinforced by a U.S. artillery battalion, moving partly by road and partly by rail, assembled at Souk Ahras on November 17–18. Blade Force and the 11th Infantry Brigade would both be split between the Souk Ahras-Souk el Arba-Beja-Sidi Nsir-Mateur and the Medjez el Bab-Djedieda routes. Two Spitfire squadrons had moved up to Bone, though they suffered heavy losses on the ground to Luftwaffe attacks. The Germans themselves were probing westward on the trail of General Barre's Frenchmen. On November 17, the Germans met Hartforce on the coast road near Djebel Abiod; the Germans committed tanks and infantry, hoping to drive the British back to Bone, while the British brought up the 36th Brigade. Both sides suffered heavy losses. It was the first land fighting between the Axis and the Allies in Northwest Africa. On November 18, British paratroops coming from Souk el Arba ambushed and destroyed a German armored reconnaissance force near Sidi Nsir. Anderson ordered the 78th Division commander not to advance farther until his whole force was concentrated in the forward area.

The Germans' immediate concern was settling with Barre's force, now concentrated around Medjez el Bab. Vichy, now just a German puppet, told Barre to join the Germans; he ignored the order. (French collaboration with the Nazis in Tunisia was finally ended by the latter's mistrust; on December 8, the Germans ordered Derrien's forces, which were still manning coast defenses at Bizerta and Tunis, to disarm. They surrendered their equipment and a large number of ships, intact.) A 36th Brigade liaison officer established contact with Barre, who had retreated as far as he cared to. Blade Force sent its American artillery battalion to support him.

On November 19, General Nehring sent Barre an ultimatum, demanding free passage to the west. Trying to play for time, Barre ignored the ultimatum. On the morning of November 19, German troops, supported by Stukas, attacked. Supported by the American gunners and small British tank and infantry units, the poorly armed French held off the Germans for a time, but they had to abandon Medjez el Bab during the night of November 19–20. Small-scale fighting continued between Allied and Axis patrols and security detachments. Anderson planned a major attack on Tunis for November 21–22 but decided to postpone it until November 24. He already doubted his ability to take Tunis, noting that the enemy buildup had already exceeded the preinvasion estimates. He hoped to strengthen himself with more U.S. units and straighten out the supply and air situations, to some extent, during the pause. Supplying units of any sort was hard, and he lacked air support. Intelligence and communications were poor. The Allies lacked enough trucks and labor, and railroad facilities were in bad shape; the roads were already deteriorating under heavy traffic. Trains were slow and unreliable; supplies were often stolen. Every effort was made to use the forward port of Bone, but it, and the nearby airfield, remained under heavy air attack. Bone's facilities were damaged, and the enemy laid mines as well as dropping bombs and torpedoes. Anderson was impressed by the enemy's air effort. The Germans enjoyed the use of several all-weather airfields near the front line at Bizerta, Tunis, Sousse, Sfax, and Gabes.

By December 1, the Germans had ninety-five single-engined fighters, twelve tactical reconnaisance models of the Messerschmitt 109, and thirty Stukas based in Tunisia. The Allies supposedly had nearly 200 fighters and light bombers to face them, but this was not reflected in their real strength. The long-obsolete Stukas proved remarkably effective; there were too few Allied fighters to interfere with them. The Allies had only a few, poor airfields in the forward area. Bone, the nearest all-weather field, was 115 miles behind the front line. Their other bases, at Youks and Souk el Arba, were vulnerable to bad weather. All three lacked adequate dispersal space; supplying them with gasoline and ammunition, much less improving them, was difficult. The AAF and RAF had had too few vehicles to begin with, and many of those had been grabbed by the ground forces. Most Allied planes had to fly from Algiers or even more distant bases. With considerable difficulty, they managed to support a pair of Spitfire squadrons and one of Hurricanes at Bone; the latter's obsolescent planes were the only available fighters that could carry bombs. Two more Spitfire squadrons were based at

Souk el Arba, which proved costly; eleven Spitfires were lost in the air or on the ground on November 22 alone.

On November 21, the Americans sent a squadron of the 14th Fighter Group forward to Youks, but six planes were lost there the first evening. Returning from a strafing mission in support of Raff's men, they crashed trying to land after sunset. The DB-7s of the 15th Bomb Squadron joined them soon afterward. Bisley light bombers, flying from distant Blida near Algiers and later from Canrobert, gave very limited support, attacking vehicles and troop concentrations. That was just about all the direct support Anderson could expect in the battle area. The few available heavy and medium bombers and the other P-38 units, all flying from distant bases, concentrated on hitting the enemy's airfields. (Their operations will be described in more detail in the next chapter.) General Doolittle had readily junked the original plan to maintain a separate U.S. air effort in the west, but there was no adequate command arrangement for the air forces. Eisenhower gave control of tactical air power to Anderson, and he concentrated it on defense and ground support. The airmen, whose own doctrines of how to provide tactical air support were not yet clear, felt that Anderson did not understand air power and misused their planes in a futile attempt to maintain a defensive "umbrella" over the front instead of concentrating them in effective attacks. They blamed him for not allotting enough transport for the forward airfields. The air problem was related to difficulties with intelligence. A German air attack on Maison Blanche airfield at Algiers had effectively eliminated the Allies' photo-reconnaissance capability. Arrangements to pass Ultra information onto Anderson were poor; he did not receive notice even of known enemy movements. The Germans also had changed the key to one of the most productive ciphers at an awkward moment. It was not broken again until the end of November.[11]

THE ALLIED TUNIS OFFENSIVE

General Evelegh, the commander of the 78th Division, was responsible for planning the Allied offensive. He planned to drive a wedge between Tunis and Bizerta, take Tunis, and then reduce the Bizerta bridgehead. The latter area was tougher to take, but Tunis was the decisive objective; once it fell, the enemy in North Africa would be finished. Evelegh planned to reach Tunis in two stages. In the first, he would reach the line Mateur-Tebourba, then strike toward Tunis. The Allied forces were split between three widely separated columns. On the left, the 36th Brigade, reinforced with a U.S. tank company and artillery, was allotted the least important role. It would drive along the coast road to reach a road junction northwest of Mateur and a bridge over the Sedjenane river north of that. Blade Force, in the center, now reinforced with a U.S. tank battalion, would push up the Beja-Sidi Nsir-Mateur road. It would grab Mateur if a chance appeared to do so, but its main job was to turn east, cross the Tine river, and drive over the Chouigui pass and take Tebourba and the bridges over the Medjerda at El Bathan and Djedeida. On the Allied right, the 11th Brigade, also supported by U.S. tanks and artillery, would drive down the Medjerda valley. It would take Medjez el Bab and converge with Blade Force on Tebourba. Once Tebourba fell, Blade Force would go into reserve, and the 11th Brigade would take Mateur.

The plan was not a good one. It spread the Allied forces on too wide a front in positions in which they were not mutually supporting and committed units to terrain to which they were not suited. A U.S. tank company was wasted in support of the 36th Brigade, where the ground did not let it operate effectively. Blade Force lacked infantry and was committed to a worse road than the 11th Infantry Brigade. The U.S. official historian later commented that it might have been better to make only a holding attack on the coast road and shift part of the 36th Brigade to the Blade Force sector or, better yet, shift the whole effort all the way to the right, committing most of the Allied force to a direct blow down the south bank of the Medjerda river, leaving the 11th Brigade on the north bank.

The attack finally started on November 25, and the plan soon went awry. The 36th Brigade found that the enemy had pulled back a bit but hit fairly tough resistance west of Djefna on November 27. On the other flank, the 11th Brigade, starting behind schedule, had a terrible time. It was pinned down with heavy losses, and it suffered greatly from the Luftwaffe and a mistaken attack by U.S. P-38s.

Blade Force, however, had a surprising success. Part of it pushed toward Mateur; the rest plunged over the Tine. A battalion of American light tanks crossed Chouigui pass, where it was held up by Germans and Italians at a French settler's walled farm. One tank company, however, broke away and got onto the road to Tebourba and deep into the Axis rear. Bypassing the enemy at Tebourba, it overran the German air base at Djedeida. The Americans destroyed twenty Stukas there for the loss of one tank before returning to Chouigui. Nehring, not realizing that this was just a raid, was in a near panic. On the night of November 25–26, he ordered a retreat, abandoning both Medjez el Bab and Tebourba. An attempted counterattack in the Chouigui pass area, near the walled farm, led to the first tank battle between the Germans and Americans. The Germans blundered into an ambush and were beaten, although inflicting heavy losses on the U.S. light tanks. The Allies occupied Tebourba early on November 27. A counterattack in which the Germans used two of the new Tiger tanks failed to throw the Allies back, but hurt them severely.

Evelegh now switched plans and regrouped. He decided to seize Djedeida, Mateur, and Tunis in quick succession, reversing the roles allotted to the 11th Brigade and Blade Force. The 11th Brigade and the 2nd Battalion, 13th Armored Regiment, would take Djedeida and Mateur. Then Blade Force would thrust to Tunis, along with the newly arrived Combat Command B, 1st U.S. Armored Division, which was to cross the Medjerda at El Bathan and thrust south through St. Cyprien and into Tunis. Two supplementary operations were planned. The British 3rd Parachute Battalion would drop at Depienne, south of Tunis, on November 29. It would move overland to take the Oudna airfield and protect the Allied southern flank. A British commando unit, accompanied by some U.S. soldiers, would land on the northern coast on December 1, near Sidi el Moudjad, harass the enemy facing the 36th Brigade, and finally join with the 36th.

On November 28, the 36th Brigade ran into a terrible ambush between Djebel Azag ("Green Hill") and Djebel Adjred ("Bald Hill") and was stopped with heavy losses. On the same day the main attack on Djedeida by the 11th Brigade and U.S. medium tanks was stopped by heavy artillery and antitank fire from well-hidden positions and Stuka attacks. The Allies brought up reinforcements and renewed their attacks on November 29. This was the climax of the Allied drive; they were stopped again. So were renewed attacks by the 36th Brigade on November 29 and 30. Evelegh suspended the offensive, but the subsidiary operations went ahead anyway. The paratroops went in as planned, only to find that they were on a wild goose chase. The enemy was not using the Oudna airfield. They wrecked the airfield installations and "exfiltrated" through the enemy front, with heavy losses. Over half of the battalion was killed or captured. The commandos got ashore all right. For a time, the Germans, hearing exaggerated Arab reports of their numbers, were again near panic. The commandos cut the Bizerta-Mateur road but were unable to establish radio contact with the 36th Brigade. Running out of supplies, they too "exfiltrated" out, suffering considerable losses.[12]

THE GERMAN COUNTERATTACK

The Allies did not realize that a turning point was past. They were still bent on renewing the attack on Tunis, perhaps in only two or three days. But the enemy was about to seize the initiative. On November 28, Field Marshal Kesselring, angry at Nehring's decision to retreat (he also blamed Nehring for slowness in unloading supplies in Tunisia), ordered the Tunisian commander to take the offensive.

The Allies were bringing up more U.S. troops and were somewhat stronger in the air. On November 25, another P-38 squadron from the 1st Fighter Group joined the 14th Fighter Group at Youks; two days later, a U.S.

Spitfire squadron from the 52nd Fighter Group reached Bone. More B-17s, along with small forces of medium bombers from the 319th and 310th Bomb Groups, got into action, hitting enemy airfields and, for the first time, port installations. The bombers caused the Germans serious problems, but neither they nor the fighter reinforcements were enough to gain control of the air or stop the enemy's supplies. They might not have done so even if they had been better managed. Right up until February 1943, the ground commanders still regarded planes as either defensive weapons or as a sort of artillery. At their behest, the few available sorties were wasted either on trying to maintain defensive patrols over the Allied forces or attacking enemy positions within artillery range. Close air support of that sort was indeed desirable but was not the best way to use the limited air forces available. Nor were Allied airmen then well trained in hitting targets close to their own men.

Unfortunately the Allied ground units were in a vulnerable situation. Their positions were individually strong but widely scattered and formed an awkward salient. Two battalions held the nose of the salient; they were dug in near Djedeida, on successive ridges, one behind the other. A British infantry battalion, a U.S. tank battalion, and an artillery battalion were stationed in and around Tebourba village. Blade Force, minus an armored regiment, guarded the Chouigui pass and the approach from the north. Its detached tank regiment and the 11th Brigade Headquarters were at Tebourba gap, a narrow strip of flat land between high ground and the left bank of the Medjerda, four miles southwest and upstream of Tebourba village.

Nehring left the planning of the attack up to General Fischer, the commander of the 10th Panzer Division. Although hampered by poor communications and a jumble of mixed units, he ably planned an encircling operation whose main aim was to crush Blade Force. Group Koch, a mix of paratroops, regular infantry, antitank guns, and artillery, including some Italians, would launch a holding attack on the right or south bank of the Medjerda. It would try to seize the bridge at El Bathan and then reach the Tebourba gap. Group Djedeida, mostly infantry but supported by tanks, including two Tigers, would hit the nose of the Allied salient to force the British away from the Djedeida airfield. If the main attack was a complete success, it would pursue the Allied force. The main blow was to be delivered by two armored groups, Luder and Hudel, attacking from the north; Fischer accompanied the stronger Hudel group. The groups were to destroy the Allied armored force at Chouigui and attack Tebourba, or the Tebourba gap, to intercept the Allied retreat. The plan had a certain resemblance to that used, on a larger scale, in the opening stage of the more famous battle of the Kasserine Pass in February 1943. But the fall battle before Tunis arguably had more effect on the course of the war.

Blade Force, initially focusing its attention on the attack of Group Luder, fell back toward Tebourba to avoid being outflanked. Then Group Hudel tore into it. The British 17/21 Lancers tried to rush to its aid but ran into a deadly antitank ambush. British armored cars that covered the retreat, very heavy British and American artillery fire, and perhaps excessive caution prevented the Germans from overrunning the fleeing units and the Allied artillery positions. The Germans cut the main road between Tebourba and the Tebourba gap, but they were unable to enter the gap itself. The British had held off the Koch and Djedeida groups, but the situation was bad. The Germans had wrecked Blade Force and almost sliced off the Allied salient; the Allies held only a narrow strip of land, carrying a dirt track, between the enemy and the north bank of the Medjerda. Only the swift shift of one British battalion to protect the artillery at the Tebourba gap and the arrival of the American Combat Command B, prevented a disaster. A German attempt to rush the Tebourba gap during the night misfired. Anderson naturally postponed his offensive. The Germans planned to resume their attack on December 2; the Hudel and Luder groups would hit Tebourba from the west, while the Koch and Djedeida groups renewed their attacks.

Evelegh ordered Combat Command B to attack the Hudel and Luder groups, resulting in a large tank battle. The Germans, although outnumbered in tanks and antitank guns, performed better and had air superiority, while the Allies used their well-placed artillery effectively. The Allies prevented the Germans from gaining much ground but suffered heavy losses; many American tanks were destroyed. Group Koch managed to advance and force the British to leave El Bathan, although the bridge there remained covered by antitank guns. It was now clear that the Allies would not be able to resume their offensive on Tunis soon. The Germans struck again on December 3. Group Djedeida, reinforced by panzer grenadiers just off the transport planes, made the main effort as the Hudel and Luder groups tried to pinch off the Allied withdrawal. The Allies managed to prevent that, but Group Djedeida finally broke through. The two British battalions opposing it suffered very heavy losses. Abandoning their vehicles and guns, the men broke up into small groups and slipped away.

Despite this bloody nose, the Allies still expected to resume the offensive, after yet another breathing space. Eisenhower warned the Combined Chiefs of Staff that "we have gone beyond the sustainable limit of air capability in support of ground forces." The air forces lacked even minimal repair and supply facilities and could not stop enemy strafing and bombing, which Eisenhower deemed largely responsible for breaking up Allied ground advances. On December 7, he wrote to Thomas T. Handy that troops lacked mobility and supplies due to lack of vehicles and the miserable functioning of the railroad.

The air forces were not doing well. On December 4, in an incredible blunder for which the airmen blamed General Anderson, nine Bisley bombers went out in broad daylight without escort to hit an enemy forward landing ground. Me-109s shot all of them down. Only three crews survived. Air Marshal Welch warned after this that his four Bisley squadrons were short 30 planes, and in any case the Bisley was obsolete and should only be used at night in "very favorable" conditions. The next day an Allied attempt to use a forward landing ground themselves at Medjez el Bab flopped. Six Spitfires, coming into land, were jumped by Me-109s. Two went down, and the rest were badly shot up.

The Allies brought up reinforcements and once more unscrambled the British and American units. Evelegh turned over control to the newly arrived V Corps under Lt. General Gordon Allfrey. Allfrey now had the whole of the 6th Armored Division as well as the 78th Division, Combat Command B, and commando and paratroop units. Combat Command B took over the area on the right bank of the Medjerda; French units held a line farther south. Allfrey could not do much before the Germans struck again, on December 6. They planned to take Medjez el Bab after first attacking south of the Medjerda to drive Combat Command B off a line of hills dominating the Tunis-Massicault-Medjez el Bab road. Paratroops and panzer grenadiers attacked, supported by tanks and divebombers. With their line of withdrawal threatened, the Americans pulled off the important Djebel el Guessa (Hill 145) with heavy losses. The Germans got ready to hit the next important position on Djebel el Aoukaz. Two understrength American tank battalions and an armored infantry battalion, which had arrived too late to relieve Djebel el Guessa, were nevertheless committed in a counterattack. They were stopped, with heavy losses, and badly shaken V Corps headquarters was quite nervous. Allfrey still expected to launch a winter offensive, now slated for December 24, but decided to pull back to a stronger line in the meantime. He was willing to abandon Medjez el Bab, but Eisenhower, egged on by the French, fortunately insisted on holding a line farther east. Heavy rains began December 7; they should have made it clear that a winter offensive was not likely.

The planned withdrawal was to take place during two nights, starting December 10–11. It coincided with a renewed German effort to capture Medjez el Bab. The Germans struck on both sides of the Medjerda, making their main effort south of the river, and they threatened to trap Combat Command B. The Germans' attack was stopped—they found that their tanks could not deploy off the roads in the morass—but once again they inflicted heavy losses when the Americans counterattacked with outgunned light tanks. Combat Command B went ahead with the planned withdrawal. It was to cross to the left bank of the Medjerda over a bridge. But confusion led to disaster. The Americans mistakenly got the impression that the Germans had cut the planned withdrawal route, or were about to do so, so Combat Command B turned off onto a narrow dirt road to Medjez el Bab, running on the right bank of the Medjerda. There it became bogged down in mud so thick that even the tanks were helpless. A mass of equipment had to be abandoned as the men got out on foot. Combat Command B later recovered a few of its vehicles and was quickly reequipped.

The Germans, noting the deteriorating weather, dropped plans to take Medjez el Bab. The Allies, misled by a brief spell of nice weather, were more optimistic. They planned to make their main attack south of the Medjerda on the Massicault-Tunis road with the 6th Armored and 78th Divisions, the latter with the 18th Regimental Combat Team of the 1st U.S. Infantry Division attached. Combat Command B would be in reserve; other forces would threaten or make holding attacks on the Sidi Nsir and coast roads.

In a preliminary move, beginning on the night of December 22–23, the Allies planned to take Djebel el Ahmera or Longstop Hill (Hill 290), an eminence seven miles northeast of Medjez el Bab, which dominated the Medjerda valley, and drive as far as Tebourba. The 2nd Battalion Coldstream Guards was to take Longstop and a railroad station at its base, while a reinforced company advanced south of the Medjerda to take Grich el Oued village. A battalion of the 18th RCT would relieve the Guards once Longstop was taken. Meanwhile, the 5th Northamptonshires started a long roundabout march through the mountains to the north to fall on the German flank and to take the Tebourba gap. The Guards took Grich el Oued and most of Longstop but lost the railroad station to a German counterattack. There was a double foul-up. The British wrongly thought that they had taken all of Longstop. But in fact the Germans were still on Djebel el Rhar, a point separated by a ravine from the main hill; and the Americans were delayed and poorly guided during the relief. They were driven off of Longstop, and an attempt to retake the railroad station led to a small disaster. Eisenhower postponed the main offensive again as the Guards returned; the Germans also fed in reinforcements. The Allies could not recall the Northamptonshires, who continued their perilous march, which the Arabs disclosed to the Germans. On December 24, the Germans counterattacked the isolated unit, which was lucky to return to the Allied lines.

The Guards managed to take the main hill at Longstop but could not gain all of Djebel el Rhar. Then, on December 25, German tanks and infantry, moving over the low ground, enveloped Longstop from both sides. The Allies were driven out with heavy losses. Longstop would stay in Germans hands until spring. That day, Eisenhower, driving up to the front, had seen how bad the weather was. He cancelled the winter offensive.[13] It was now clear that there would be a prolonged campaign for Tunisia, lasting well into 1943. How long it would last and how many lives it would cost would depend greatly on the effectiveness of the Allied war against the Axis supply lines. The Allied failure, however, had a fortunate consequence. A prolonged Tunisian campaign would ensure that more and more Axis resources would be poured across the Mediterranean. If—or more accurately, when—those forces could no longer be sustained or withdrawn, the Allies would be handed an immense but cheap victory, after which the Axis would be hard put to defend the European shore of the Mediterranean. The failure to take Tunis in 1942 would turn out to be one of the most important small battles and one of the few fortunate Allied "defeats" of World War II.

Many reasons have been adduced for the defeat; there has been much argument about whether it was a "near thing."[14] On the whole, given French behavior and the limited Allied strength on hand, it does not seem that the Allies ever had a good chance of capturing Tunis quickly, although they might have used their forces more effectively.

Eisenhower laid the principal blame on the French failure to cooperate promptly and effectively, a general shortage of troops, the lack of adequate motor transport, coupled with the inefficiency of the railroads, and the enemy domination of the air. While the last problem was inherent in the situation, he conceded the arguments of later critics that the air command arrangements were bad; especially their criticism of the lack of an overall air commander and the poor training for Army–air cooperation. Another factor which he did not stress was the inexperience of the Allied troops and the generally greater efficiency of the Germans, who were mostly Russian-front veterans. At the tactical level, the Allies made many simple mistakes. It is noteworthy that Allied troops often suffered severe losses, even when they were successful in taking their objectives (and many of their attacks failed), while German attacks, even when they failed, consistently inflicted heavy losses on Allied units. Those things could not easily have been avoided. There were, however, a number of mistakes, notably the air command arrangements and the poor system for passing on communications intelligence that could have been prevented. The chances of capturing Tunis were prejudiced by two mistakes at the high command level: Evelegh's poor plan in late November and the failure to switch the effort against enemy supplies from the Tripoli route to the new run to Tunisia.[15]

CHAPTER 4

Attacking the Tunisian Buildup: November–December 1942

O n December 26, Eisenhower told Washington and London that, "The continued rains have made impossible any decisive attack in the near future." He intended to take the initiative, with decent weather, in the area southeast of Tebessa, but probably in not less than two months. In the near term, he planned to improve his line of communications and to maintain air attack at the "maximum intensity permitted by the weather and our resources." Three days later, he assured them that he would maintain an aggressive defense, especially on his right. He hoped to ultimately attack toward Sfax on the coast and split the enemy force in Tunisia in two.[1] The Axis powers were well aware of the Allied ambitions along this line and planned to forestall them.

AXIS STRATEGY AND COMMAND ARRANGEMENTS

Hitler, for a time, nursed even bigger hopes; on November 20, he wrote to Mussolini about an eventual advance westward to destroy the whole Allied position in North Africa and the Mediterranean—a fantastic idea, given the Axis powers' real situation. The disastrous defeats in South Russia, where the Soviets surrounded the entire Sixth Army at Stalingrad on November 23, imposed another major drain on German reserves and air transport and made it even more certain that a grand counteroffensive was out of the question. It also became clear that Vichy cooperation would not mean much; few Frenchmen would fight alongside the Germans. The admiral commanding the French fleet at Toulon stupidly refused to take his ships over to the Allies while there was still a chance to do so, but he scuttled them on November 27 rather than let them fall into Nazi hands. On November 30, Hitler ordered even the so-far-cooperative French forces in Tunisia disarmed. The Axis powers were on their own. Still, it seemed not only desirable but possible, even easy, to maintain a long-term Axis bridgehead in Tunisia. (As we shall see, however, the commanders who would actually have to defend it took a very different view.)

Admiral Raeder, the head of the German navy, argued that such a position would keep the enemy force in the Mediterranean theater divided, prevent the Allies opening the Mediterranean to their shipping and force them to use the much longer Cape route, and prevent the Allies from invading southern Europe. Raeder insisted that Tunisia was the decisive position in the Mediterranean; he almost seemed to think that the Axis was better off now that it was finally in their hands. As late as December 22, Raeder advocated a drive through Spain to trap the Allied forces in the Mediterranean. Despite the difficulty of supplying Libya, Raeder and Field Marshal Kesselring were optimistic about the problem of supplying Tunisia. They noted that the route from Sicily to Tunis (about 130 miles) was just a third as long as that to Libya; ships and planes should have a much shorter, easily defended passage. They also seemed to think that the chastened Italians would be more receptive to German suggestions about how to employ their resources more efficiently. Later, when it was clear that such hopes had been more than a trifle optimistic and that Tunisia and its defenders were doomed, the Germans contented themselves with the thought that they had at least seriously delayed the opening of the Mediterranean to Allied shipping and the invasion of Italy and had deferred an invasion of France until 1944.

Mussolini, while as prone to illusions as Hitler about the chances of reversing the military situation in the Mediterranean, had a greater appreciation of the overall odds facing the Axis. He and other Italian leaders recognized the need for a radical change in policy. Many in the Italian government (unlike Mussolini) were desperate to make peace with the Western powers, with or without the Germans. Even after the Allies announced their demand for "unconditional surrender" in January 1943, they remained under the illusion that the Western democracies would make a deal with them, especially if Italy could take the whole bloc of southeastern satellite countries (Hungary, Romania, and Bulgaria) out of the Axis with it.

Preparations for such a move occupied Italian diplomats for much of the first half of 1943, but Mussolini reluctantly authorized a peace feeler to the Western powers only in July, just before he and the whole Fascist regime were overthrown. Mussolini held a different view from most of his followers. Perhaps he just hated the democracies more; or perhaps he held a genuinely more realistic view and saw that the British and Americans would never deal with Nazis or Fascists. But Germany and Italy might be able to make a separate peace with the Soviets—an idea the Japanese had already proposed. In that case, only Stalin, not exactly a man of unswerving principle, had to be persuaded; and success would free immense forces for the struggle with the West. That was the only course that *might* have saved the Axis powers, although it seems more likely that it would merely have prolonged the war long enough so that the first atomic bombs would have fallen on Germany instead of Japan. In any case, Hitler would not listen to suggestions for a deal with the Soviets, or even to proposals that the Axis stand on the defensive in the east to release resources for the defense of Italy.[2] The Axis would remain in a two-front war.

How to handle things in North Africa was a bone of contention both among the Germans and between them and the Italians. Field Marshal Rommel favored a rapid retreat to the "Gabes gap" or "Chott position" in Tunisia. From there he would strike at the approaching Allied armies in succession, first at the American and British forces coming from Algeria and then at the Eighth Army coming from the east. But all that must be simply a delaying action. In the end, and sooner rather than later, the Axis forces must evacuate Africa. In the long run, they just could not be maintained there in the face of Allied air superiority. He flew to Hitler's headquarters in East Prussia to argue his case. But Hitler came down on the side of the Italians, who insisted on a much more gradual retreat through Libya, to enable forces to build up in Tunisia, and a stand farther south on the Mareth Line. This issue consumed so much time that Rommel was unable even to present his complete views to Hitler. Returning to Italy, he accompanied Herman Goering, who was to meet the Italians to straighten out supply arrangements.

Goering remained optimistic and unreceptive to Rommel's views. In a series of conferences and inspection tours December 2–5, Goering discussed ways to improve the air defense of ports and to use shipping more efficiently and the distribution of the enormous amount of shipping and the few badly damaged warships that had been seized when the Axis overran southern France. It was agreed that the Germans would provide mines to complete a double set of antisubmarine minefields between Sicily and Tunisia, forming a protected corridor for ships that should be immune to attack by surface ships as well. Hitler had already strengthened Kesselring's powers as Commander-in-Chief South on November 16. Regarding Nehring as a "defeatist," he appointed Colonel General Hans-Juergen von Arnim, who had been an effective corps commander in Russia, to replace Nehring, whose corps was renamed "Fifth Panzer Army." This force was to be built up to seven divisions (three panzer). Von Arnim, a Prussian Junker from a distinguished military family, was quite different from Rommel. (As junior officers, the two men had known and disliked each other.) Like most men of his class, he did not like the Nazis, although he was in no way actively anti-Nazi. Fortunately for the Allies he was, although very courageous and a competent tactician, a jealous man who found it hard to cooperate with Rommel, something the faulty Axis command structure made more important than it normally would have been. Until March 1943, there was no overall Axis ground commander in Africa. Von Arnim did share one important characteristic with Rommel; he bluntly told Berlin what was going on, whether or not it wanted to hear it.

Inter-Axis jealousies prevented a rational command structure. Hitler at first wanted to explicitly maintain German command of the forces in Tunisia, but in a conference with Italian representatives on December 18–22, he conceded that operations there would be the responsibility of the Italian high command. Kesselring, who controlled all German forces in the Mediterranean, would attach a German operations staff to the Italian headquarters. Hitler also conceded that once Rommel's "German-Italian Panzer Army" stood on the Mareth Line, it would be renamed the "First Italian Army" and put under an Italian general. Hitler failed to press his own advisers' suggestion that a (German) Army Group should then take control of both armies. The Italian "Commando Supremo" would continue to direct them—from Rome! The Germans could not resist trying to outmaneuver their allies; Kesselring attached almost his entire staff (which outnumbered the Italian staff) to Commando Supremo. The Italians took this badly.

As the retreat into Tunisia loomed, they designated Giovanni Messe, a competent officer and one of the few Italian generals the Germans respected, to command First Italian Army. But Rommel's relief was repeatedly postponed. Finally, *after* the major counteroffensive against the Allies in the west had taken place, Hitler stepped in. Playing the role, rare for him, of the voice of reason, he unilaterally appointed Rommel the commander of "Army Group Afrika" on February 23.

In contrast to the overall command muddle, the control of the Axis air forces was fairly efficient. As the forces in Libya pulled back, the Tunisian and Libyan air commands were consolidated under one "Fliegerkorps Tunis," which controlled the Italian air units, which the Germans deemed only a minor, auxiliary force.

By December, "Fliegerkorps Tunis" had about half a dozen bases, a sizable force of single-engine fighters, and a small ground attack force of Stuka dive-bombers, Henschel 129 "tank busters," and Focke-Wulf 190 fighter-bombers. The Allies considered the maintenance of the ground attack force in Africa a real achievement, given the problems the Germans faced. The core of the German fighter force was Jagdgeschwader 53, equipped with Me-109s. It maintained its headquarters at Bizerta. At any one time, two of its three groups were stationed at Mateur, with a single squadron at Gabes in the south, while another group rotated to Sicily. Individual groups and squadrons from other geschwader filled out the force. The Me-109s of II Gruppe/Jagdgeschwader 51 operated from La Sebala (near Bizerta), along with the Stukas of II Gruppe/Stukageschwader 3. II/JG 53 and II/JG 51 absorbed two squadrons rushed to the Mediterranean from JG 2 and JG 26 in Western Europe; the squadron transferred from JG26 had suffered very heavy losses en route or after reaching Tunisia. JG 2's whole IInd Gruppe, equipped with Focke-Wulf 190s, was transferred from France to the Tindja South airbase. Another Focke-Wulf group, III/Zerstorergeschwader 2 (Zerstorergeschwader were usually composed of twin-engine fighters), was based at Sidi Ahmed. El Aouina was principally a terminus for transport flights, but a squadron of FW-190 figher-bombers (5/SG 1) and another (8/SG 22) of Henschel 129s (twin-engined planes armed with heavy cannon to attack tanks) were based there. As the campaign proceeded, the Germans brought in another Stuka group and increasingly dispersed their fighter and fighter-bomber units to a mass of smaller, newer fields: La Marsa near Tunis (which also acted as an alternate transport terminus), La Smala de Souassie, Kairouan, La Fauconnerie, Fatnassa, and Matmata. The Me-109s of Jagdgeschwader 77, falling back from Libya, occupied the last three bases. Later on, even more temporary landing grounds came to use. (In the last stages of the campaign in the spring of 1943, however, the Allied advance forced the Axis to concentrate on fewer, more vulnerable bases.) Three Italian groups of Macchi 202s and one of Re-2001 fighters supported the Germans; although their operations were poorly recorded, they were by no means wholly ineffective, despite their inferior aircraft. The approximately 150 operational German planes based in Tunisia itself in late 1942 were but a small fraction of some 1,350 operational German planes in the Mediterranean. The twin-engined groups of III/ZG 26 and III/ZG 1 usually stayed on Sicily, with a sizable force of medium bombers, reconnaissance and transport planes, and one single-engine group from JG 53.[3]

THE AXIS SUPPLY SYSTEM

It soon became clear that hopes that Sicily's proximity to Tunisia assured an easy solution to the Axis' supply problems were illusory. To be sure, the Axis never could have supplied Tunisia without Sicilian ports and airfields, but most of their logistics effort had to be based much farther back. Indeed, most of the factors that had initially seemed to favor the Axis supply effort, even when real, proved wasting assets. The problem was basically insoluble. There were not enough ships nor escort craft or planes to defend them. But partly because of Allied mistakes, partly because of conditions beyond anyone's control, and also because the Axis used what they had intelligently, the struggle to cut the Axis supply route to Tunisia was neither short nor easy. The Axis managed to parry some sorts of attacks, even if they lost in the end.

In theory, the Italians and the Germans (who had a surprising number of merchant ships in the Mediterranean) had access to enough tonnage to supply Tunisia. But so much of this was damaged, of an unsuitable type, or tied down by other commitments that finding ships was a chore from the start. Huge numbers of damaged warships and merchant ships cluttered Italian shipyards, which were increasingly bombed by Allied planes. The Axis had to supply not just Tunisia but Sicily, Sardinia, Corsica, and the islands of the Aegean. The poor railroad system of southern Italy prevented Sicily from becoming the main supply base for Africa. Although the Germans introduced their own personnel and communications equipment to increase the railroads' efficiency, the Axis allies quarreled over the allotment of trains; and in the later stages of the Tunisian campaign, movements were increasingly hampered by the bombing of Naples.

Keeping Sicily's civilian economy and vital bases going was a heavy drain on shipping. Sicily alone needed 200,000 tons of coal a month, and only a fifth of that could be brought by rail and ferry across the Strait of Messina. The rest had to go by seagoing ship. When possible, men and heavy weapons went to Africa via Sicilian ports, but most supplies had to come from the Italian mainland. Guarding the inadequate Messina bottleneck was a source of anxiety. Much depended on the smooth operation of the Messina ferry terminal, a concrete building that housed machinery that unloaded complete trains from six specially built train ferries; 4,000 cars a day crossed the Straits. The Messina area became one of the most heavily defended places in Europe. In February 1943, the Germans began to supplement the large ferries with small coastal ships as a precautionary measure. But the terminal and the special train ferries proved unexpectedly tough targets, or perhaps were not dealt with in the right way. The last Messina train ferry was only knocked out during the evacuation of Sicily in August 1943.

Perhaps only thirty-seven ships, totaling 150,000 tons, supplemented by about twenty small so-called "ferries" (not to be confused with the Messina ferries), which will be described later, were immediately available for the Tunisian run. The Germans were in the process of securing 450,000 tons of shipping from Vichy France (which greatly worried the Allies), but many of the French ships needed major refits. Under 100,000 tons proved usable on the Tunisian route. The bombing of repair facilities ensured that much of this would not go to sea. From January to May 1943, only 30,000–50,000 tons of shipping were actually available at any one time for Tunisia. Most of Italy's biggest and fastest ships were long since gone; most of those that were left could average only eight to ten knots an hour, dangerously lengthening the already perilous trip to Africa. The situation in Tunisia and en route placed a premium on small, fast ships; really fast ships could cross from Sicily to Tunisia almost entirely in darkness during the winter.

The Germans and Italians learned the hard way that Arab dock workers simply vanished with Allied air attacks; attempts to mobilize Tunisian Italians for the job failed. The local French and the Tunisian Jews were often used as slave laborers to dig defenses, and the latter especially were plundered by the Germans, but the Germans did not want them near German equipment and supplies. (Since Tunisia was nominally an Italian theater, and the Italians opposed Nazi policies toward the Jews, the Tunisian Jews were only exploited, not murdered.) It became routine to hold combat troops arriving in Tunis and Bizerta for days to unload ships. Ultimately, the Germans brought in special labor troops and civilian longshoremen from Hamburg. Power cranes were repeatedly damaged or destroyed. The first set of replacement cranes was sunk en route. Experience showed that a ship could be unloaded at the rate of 1,500 metric tons a day. A large ship had to stay in port for more than a day, and Allied bombers were liable to ensure that they stayed there permanently.

With many of the remaining escorts tied down elsewhere, or under repair, along with the few naval craft taken in France, the Italians had an average of only ten destroyers and ten torpedo boats available for convoy duty from late 1942. The large escorts often were supplemented by smaller craft, particularly motor torpedo boats. Fuel oil also was scarce. The destroyers themselves often were diverted to transport work. The Germans finally assigned a force of forty-five Messerschmitt 110 and 210 "destroyers" (Zerstorer), twin-engined "heavy fighters" as permanent convoy cover; they were increasingly bolstered by diverting bombers to such duties. Unlike the Me-109 and FW-190, such planes could patrol over a convoy for a long time, but none were a match for Allied fighters.

Even before logistic realities sank in, Allied air attacks discouraged continuance of an initial attempt to make Palermo the main supply port for Tunisia. That dubious honor went to Naples. Sometimes, after a series of damaging bombings, Palermo replaced Naples for a time, but not for long. In all, two-thirds of the merchant ships destined for Tunisia loaded at Naples, the rest at Palermo. The voyage to Africa was tedious as well as dangerous. Even convoys departing from Naples usually stopped at Palermo, and sometimes at Trapani or Pantellaria, to make repairs or to assemble escorts. A stop at Palermo lengthened the trip from Naples from 300 to 360 miles. For a time, in January 1943, some convoys tried to escape the British submarines by steaming right up against the Italian coast to Messina and then to Palermo. That did not work and added 130 miles to the trip. Leaving Sicily, the convoys entered the most dangerous part of what the Italians began to call the "death route."

It was deadly in spite of a highly successful countermeasure that largely checked British surface and submarine operations between Sicily and Tunisia. The Italians had long been laying mines in the Strait of Sicily, partly as a measure against the Malta convoys and partly to guard their own shipping lanes. By late 1942, a continuous mine barrier ran from the vicinity of

Cape Bon, the northeast tip of Tunisia, to the Aegades islands, within thirty miles of Trapani in western Sicily, making it very hard for surface ships from Malta or submarines coming from the eastern Mediterranean to get at traffic en route to Tunis and Bizerta. In late November, the Italians decided to block attacks from the west with another huge minefield. The Germans were eager to help. Despite limited resources, the Italians had a minefield running from Bizerta to the Skerki bank, a distance of eighty miles, in an amazingly short time. (Beyond the Skerki Bank, the sea bottom fell off sharply, making minelaying, at least with the weapons then available to the European Axis, impractical.) Although too late to prevent one very costly surface attack in early December, the Axis had a safe corridor fifty miles wide for most of the way to Tunisia. But the Allies soon managed to turn this feat against the Axis to some extent. Fast British minelayers entered the corridor at night—a delicate and dangerous operation—to lay mines inside it. The Italians were reluctant to expose their already too few minesweepers to air attack and soon gave up trying to sweep the accumulating British fields, which finally constricted the Axis sea corridor between the Aegades and Tunisia to a width of little more than a mile. Ships had to stay within this narrow, unmarked alley despite air attack and bad weather. For a time, in early 1943, the Italians routed some convoys completely outside of the corridor; they sailed east of the Cape Bon-Aegades minefield and (at night) threaded a narrow passage, in some places just three-quarters of a mile wide, between Cape Bon and the eastern mine barrier. But this route soon became as dangerous as the other. Whatever route they took, as we shall see, even ships that reached Tunis and Bizerta stood an excellent chance of never putting to sea again. The smaller Axis ships made some use of the shallow ports of Sousse and Sfax on Tunisia's east coast, early in the Tunisian campaign, but they had a very limited capacity to unload ships, and only coastal craft could use Sfax. Allied bombing closed them in February 1943.

Standard merchant ships were not the only means of maritime supply. Despite the desperate need for escorts, the Italians made considerable use of destroyers to carry personnel. After an entire convoy was lost on December 2, troops going by sea to Tunisia usually embarked on destroyers at Pozzuoli in Sicily; each destroyer could carry 300–350 men to Africa in less than a day. In all, destroyers made 155 troop runs, taking almost 52,000 men to Tunisia. (In all, some 172,000 or more Germans and Italians were shipped to Tunisia during the period 1942–1943; the exact number of Italians is uncertain.)[4]

THE FERRIES

An important though subsidiary role was played by an assortment of smaller craft the Allies lumped together as "ferries." The largest of these were the

German navy's numbered "Kriegstransporter" or "KT boats," actually small, coal-powered ships of 850 tons, able to carry 600 tons of cargo. Thirty of them were built in sections and assembled in Italian and Yugoslav ports during the period 1941–42. They were somewhat comparable in capacity to, but faster than, the later Allied Landing Ship Medium. They were armed with a quadruple 20 mm flak gun; sometimes they also carried an 88 mm gun, a twin 37 mm flak gun, and three single 20 mm guns, and depth charges for use as an escort craft. With a 14.5 knot speed, they could make the run from Sicily to Tunisia almost entirely at night during the winter. A smaller, slower German navy landing craft, the diesel-powered Marine-fahrprahm (MFP), called the "F-boat" by the Allies, was approximately the equivalent of the Allied Landing Craft Tank. Equipped with a bow ramp, it came in two versions, displacing 200 or 280 tons, and it could carry 80 to 100 tons of cargo or up to three tanks, at seven to ten knots. It was heavily armed with an 88mm gun, one 37 mm, and two 20 mm auto-cannon. A still-smaller craft, the Siebel ferry, was perhaps an equivalent of the Allied Landing Craft Medium but was unorthodox in configuration. It had been designed in 1940 by an aircraft designer, Fritz Siebel, for use in the invasion of England. A double-ended catamaran powered by two airplane engines, it was built of two army engineer pontoons held together by steel girders that supported a platform carrying the crew, passengers, and cargo. Various models displaced 137 to 170 tons and could carry forty-five tons of cargo on the open sea or ten to twelve trucks at 7.5–8 knots. As a transport it carried a standard arma-ment of one 40 mm flak gun, a twin 20 mm mount, and rocket launchers. Some Siebel ferries were turned into antiaircraft escort craft, by adding two or even three 88 mm guns. They were particularly formidable opponents and greatly feared by Allied pilots.

The Italians employed more orthodox landing craft of comparable size "motozattere," which had been developed for the invasion of Malta. The fer-ries were based at Trapani and Palermo, and from March 1943, at Marsala. Later, some KT ships picked up their cargoes at Reggio in Calabria, elimi-nating the need to take those loads across the Strait of Messina to Sicily. The ferries' cargo capacity was small, but they had important advantages. They were hard to hit and less vulnerable to torpedoes, mines, and near misses by bombs than large ships. (Only six KT ships were sunk at sea during the course of the campaign.) The ferries were easily unloaded, classic "roll-on and roll-off" craft. The Axis forces increasingly used them to carry the most valuable cargoes.

By January 1943, the Germans had three KT ships, forty-five MFPs, and forty-five Siebel ferries on the Tunisian route. In that month, Hitler ordered that tanks be shipped only via Sicily and the ferries; in February, personnel movements were switched from the destroyers to the ferries for a time. The ferries were a nuisance to the Allies, but as valuable as they were, there were never more than fourth of the number needed to supply Tunisia. Even if enough had been built to replace conventional ships, it seems unlikely that they could have been supplied with cargo, berthed or fueled in the Sicilian ports. Nevertheless, Kesselring's headquarters calculated that when all large ships were lost, a fleet of ten KT ships, 200 MFPs, and 200 Siebel ferries could supply Tunisia, and urged a major construction campaign. In the interim, they tried to press the Italians to supply 300 to 500 sailing craft with auxiliary engines and to launch a program to build 300-ton wooden motorized sailing vessels. These efforts started too late and were unsuccessful. The Germans themselves grabbed some 200-ton Greek motorized sailing ships, planning to provide them with new engines and to put a German in charge of their Greek crews; they would be transferred to Italy to sail from there. But few engines were available, the Italians proved obstructive, and the Greek sailors mutinous. Little came of the effort. The wisdom of the motorized sailing craft projects is doubtful; British submarines found similar vessels easy targets for their deck guns. An attempt by German army engineers to build concrete boats at Athens also misfired. A somewhat more successful project was devised to transfer river craft from France and Germany to the Mediterranean; but the first of there reached Marseilles only in March 1943. They then had to be modified for sea work and became available too late for Tunisia. They did, however, prove useful in supplying Sardinia, Corsica, Sicily, and southern Italy.[5]

AIRLIFT

Although most supplies and equipment went to Tunisia by sea, the airlift that began in November was extremely important to the Axis war effort. The Germans rapidly built up a large air transport force. In November, no less than 15,273 Germans reached Tunisia by air (only 1,900 came by sea.) By the end of the year, they had flown 41,768 men and 8,651 tons of cargo to Africa. The standard German transport plane was the old but reliable Junkers 52. With its three engines, squarish fuselage and wings, washboard skin, and fixed landing gear it looked like a low-wing version of the Ford Tri-motor. Unlike Allied transports, it was lightly armed. It could carry 1.8 metric tons of cargo or eighteen passengers. Although the Germans would have done well to follow the example of their Japanese allies and the Soviets and simply copy the newer Douglas DC-3, the Ju-52 served them well. At the other end of the scale was a most peculiar aircraft, the Messerschmitt 323, which had been turned into the biggest transport plane in the world by adding six engines to the huge Messerschmitt 321 glider. The result looked a bit like an anvil with wings; it was an awkward, vulnerable plane, difficult to fly in formation, but it could carry 100–120 men or up to twenty tons of cargo. In the first phase of the Tunisian airlift, in late 1942, the Germans had some 400 Junkers 52s and 20 Me-323s. They had a few giant six-engine Blohm and Voss 222 flying boats with a ten-ton load, and an assortment of four-engine land planes, including the Focke-Wulf 200, a modified prewar airliner that somewhat resembled the American DC-4/C-54; it could carry 10,800 pounds or twenty-five to thirty men. There also were a few Junkers 90 and 290, abortive heavy bombers used as transports, supplemented by bombers discarded as obsolete or temporarily diverted from combat missions: Heinkel 111s, Junkers 86s, and Italian Savoia-Marchetti SM 75s and SM 81 tri-motor bombers.

Most of the airlift force was based at Naples and Palermo, with a few flying from Bari and Reggio. The Ju-52s based in Sicily could make two flights a day to Tunisia, one in the morning and one late in the afternoon. The main force, flying from Naples, timed its flights to land in Africa at noon when experience showed the Allied air forces were least active. Naples-based planes had to refuel on one leg of their flight and usually stopped in Sicily en route, or sometimes on the way back, to avoid consuming fuel stocks in Africa. The Ju-52s flew in large formations called "pulks" (the Polish and Russian word for "regiment," which became German slang for a variety of military formations) low over the sea, rendezvousing with a squadron of escorting fighters at Trapani. Once in sight of Africa, the "pulks" split up to head for El Aouina and Sidi Ahmed. Tunisian-based fighters took off to cover their landing, unloading, and getaway.

By the end of 1942, the Germans had scaled down the airlift for a time, withdrawing some transports for Stalingrad. Landings in Africa fell to just twenty to fifty a day; they rose in January to seventy a day. In January, they flew 14,250 Germans and 4,000 tons of cargo by air, while 15,000 Germans and 70,000 tons of equipment and supplies came by sea. In February, 12,800 Germans and over 4,000 tons of cargo were flown in. Many Italians also went by air, but the number is uncertain. Ultimately, the Germans delivered 137,149 of their own men and 31,686 tons of supplies by air from November 1942 to May 1943. While small by comparison with later wartime airlifts— in one month, July 1945, the American "Hump" airlift over the Himalayas hauled 71,000 tons from India to China over a longer route with more natural hazards—the Tunisian airlift, given the Axis' equipment and problems, was a real achievement. It also was costly, even at first. The Germans lost 128 Junkers 52s in November and December 1942; the effort to keep the Tunisian and Stalingrad airlifts going forced the Luftwafe to close its instrument-flying and bomber-transition schools.[6]

Sea and airlift together kept the Axis forces in Tunisia going, but on very short rations. As early as December 15, von Arnim warned that the rate at which supplies arrived was far below his minimum needs. He currently needed 12,000 tons a month for his Fifth Panzer Army and an equal amount for Rommel's force; and only half his projected force had reached Tunisia. He warned that he needed more transport to complete the assembly of the Fifth Panzer Army, and that there was only a limited time to do this and reach the 24,000 tons level of supply; the Axis had six to eight weeks, while the winter rains kept the Allies off their backs.

On January 8, von Arnim submitted a far higher estimate of his and Rommel's joint requirements at no less than 150,000 tons a month actually delivered in Africa, if they were to wage an active defense, including major counteroffensives against the First and Eighth Armies. On later occasions, he and Rommel cut this down to 140,000 tons, with an absolute minimum consumption of 69,000 tons a month. Kesselring, a notorious optimist, apparently discounted their assessment; on January 12, he gave Berlin an estimate of their needs of only 60,000 tons a month and professed to believe that with the rehabilitation of confiscated French shipping, there should be no problem getting the supplies to Tunisia. He does not even seem to have made an allowance for the inevitable losses in transit. Hitler seems to have accepted this; he did not take much interest in the supply problem until March, a fatal lapse. The Italians had no such illusions. As far back as November, they estimated that 70,000 tons of supplies and 6,000 vehicles could be shipped to Tunisia. In early February, Commando Supremo's top transport officer estimated that, at best, 70,000 tons to 82,000 tons might be shipped out each month, but that 25 percent would be lost en route, so it was unlikely that enough would get through even to cover Kesselring's optimistic assessment of needs. And, in that month, the total amount of cargo landed in Africa began to drop sharply.[7]

FIRST BLOWS AGAINST THE AXIS SUPPLY LINE: MALTA AND THE SURFACE STRIKING FORCE

Despite generally excellent intelligence, the Allied commands were slow to react to the Axis move into Tunisia at the strategic level. They were sluggish in redirecting the admittedly limited striking forces then available from the Libyan route to the newer Tunisian one. Moreover, there was, at that time, no one closer than London to coordinate Eisenhower's command, the long-established striking force on Malta, and the eastern Mediterranean. On November 11, the British ordered the submarines stationed in the central Mediterranean, which had been disposed to counter any interference by the Italian fleet with the North African landings, to concentrate on the Tunisian route. On November 20, the British Chiefs of Staff ordered Malta-based bombers to shift their efforts to the Tunisian route and airfields supporting the Axis effort in Tunisia. On November 22, a decision was made to reinforce Malta with more torpedo bombers. A Fleet Air Arm Albacore squadron would join the Albacore squadron and the Swordfish squadron already there; the RAF's 39 Squadron, with new Beaufort IIs, would return to the island. The new units, however, only began operating in December. The Admiralty also ordered the early formation of a surface striking force, Force Q, at Bone, as soon as minimal air protection could be provided, instead of waiting for a much better air situation as earlier planned. Shortly afterward, it was decided to reform Force K, the old surface striking force at Malta.

The effect of all these measures was limited. The British submarines were hampered by the shortness of the passage to Tunisia, already heavily protected by mines and covered by heavy antisubmarine patrols, while the Axis ships were aided by the longest nights of the year and bad winter weather. The first sinking by a submarine, the German ship *Suelberg*, came on December 9. Malta not only had little to attack with but was still in bad shape in November. It had been nearly four months since the August convoy had brought in just enough to prevent collapse. The tired garrison, which had endured another Axis air onslaught in October, was still on siege rations; fuel, ammunition, and torpedoes were scarce. A new "deadline" loomed; in mid-December, food would run out. The timely capture of airfields in Libya let the British provide air cover for a convoy from the east. Four vital supply ships reached Malta on November 20. The island's air force was still largely oriented toward defense; it had four single-engine fighter squadrons and one Beaufighter squadron and part of another. A single Wellington squadron and detachments from two others based in Egypt served for reconnaissance as well as strike purposes, along with the two Fleet Air Arm torpedo squadrons.[8] Reinforcements would shortly arrive, but despite the new orders from London, the command at Malta stills seems to have focused on the Libyan route. Like a boxer swinging after the bell, it kept on hitting the route to Tripoli it had been attacking for more than two years, hounding the beaten forces fleeing the Eighth Army rather than those facing Eisenhower's command. Still, Malta and the surface striking force based at Bone struck the first, limited blows against the Axis support of Tunisia.

Malta-based planes proved more effective against enemy air transport than shipping. Just before the North African invasion, 227 Squadron on Malta got new crews and the new Mark VIC version of the Beaufighter. Joined by the new 272 Squadron, it was assigned the task of intercepting planes flying between Sicily and Tunisia. Going out in small numbers, occasionally accompanied by a few Spitfires when operating near Malta, the

Beaufighters sometimes strafed the air terminals on the African end; on a few occasions, they attacked ships, mostly on the Libyan run. They scored their first big success on November 12; a half dozen Beaufighters ran into as many Savoia-Marchetti 75 transports near Pantellaria and wiped them out. The next day, eight of the big twin-engine fighters caught a Dornier 24 flying boat off the coast of Tunisia. They went on to shoot down six Ju-52s and SM 81 troop carriers, which were armed and far from sitting ducks; the soldiers aboard also fired from the windows. One Beaufighter went down, others were damaged; one had to be written off when it returned to Malta.

On the same day, a seven-plane mission downed a Heinkel 115 seaplane en route to Tunisia. Diving through intense flak, the Beaufighters destroyed several Ju-52s on the ground at El Aouina. One Beaufighter crew was killed by enemy fighters. Another bellied in on a nearby beach; surprisingly, the crew evaded capture and made its way to the Allied lines. Such strafing missions were costly and not always successful; a similar mission to Bizerta on the next day failed, costing two planes. Sweeps to the Tunisian coast—"Messerschmitt Alley"—remained dangerous, for the Beaufighters were no match for single-engine interceptors. There were several strafing and bombing missions against ships in late November; the Beaufighters sank a small naval auxiliary en route to Tripoli and an ammunition carrier running along the Libyan coast with relatively light 250-pound bombs. The Wellingtons of 40 Squadron flew from Egypt to Malta and on November 26 began night attacks on Tunisian and Sicilian harbors, sometimes flying two missions in one night. By the end of November, the RAF units based on Malta had destroyed fifteen German transport planes, twenty-three bombers, twelve fighters, and two flying boats. In December, the Beaufighters began scoring more successes against enemy transport planes. On December 8, three planes seeking enemy shipping ran into no less than fifty tri-motored German and Italian transports. Despite the escort of Ju-88s and Me-110s, the Beaufighters managed to down three transports while losing one of their own. Similar encounters between Beaufighters, and sometimes Spitfires, and Ju-52s followed the next week. Beaufighter losses were heavy, and it was common for the survivors to return to Malta on one engine. The Wellingtons of 40 Squadron did not suffer great losses in the air, but the enemy did not suffer their attacks passively either. On December 18, a surprise dive-bombing attack destroyed seven Wellingtons on the ground.

Malta-based planes had failed to sink any ships at sea on the Tunisian run during November; in fact, only one Axis ship was lost on that route. On November 28, the 5,418-ton *Citta di Napoli*, upon its return to Palermo from its third trip to Bizerta, hit a mine and sank. But mines were notoriously indiscriminate; they were apt to cause unwanted destruction. One sank the hospital ship *Citta di Trapani,* en route from Naples to Bizerta, on December 1.[9]

The Royal Navy was about to make things much more difficult for the Axis. On November 27, Force K was reconstituted at Malta with three cruisers, *Cleopatra, Euryalus,* and *Dido,* and four destroyers. Three days later, Bone seemed just safe enough to permit the assembly of Force Q, with three cruisers—*Aurora, Argonaut,* and *Sirius*—and a pair of destroyers. In the first few days of December, several Axis convoys, some unusually large, were en route to Africa, and that gave the surface forces their one big chance to strike during the Tunisian campaign.

Force Q put to sea on December 1 to intercept Italian convoy "H", which had left Palermo for Bizerta. The convoy consisted of three merchantmen, *Aventino, Puccini,* and *Aspromonte,* and the German KT 1, carrying troops, 88mm guns, tanks, and other vehicles, escorted by three destroyers and two torpedo boats. A German plane spotted Force Q off of Bone, and the Italians intercepted a message indicating that British planes were tracking convoy "H." They alerted the convoy. That did not save it, though perhaps the warning prevented complete surprise and the total destruction of the escorts as well as their charges. Shortly after midnight, Force Q closed in on the convoy sixty miles northeast of Bizerta. The supply ships hastily turned east, shepherded by the torpedo boats, while the Italian destroyers boldly sailed into the much stronger British force with torpedoes and gunfire. The British nevertheless sank all four supply ships and the destroyer *Folgore,* another destroyer and a torpedo boat were badly damaged; and 2,200 of the 3,300 soldiers and sailors aboard the convoy were killed. It was one of the worst losses of life the Axis suffered at sea in the Mediterranean. Force Q suffered no loss in the sea battle, but just after dawn, as it returned home, a German torpedo plane sank the destroyer *Quentin.*

On the same night, December 1–2, Malta-based Royal Navy torpedo planes had achieved their first success on the Tunisian run. Yet another small convoy had been en route from Palermo to Tunis; it consisted of the tanker *Giorgio,* escorted by the destroyer *Lampo* and the torpedo boat *Climene.* The two understrength Albacore squadrons on Malta combined forces to send out three torpedo carriers, guided by another Albacore equipped with radar. The old biplanes found and attacked *Giorgio,* south of Marettimo island; a torpedo hit set her on fire. The tanker had to run aground on the coast of Sicily; she was saved, but her cargo would never reach Africa.

The next night, near Kerkenah Bank, the Axis suffered another serious loss. One of two cargo ships en route to Libya was sunk by a torpedo from an Albacore; one of the five attacking torpedo bombers was shot down. Force K destroyers interrupted rescue operations and sank the torpedo boat *Lupo*, one of the finest small ships in the Italian navy. (The British, evidently wrongly, according to Italian records, credited Force K with finishing off the cargo ship too.)

Some days earlier, the fast British minelayer *Manxman*, guided by deciphered enemy messages, had slipped between two Italian minefields near Cani Rocks and unloaded her cargo in the gap; she got home, though damaged by the German U-375. On December 3, convoy "B," with five cargo ships, was en route from Naples to Bizerta and Tunis; the German ship *Menes* hit one of *Manxman*'s mines and took thirty-four tanks right to the bottom. Two more German ships were lost to mines two days later. A very small tanker, *Noroit*, leaving Tunis for Trapani, hit a mine getting out of La Goulette channel. The small hospital ship *Gratz*, en route from Naples to Bizerta, sank in the same area that *Menes* was lost.

Although too late to affect the critical struggle before Tunis, these disasters had an important impact. All Axis troops going by sea to Tunisia henceforth went only in destroyers or ferries. Night movements between Sicily and Tunisia stopped until the mine barriers were finished, no more convoys went to Libya at all, although single ships continued to chance the trip.

The disaster to convoy "H" showed that surface ships, if they got within gun or torpedo range, could annihilate a whole convoy in a way that planes and submarines rarely could. But it was an isolated success. Reinforced, Force Q continued sweeps. But the Axis' greater caution, and the mine barriers, prevented the British ships from sinking anything. On December 14, an Italian submarine badly damaged the cruiser *Argonaut*. Only much later in the Tunisian campaign did surface craft—motor torpedo boats—have some effect; only in late April 1943 did the heavy ships score again, on a smaller scale, sinking three more ships.[10] Conditions in the Sicilian Straits were unusual in some ways, but the fighting there pointed toward a general lesson. The big surface ships on which the world's naval powers lavished so much money increasingly played second fiddle to planes, submarines, and even mines. It would be aircraft, aided by submarines, that would be decisive in the war against the Tunisian supply line.

THE TWELFTH AIR FORCE GOES INTO ACTION

Many single-engine fighters and light bombers of the U.S. Twelfth Air Force and the RAF's Eastern Air Command had assembled at Gibraltar before the North African invasion. These planes quickly flew into newly captured bases; some helped finish off the last French resistance. As the French crumbled, the Twelfth's heavy and medium bombers and escort fighters began trickling into the new theater, making the long flight from England around France and Spain to Gibraltar. They quickly encountered the conditions that would hamper their operations for months: miserable weather, lack of supplies, inadequate and vulnerable bases, and muddled command arrangements. Much of their efforts, initially, would be devoted to warding off a superior Luftwaffe rather than striking at the enemy's rear.

Some of the 97th Group's B-17s had already been pressed into service as command transports. One Fortress, taking General Doolittle to Eisenhower's headquarters, was attacked by four Ju-88s over the Bay of Biscay and was lucky to escape with a few hits. The rest of the Group's air echelon began leaving their old base at Polebrook on November 10. Stopping at Gibraltar to remove the vulrterable bomb-bay auxiliary tanks and refuel, they went on to Maison Blanche airfield outside of Algiers. The heavies had a relatively easy time, though on November 17 one B-17, carrying Brigadier General Asa Duncan, the Eighth Air Force's Chief of Staff, caught fire over the Bay of Biscay and was lost with all hands. The twin-engine planes found the trip more difficult. The P-38s of the 1st and 14th Fighter Groups, sometimes led by B-26s of the 319th Bomb Group, began leaving England on November 12, staging through an RAF base at St. Eval in Cornwall. Even the medium bombers had a tough time. They were heavily overloaded and hampered by bad weather and poor navigation. Of thirteen B-26s that took off from England on November 12, five were lost and three others suffered major damage. Some strayed over Cherbourg in enemy-held France; Lt. Colonel Alvord Rutherford, the commander of the 319th Group, was shot down. The B-26s and P-38s that completed the trip were fired on from Spanish Morocco as they passed Gibraltar, en route to Tafaroui near Oran. A few P-38s fell out and had to refuel at Gibraltar. One Lightning of the 1st Fighter Group was lost. Another force landed in neutral Portugal, where the pilot was interned for months. As the 310th Medium and 301st Heavy Bomb Groups followed on the road to Africa, the units were sorted out. The ground echelons of the P-38 groups and the 319th had sailed with the invasion force, and these units were soon more or less complete in personnel, but the ground men of the heavy bomber units arrived only gradually on the follow-up convoys. For some time, B-17 combat crews had to maintain and service their planes in miserable conditions. The same thing sometimes happened in other units because they were shifted from base to base within North Africa, so often that the ground echelons were separated from the planes for considerable stretches.

The 319th Bomb Group, which had left some planes behind in Britain and along the northern ferry route, was badly understrength in planes, and remained so for the rest of its participation in the North African campaign. By some accounts, it never had more than twenty-three planes and never flew more than twelve on a single mission. The 319th and the 14th Fighter Group stayed at Tafaraoui for some time; the 1st Fighter Group moved to Nouvion, forty miles east. The first few B-17s of the 97th Group began operating from Maison Blanche, joined by the 14th Groups 48th Squadron. Two squadrons of the 319th Group that had no planes and were not likely to get any soon went to Algiers by train to provide maintenance for the heavy bombers.[11]

Living conditions in North Africa were miserable. Men lived in tents; sometimes they did not have even that. Many Americans were surprised to find that North Africa could be quite cold at night; A. J. Liebling wrote, "If there is any way you can get colder than you do when you sleep in a bedding roll on the ground in a tent in southern Tunisia two hours before dawn, I don't know about it."[12] Water, especially drinking water, could be scarce. Food was often insufficient or bad, although the Allied soldiers gradually learned how to barter with the Arabs for fresh fruit and other items. Although American soldiers generally did not like British food, some found the British "Compo" ration better than its American counterpart, the C ration. At least it was a change. Some P-38 units, stationed at forward bases, received only two meals a day.

Few Americans were favorably impressed with North Africa. Most were shocked at the natives' poverty, although the well-traveled Ernie Pyle thought that North African cities like Oran compared favorably with some places he had seen in Latin America. Even he did not think much of the people; and, on the whole, relations with the French and the natives were poor. The Americans—General Eisenhower as well as the rank and file—were taken aback by the attitudes of many of the French "colons" and military officers. Neither group fit well with the stereotypes most Americans had of the French, or the general impression that, except for a few Fascists and opportunists, just about everybody outside of Germany, Italy, and Japan was solidly on the Allied side. Many were still pro-Vichy, if not pro-German, or at least seemed to resent being "forced" back into the war. After contemplating North Africa, the liberal Ernie Pyle wrote, "In all my traveling both before and during the war, I was frequently revolted by the shriveled greediness of soul that inhabits so much of the world. The more I saw of us Americans and British, the more I liked us. And, although Germany was our bitter enemy, at least the Germans seemed to have the character to be wholly loyal to their own country." That was a remarkable thing to write in 1943!

Vehicles, equipment, tools, and supplies of all sorts were scarce in late 1942. Bombs often were loaded by hand, and there were no gasoline trucks. Planes were tediously fueled by hand with five-gallon cans. (It took more than 500 cans to top off a B-17.) The 1st Fighter Group rejoiced to get fifty-five-gallon drums fitted with pumps. Bases were crowded and messy. Maison Blanche had one complete macadam runway, surrounded by a sea of mud. Tafaroui had two incomplete concrete runways—finishing them was one of the first tasks of American aviation engineers—also increasingly surrounded by mud. In a wartime rhyme, Tafaraoui was the place where the "mud is thick and gooey." The 1st Fighter Group insisted that Nouvion was, if possible, even worse. The U.S. engineer units—five battalions of aviation engineers, an airborne engineer company, and a special new airborne aviation engineer company—were mostly new and poorly equipped. Part of their equipment had been sunk en route to Africa, part diverted or mistakenly shipped to the wrong places, nor were they wisely used. After repairing damaged airfields and completing unfinished construction at Tafaraoui, most were assigned to build airfields west of Algiers in accordance with the pre-invasion emphasis on guarding against an attack through Spain.[13]

On November 16, Air Marshal Welsh's Eastern Air Command informally "requested" that the 97th Group attack the Sidi Ahmed airfield whenever it could. Lt. Colonel Paul Tibbets, who would later become famous as the pilot of the B-29 that dropped the atomic bomb on Hiroshima, responded eagerly. The B-17 crews tediously fueled six Fortresses, loaded them with British bombs, and took off without escort. Tibbets later ruefully admitted that "we did everything wrong," but the sloppily prepared mission, the first American blow against the enemy in Northwest Africa, was successful. Going in at 6,500 feet, far lower than their normal altitude, the B-17s hit Sidi Ahmed hard, killing much of a Luftwaffe squadron in the mess hall and destroying several aircraft—some French—on the field. The B-17 gunners claimed one Me-109 shot down. Three of the B-17s were hit by flak; they were hastily patched up with flattened-out tin cans and adhesive tape.[14] Airfields would remain the main target for Allied bombers for some time; on November 23, it was decided to switch some of the bomber effort to ports, but circumstances prevented putting that decision into effect for some days. Later attacks were far more formally planned and prepared than Tibbets' first strike, but the command machinery worked creakily for a time.

On November 16, the 48th Fighter Squadron moved up to Maison Blanche, which was crowded. That night, the Luftwaffe attacked and badly damaged seven Lightnings. Nevertheless, the P-38s managed to mount their first combat mission, escorting transports to Constantine on November 18. On November 19, 48th Squadron Lightnings escorted six B-17s to Tunis in a conventional, high-altitude attack that claimed the destruction of eight planes on the ground at El Aouina. Apparently they actually destroyed four Ju-52s and three Me-109s. On the night of November 21–22, 39 Ju-88s and Ju-87s hit Maison Blanche. A direct hit destroyed a B-17, killing nine of the ten crewmen sleeping under it; the tenth man was later found wandering in a state of shock. (According to the 97th Group's War Diary, another B-17 also was destroyed, something not mentioned in other sources.) A pair of P-38s, five Beaufighters, and four Spitfire fighters also were destroyed, along with a complete RAF photo-reconnaissance unit and three camera-equipped Spitfires. The last loss probably had the biggest effect on the Tunisian campaign; lack of photographic intelligence was a serious handicap to the Allied command. The Algiers area was poorly defended; there were no ground control intercept radars to guide the night fighters, which had left their own airborne radar sets back in England. (Algiers was exposed in other respects too; on December 12, three Italian "human torpedoes" and ten frogmen with explosive charges entered the harbor. All sixteen men were captured, but they sank two merchant ships and damaged two others.)

On November 21, the 97th Group "retaliated" against El Aouina (the attack of the night before had in fact come from Sardinia) with a dozen Fortresses. Doolittle flew in one bomber. Lt Carl Williams, flying one of the six escorting P-38s from the 14th Group, shot down a Me-109. The Americans counted five planes left burning on the field; one P-38 crashlanded up on its return to base. That night, however, the Luftwaffe smashed another B-17 on the ground at Maison Blanche. Algiers was just too exposed; on November 22, the heavy bombers were removed to Tafaroui. There the force was gradually swelled by the arrival of the remaining planes of the 97th Group and the 301st; the ground echelons gradually caught up with them. The Twelfth was able to mount increasingly larger strikes. In the prevailing conditions, getting anything done was a feat. The men at Tafaroui at first did not even have tents; later the luckier ones found relatively dry spots on high ground for their two-man pup tents. The weather got worse and worse; water on the runway was sometimes so deep that the lighter planes could not take off. The clinging mud was like wet cement. After a B-17 was slowly dragged to the runway, its landing gear had to be scraped clean so that the wheels would roll properly and they could be retracted. Attempts were made to lay Somerfeldt track and steel matting around the runways at Tafaroui and other bases so that planes could park on solid surfaces, but the stuff simply sank out of sight.

A further scrambling and scattering of units accompanied the shift of the heavy bombers. The 14th Fighter Group moved up to Youks-les-Bains in Tunisia to provide forward-based support for the ground forces, a task in which it took heavy losses. It also escorted bombers to the ports and airfields on Tunisia's east coast. The 1st Fighter Group took over the job of escorting the B-17s. It soon parted with its 94th Squadron, which reinforced the 14th Group (which, it will be recalled, had just two squadrons) at Youks. Escort missions from Nouvion to the Tunis-Bizerta area were long and nerve stretching, near the limit of even the P-38's then-practical radius. Tired pilots anxiously watched their gas gauges. That and the poor state of Nouvion led to the movement of the 71st Fighter Squadron and most of the 27th up to Maison Blanche in early December.

There was an attempt to vary the pattern of concentration on Tunis and Bizerta. On November 23, fourteen B-17s and twelve P-38s set out for Elmas airfield on Sardinia, the source of the dangerous enemy attacks on Algiers and Bone. This would have been the Twelfth Air Force's first attack on a European target, but the weather was so bad that the force had to turn back. The same thing happened the next day to the first mission sent against the port area at Bizerta. The heavy bombers stayed on the ground for three days. On November 28, the 97th Group and the newly arrived 301st Group, in its first operation in Africa, then put up thirty-seven B-17s for an attack on Sidi Ahmed and the Bizerta dock area. But the mud at Nouvion was so bad that the P-38s could not take off; the B-17s went in alone. The bomber gunners claimed ten fighters downed, but the 301st Group lost two planes—the first B-17s lost in the air in Northwest Africa. It was a lesson in the value of fighter escort and the state in which the air bases were getting. The B-17 strike unfortunately failed to coincide with the two visits to Bizerta by the forward-based 14th Fighter Group that same day. A sweep by eight Lightnings claimed six Ju-52s shot down, but Me-109s jumped them and shot down two P-38s. Later, a dozen fighters escorted as many DB-7s from the 15th Bomb Squadron to Bizerta; again, the U.S. fighters lost two of their number to German interceptors.[15]

On the same day, the first medium bombers got into action. The 319th Bomb Group's B-26s had moved up to Maison Blanche on November 24. It was still overcrowded; mud made taxiing and parking difficult, and ground equipment was still lacking. Aircrews had to help with repairs and even guard planes at night. The Algiers area was becoming safer, as radar-equipped night fighters and ground radars arrived; on the night of November 27, Beaufighters downed three German bombers. The 319th had been trained and equipped for low-level strikes of the sort increasingly in demand in the Pacific, but which proved inappropriate, at least against land targets, against German flak. The B-26s would join the heavies against Tunis and Bizerta and inaugurate attacks on the smaller ports, airfields, and railroad installations of central and eastern Tunisia.

In their first mission, nine B-26s led by a veteran of the Doolittle raid set out for the Kairouan airfield, unescorted and carrying obsolete 300-pound bombs. Finding no planes or anything else worth attacking there, they continued to Sfax. Flying out to sea, they came in at 1,000 feet to hit docks, warehouses, an oil tank farm, and the railroad yards. Despite intense flak, they made several careful bomb runs and then went down to strafe, setting many fires and causing considerable damage. One plane was hit by flak; the turret gunner was wounded in both legs. On November 30, nine mediums set out for Gabes, carrying 100-pound bombs; this time they were covered by eight P-38s. They bombed from just 300 to 500 feet, attacking the airfield, military camp, and railroad installations, again encountering intense flak. While the bombers did a good job hitting hangars and a fuel dump, they paid heavily. One B-26 was badly hit; its tail gunner was killed. It returned to base, but another crew went down and had an unusual rescue. Lt. David Floeter's B-26, badly damaged by flak, dropped out of formation on the return flight. Floeter found a level area and made a good crash landing. One of the P-38 escorts circled overhead and summoned help. A DB-7 from the 15th Bomb Squadron, covered by a pair of Lightnings, managed to land nearby. After salvaging the nose glass of their Marauder—a scarce item, badly needed to repair another B-26—they burned the plane, and all six men piled aboard the DB-7.[16]

BOMBER ESCORT

In attempts to strangle the enemy supply effort and counter enemy control of the air, the Americans alternated between hitting ports and airfields. On November 29, the B-17s concentrated on the Bizerta dock area for the first time; they returned to it the next day, trying to smash the North quay there in a mission Eisenhower regarded as especially important. The 97th Group put up eighteen B-17s, escorted by twelve P-38s from the 1st Fighter Group. Overcast skies prevented most of the bombers from dropping, and flak killed a B-17 gunner. The 1st Fighter Group scored its first kill on a bomber escort mission. (The squadron operating with the 14th Group at Youks had gotten a Me-110 a day earlier during a strafing mission in the Gabes area.)

The P-38s had rendezvoused with the bombers over Nouvion, taking a position "up sun" of the bombers. The 27th Squadron leader led two flights out of four—half the squadron—as a close escort just 500–700 feet above the bombers, much too close by later standards. A "support flight" flew higher to prevent the close escort from being "bounced" by enemy fighters; a top cover of four more flew 1,200–1,500 feet above the support force. Only the top cover, led by Captain Joel Owens, was able to engage. The enemy fighters intercepted only after the bomb run was over. Owens spotted a Me-109 climbing through the hole on the clouds that had let some B-17s bomb; he dived on it, and hit it with a single short burst, but his P-38 was going so fast it was almost uncontrollable. The German pilot used the standard method of escape (which worked well against the P-38 and the Spitfire, but would become suicidal against P-47s and P-51s) of a half-roll and dive and vanished into the cloud cover. Owens and his wingman were climbing to rejoin the rest of the formation when he spotted another Me-109 below, climbing to get at the bombers. He jumped it, closing unseen to within 200 feet, and blew its tail off.[17]

At this time, AAF escort doctrine was not well developed; not that there was much to escort with. It was a matter of how best to stretch the few fighters available to cover the few bombers. Ideas about how to protect bombers tended to polarize between two extremes. Bomber units especially wanted very close escort, with fighters very near and directly interposed between the bombers and any attackers. This, however, gave the enemy the initiative and forfeited the fighters' main advantages of speed and maneuverability. At the other extreme, some fighter officers practically ignored the bombers, favoring "fighter sweeps" ranging on their own to seek out and destroy enemy fighters. Although British experience with such sweeps over Western Europe was discouraging—the Germans refused to engage unaccompanied fighters unless an unusually favorable situation developed—this idea distracted the Eighth Air Force until well into 1943. (Much later, when plenty of fighters were available, cutting most fighters loose to roam freely came into its own.)

In Africa, the sweep idea had less appeal, although ground commanders' desire for an "air umbrella" over their units played a similar role in dispersing the available air power. The RAF's experience with escort was not much of a guide. It was neither particularly relevant nor much cause for rejoicing. In the Western Desert, the RAF, enjoying superior numbers, successfully escorted light bombers but rarely flew deep into enemy airspace in daylight; nor had it encountered a solidly organized defensive system. In its day operations in Western Europe the RAF used large numbers of fighters to escort small numbers of poorly armed light bombers to fringe targets in France and the Low Countries, in operations designed to get the Luftwaffe to come up and fight more than anything else. The RAF guarded the bombers well but suffered heavy losses of fighters at little cost to the Germans.

The Twelfth Air Force faced almost the opposite problem—using small numbers of fighters to protect relatively well-armed heavy bombers on major missions deep into enemy territory. Like Fighter Command over Western Europe, the P-38s often suffered heavy losses. But they did protect the B-17s. As the AAF official history described the operations of December 1942, "The Twelfth's B-17s attacked Tunis and Bizerte day after day, going in with forces which seem pitifully small in comparison with the armadas of 1944 and 1945. That their losses remained low must be attributed to the fact that they usually had P-38s escorting, not many P-38s but enough to divide the opposition's attention. Moreover the German pilots had not evolved any very satisfactory way of attacking the heavily armed B-17 and they were properly respectful."[18] German pilots over France had already found that the best way to attack the B-17 was head-on, but units in the Mediterranean seem to have been slow to copy them. Most attacks on B-17s in Africa were made from the rear, precisely the sort of attack it was best at dealing with, although head-on attacks became more common during the campaign. The U.S. fighter units experimented with various arrangements for both four-ship flights and escort formations. After trying out line abreast and echelon, the Twelfth settled on the "finger four" arrangement for four-ship flights (the planes were arranged like four spread fingers of a hand), standard with the RAF and the Luftwaffe. The P-38 units, which in any case had trouble finding enough serviceable planes, put up twelve-plane units instead of the standard American sixteen-plane squadron. Abortive tries were made at flying more open formations, 1,000 feet above and 5,000 to 10,000 feet above the bombers, with one flight as close cover and two others flying wide to guard it, but the tendency was to keep the fighters near and right over the bombers. There were even missions on which a P-38 flight was stationed line abreast under the lead B-17s in the hope that they would supplement the bombers' inadequate forward firepower and counter head-on attacks. After the African campaign, the P-38s returned to the standard sixteen-plane squadron formation, flown in a looser pattern.[19]

Operations in early December were characterized by stiffening German opposition and costly efforts to use medium and light bombers against the same targets hit by the heavies in an effort to prepare for a renewed offensive against Tunis. There also were belated moves to improve the functioning of command and intelligence.

On December 1, the DB-7s of the 15th Bomb Squadron, which had been attacking Gabes and other Tesser airfields from Youks-les-Bains, struck El Aouina ahead of the 97th Group's B-17s. The twelve P-38s of the 14th Group escorting them shot down an Italian Mc 202. The B-17s hit the hangar line and other airfield buildings. The sixteen P-38s sent out by the 1st Fighter Group as escort had plenty of trouble without any help from the Luftwaffe; one pilot crashed upon takeoff from Maison Blanche and burned to death, and two others had to turn back with mechanical problems. On December 2, the Twelfth mustered its biggest effort to date, in an attempt to blast the way open for the ground forces. The 310th Bomb Group, which had gotten some of its B-25s up to Maison Blanche, launched its first mission. Eight Mitchells, escorted by Lightnings from Youks, dropped 300-pound bombs on an ammunition dump near Gabes. The 15th Squadron's light bombers, followed two and a half hours later by the 319th Group's

Marauders, hit El Aouina, where they found fifty planes on the ground; the
B-26 crews also discovered Me-109s parked on an auxiliary field nearby. The
light bombers blasted an Mc 202 on the ground. The dozen B-26s, covered
by half a dozen P-38s, making their first strike against the hottest targets in
Africa, flew around a belt of bad weather and ran in at 300 feet against very
heavy flak, dropping hundred-pound bombs and strafing the flak emplace-
ments. They reported hitting fifteen to twenty planes and destroyed a
hangar. Three of the B-26s were hit by flak; two were only slightly damaged,
but the other crash-landed at Maison Blanche with a wounded bombardier.
The 301st Bomb Group put eighteen B-17s over Sidi Ahmed and Bizerta
harbor. The growing difficulty of just keeping operations going was shown
by the fact that of eighteen P-38s dispatched by the 1st Fighter Group, six
had to turn back with engine trouble.

On December 3, the heavies were finally switched completely to ports
and shipping. While the DB-7s again hit El Aouina, the 97th Group bombed
Bizerta harbor; eighteen B-17s scored many hits on the docks and a pair of
ships in the harbor entrance, despite heavy flak and a determined interception by a dozen Me-109s. The 1st Fighter Group's eighteen P-38s kept the
enemy fighters off of the bombers, but at a heavy cost. Although jumped
from above, the P-38s shot down three Me-109s. But no less than three P-38s
went down; another pilot was wounded but managed to get home. In all,
half a dozen Lightnings were lost or wrecked beyond repair.

On December 4, the B-17s returned to Bizerta, but they could not bomb
through an overcast. The Germans intercepted, however, and two of the
escorting Lightnings went down and another force-landed, in exchange for
just one Me-109 shot down. Half an hour late, seven B-26s—an eighth had
turned back with propeller trouble—swept over Bizerta harbor and nearby
Ferryville at 4,000 feet, dropping 500-pound bombs on ships, submarines,
oil tanks, and a railroad station. The flak was intense. Lt. Colonel Sam Agee,
Jr., who led the mission, had just replaced the group commander lost over
Cherbourg. He had the unenviable distinction of being one of the shortest-
lived group commanders in the AAF; his B-26 was shot down. (He and some
of his crew survived and eventually escaped from a POW camp after Italy surrendered.) Five more bombers were damaged—one had its tail shot to
bits—and several men were wounded by flak or flying glass. Things would
have been worse if the P-38s had not dealt with attacking FW-190s and
Me-109s, downing an FW-190. With planes wrecked and men wounded, if
not lost outright, on practically every mission, out of a small force, low-level
attacks on heavily defended land targets were hard to justify.

On December 5, eight B-25s, followed by DB-7s, escorted by P-38s from
Youks, bombed Sidi Ahmed airfield, while B-17s hit the Tunis docks. The

P-38s escorting the twin-engine bombers suffered heavy losses to enemy fighters; the 14th Group lost three P-38s for only two Me-109s. The twelve P-38s from the 1st Fighter Group accompanying the B-17s met no enemy planes, but two were lost anyway to mechanical problems. There was one more B-17 attack on Bizerta before the weather stopped operations from Algeria for several days. Even the normally eager fighter pilots, now weary, were glad to get a break.[20]

COMMAND ARRANGEMENTS, STRATEGY, AND INTELLIGENCE

On November 30, General Doolittle had written to General Arnold to warn that the fall rains had set in: "We may expect at least two periods of several impossible flying days per month from now on." He still hoped then that Somerfeldt track and steel matting would handle the mud, but he noted that his most serious problem was the loss of much heavy aviation engineer equipment and many trucks on two ships that had been sunk. Only air transport had saved the day. He had suffered "appalling" losses of planes to causes other than enemy action; but the B-17s and P-38s had done well. He noted that his only B-17 losses had occurred on the November 28 mission that had gone without escort because the fighters had been stuck in the mud. He noted that German light flak had proven extremely accurate.[21] Doolittle did not go into the organizational problems that were the element of difficulty that could be solved most quickly.

Air Marshal Sir Arthur Tedder, the commander of the RAF in the Middle East, had visited Eisenhower's headquarters in late November. He, like many others stationed there, was appalled by the poor air command arrangements. He strongly advised Eisenhower to form a fully unified air command. The British Chiefs of Staff thought Tedder himself should head that. But Eisenhower considered such a move premature. He argued that the Mediterranean and the Middle East were too large for one commander and that Tedder would be in the position of serving under two different ground commanders at once. He also may have wished to postpone such a move because he thought it would cut across tentative American plans for a "theater air force" under Carl Spaatz that would control all U.S. air units engaged against the European Axis, from England to the Middle East. (In 1944, such a headquarters, but for controlling strategic air forces only, did come into existence.) On December 3, as a temporary solution, Eisenhower appointed Spaatz, already his most trusted adviser on air matters, as "Acting Deputy Commander in Chief for Air." This position was essentially advisory, and Spaatz retained his post as commanding general of American air forces in the European theater. He arranged a reasonable division of labor between the British and American air forces. The Eastern Air Command would support the ground forces directly, while the Twelfth Air Force concentrated on attacking ports; on the same day he was appointed, Spaatz had directed the shift of the heavy bombers from airfields to harbors. Doolittle and his Chief of Staff thought the concentration on airfields had been mistaken from the start—as had the Luftwaffe, although the attacks on El Aouina and Sidi Ahmed had been quite destructive and had caused the enemy serious trouble. Between pressures to curb enemy air attacks on the Allied ground forces and to stop the enemy forces pouring into Tunisia, by air as well as by sea—the Allied commanders were not far from the dilemma of a mother deciding which of her children must die. Spaatz also got all four available aviation engineer battalions shifted east of Algiers to improve the air base situation.

At lower levels also the Allied effort had been hampered by amorphous and fluctuating organization and musical chairs commands. Doolittle had decided on November 19 that the shift of the American air forces eastward, although they still maintained considerable commitments in Morocco (where an Axis attack still seemed possible), required forming a set of composite geographical commands that would control both bombers and fighters as needed. As finally set up, on December 11, XII Bomber Command headquarters at Constantine controlled operations from Bougie to Tunisia, and XII Fighter Command controlled the Tebessa-Feriana region to the south, while its rear echelon became the Western Algerian Composite Wing, with headquarters at La Senia near Oran. The XII Air Support Command furnished the cadre for a Moroccan Composite Wing; a Central Algerian Composite Wing was supposed to be drawn from a troop carrier wing, but it was never actually formed. The XII Bomber Command, which was the main force actively engaged, had no less than four commanders, one of whom was killed in its first six weeks in Africa.

The method for choosing objectives from day to day remained inefficient. Targets were picked by a daily command conference of Spaatz, the Twelfth Air Force, the RAF, the Royal Navy, and Eisenhower's Allied Force Headquarters for the following day. That did not leave enough time to properly match the type of bombs and fuses to the planned target. Intelligence, as yet, was not too good. Ultra disclosed the tonnages being delivered to Tunis and Bizerta, but early in the campaign there were few details on what the cargoes were. The use and distribution of Ultra was not efficient. Group Captain R. H. Humphreys, the Chief of Air Intelligence at Eisenhower's headquarters, noted that he initially derived much intelligence from "Y" service work (intercepts of enemy forward communications, especially air to ground); it was a big help before the Allies established a reliable network of radar stations to track enemy attacks. Later, exploitation of "Ultra" became more intense. Special liaison units were pushed forward to First Army head-quarters and 242 Group, which controlled the forward elements of the Eastern Air Command. The EAC and the Twelfth Air Force were supplied with Ultra intercepts and interpretations by Humphreys directly at Algiers, while the Twelfth Air Force headquarters was there (Spaatz received Ultra personally). Humphreys noted that naval and air attacks on ships at sea required elaborate security precautions to guard the Ultra secret. But directing attacks against ships in port was not so tricky. There were relatively few ports in use; bombers and reconnaissance planes visited them so routinely that such attacks raised few problems of security.[22]

NEW BASES

As Spaatz and Doolittle had realized, new airfields were the key to more effective operations. Apart from rain and mud, every existing base within range of the enemy was already jammed.

After seeing their steel mats sink into the mud, British engineers learned of some sandy spots in the Medjerda valley that would provide suitable sites for forward fields for the EAC's fighters. The American engineer command looked farther south, beyond the wet coastal plain. On December 2, on French advice, it picked a suitable site for medium bombers at the village of Telergma in the Rhumel valley, in the "tell," the high, relatively dry plateau between the Maritime and Saharan ranges of the Atlas mountains. Americans stationed there later fondly described it as "a more dirty and filthy place you'll never find anywhere in the world."[23] The Americans found a base for the heavy bombers and their escorts at Biskra oasis, beyond the Saharan Atlas, known before the war for its dates and resort hotels. It was 200 miles southeast of Algiers, at the end of a rickety rail line running from Philippeville on the coast.

Although hampered by the loss or diversion of their bulldozers and trucks, the aviation engineers set to work effectively. By December 13, the 809th Aviation Engineer Battalion, helped by French troops and Arabs, had finished a dry weather field at Telergma; they then turned to building more fields in the area. Telergma would serve as a base for the 319th Bomb Group, which would be joined by the 310th and later by the 17th Medium Bomb Group and the 82nd Fighter Group. In January, the 310th Bomb Group and the 14th Fighter Group would move into Berteaux, another new field not far from Telergma.

C-47s plunked down an airborne aviation engineer company at Biskra. After four days of work, B-17s could fly in. On December 14, the 1st Fighter and 97th Bomb Groups began arriving at the new base; they were followed by the 301st Bomb Group. It was already understood that Biskra was only a temporary expedient. By March, the sirocco, the south wind off of the Sahara, would raise dust storms, making it unusable. From the start, sand was a serious problem, forcing frequent engine changes. The hotels provided accommodations for the officers; enlisted men crowded into tents and tried to dig foxholes in exceptionally hard ground. Food and water were short; Biskra was hard to supply. A shuttle of C-47s had to supplement the limited train service.

As we have noted, Telergma, although more suitable as a permanent base, was no bargain either. The Americans suspected the French officers of the local garrison of being pro-Nazi. Although the area was drier than the coast, the Telergma field could be a miserable mess when it did rain. By late December, B-26s could not take off from Telergma with a full load of gas and bombs, so part of the 319th had to fly out of Biskra for some days.

Neither Telergma nor Biskra were well defended in late 1942 and early 1943. As late as Christmas, Biskra was protected by just a dozen .50-caliber machine guns "loaned" by the aviation engineers. The 1st Fighter Group then supplemented these poor defenses by building its own, improvised radar set and antiaircraft gun, mounting a 20 mm cannon salvaged from a wrecked P-38 on a fifty-five-gallon drum filled with sand. The Luftwaffe would have been well advised to mount the strongest possible low-level daylight attacks against both bases, but fortunately it did not exploit the opportunity. It did carry out some troublesome night attacks. The strongest attacks come on January 3; six Ju-88s hit Biskra just after the departure of the afternoon fighter patrol, badly damaging three B-17s and slightly damaging ten more. Early that evening, eight Ju-88s destroyed one B-26 and damaged five others at Telergma. The Allied command then ordered a Spitfire squadron from the U.S. 52nd Fighter Group to Biskra to augment the defenses. But a week later, a dive-bombing attack on Biskra destroyed a B-17, a P-38, and a C-47.[24]

THE NINTH AIR FORCE JOINS IN

Although there was still no unified command embracing the air forces in the Mediterranean, the small U.S. air force based in the Middle East began taking part in the Tunisian struggle and, most effectively, making long-range, unescorted attacks at dusk and night deep in the enemy rear. On December 4, twenty B-24s of the 98th and 376th Bomb Groups carried out the first American air attack on Italy, bombing Naples harbor, then the main base of the Italian fleet. They sank one light cruiser, *Attendolo*, and damaged two others, *Montecuccoli* and *Eugenio di Savoia*, and four destroyers, as well as the port facilities. The damage to the destroyers probably did the most harm to the Tunisian supply effort, but the attack had other useful effects. The Italians, realizing that Naples was too exposed, moved their battleships and most of their cruisers to northern bases on December 6. After further attacks on Naples, the remaining cruisers went north too. This move was costly in precious oil fuel, and it also discouraged any thought of using cruisers to run supplies to Tunisia or to strengthen convoy escorts. Further attacks on Naples were made on December 8 and 11. On December 13, nine Liberators of the 376th Group inaugurated Ninth Air Force attacks on Tunisian targets, smashing the locomotive repair shops at Sfax.

A move originally designed to reinforce Doolittle led to a major addition to the Ninth. The Eighth Air Force had had some trouble breaking in its B-24s. It had too few to fly an effective defensive formation and found that trying to fly B-24s in combination with B-17s did not work well. On December 5, Spaatz ordered the Eighth to loan most of the 93rd Bomb Group to Doolittle for ten days; the ten days detached service turned into two months. Leaving one squadron (carrying out experimental electronically guided missions) behind in England, B-24s of the 93rd's other three squadrons, carrying a few ground crews, flew to Tafaraoui. One crashed into a mountain and was lost with all hands. Four attempted missions from Tafaraoui were foiled by mud before two small attacks were mounted on Bizerta on December 13 and 14. Then Spaatz arranged a swap with the Ninth Air Force. The 93rd Group would be loaned to the largely B-24-equipped Ninth, which would part with its 513th Bomb Squadron, which had its last nine B-17s. The Ninth would use the 93rd Group mainly against targets related to the Tunisian campaign. On December 15, the 93rd Group flew to Gambut in Libya, then the Ninth's most forward base. (Most of the Ninth was still based in Egypt.) The 513th's war-weary Fortresses and tired crews joined the 97th Group at Biskra, flying a few missions before they returned to the United States.

The Ninth attacked the Tunis, Sousse, and Sfax harbors on a small scale at night, sometimes with just two or three planes, but increasingly concentrated on the European end of the Axis supply line, hitting Naples, Palermo, and Messina. Naples was the toughest target; a B-24 was lost to flak on almost every mission there. The other heavy groups, still based in Egypt, would fly to Gambut in the morning to refuel for the second leg of their mission. The Liberators crossed the Italian coast at a spot not covered by radar, timing their flights to reach the targets just before dusk. After the attack, they flew out to sea, where the interceptors were reluctant to follow. When night fell, the bombers broke formation and flew individually to Gambut, using Malta as an emergency field. In late January, the whole of the Ninth moved up to the Libyan fields. In some ways, the Libyan bases were even more miserable than those of the Twelfth Air Force. The men lived in unrelenting heat and flies, on a pint of water a day, with shabby tents and oil drum latrines. Their increasingly ragged clothing had to be pieced out with bits of British, German, and Italian uniforms.[25]

DECEMBER OPERATIONS

In mid-December, flying conditions improved slightly, even as the Allied forces were stuck in front of Tunis. The Twelfth Air Force's heavy and medium bombers resumed operations, leaving their old bases on the Algerian coast at Tafaraoui and Maison Blanche for last missions over Tunisia and landing at Biskra and Telergma. Operations settled into a routine that would last for some months, in some respects until the end of the African campaign. The heavy bombers hit Tunis and Bizerta harbors, while the mediums, taking over the job of hitting enemy airfields, also bombed the small east coast airfields and railroad facilities, which also were favored targets for Ninth Air Force bombers. The limitations of the mediums' current mode of operations became clearer. The heavy bombers of the Twelfth also attacked the small ports when unusually important activity developed or weather forbade operations against Tunis and Bizerta. The mediums, with little success at first, began trying to catch enemy ships at sea. All of these operations were hampered by bad weather and tougher opposition. The Twelfth received some badly needed reinforcements and a trickle of replacements, while the British added an important new capability for night attack.

The weather lifted, or seemed to lift, on December 12. The B-17s went after the Tunis harbor and railroad facilities. A B-26 mission to Sousse harbor and a tactical target, a railroad bridge at La Hencha, already attacked by the 310th Bomb Group a day earlier, went sour. The bombers never met their escort and ran into terrible weather, losing two of nine planes to icing. One crew survived. The next day, the heavies began a perhaps dangerous practice of splitting their efforts between the heavily defended northern ports. Fifteen planes of the 97th Group attacked the Tunis dock area, while the 301st sent ten to Bizerta, followed by a dozen B-24s from the 93rd Group. One B-24 crash-landed on its return to Maison Blanche. While the B-26s finally hit La Hencha bridge, six B-25s, protected by a single flight of P-38s, successfully bombed Sousse harbor from 7,000 feet, attacking accurately from much higher altitudes than the mediums had been accustomed to operate. On December 14, a dozen B-24s, escorted by two forward-based RAF Spitfire squadrons (a rare move at this stage of the campaign), hit Bizerta, damaging a ship, while the B-17s attacked Tunis harbor. The B-26s ran a successful low-level mission against Sousse; six Marauders, escorted by as many Lightnings, attacked from 1,200 feet or less, claiming many hits on three ships and dock installations.

On December 15, both medium groups were sent against El Aouina, in the hope that the 301st Group's heavy bombers, going in first, might draw part of the enemy fire. The Fortresses, however, were split between Tunis and Bizerta. While a dozen B-17s struck Bizerta, seven others hit Tunis harbor. Each of the small forces was covered by a half-dozen P-38s; the Bizerta strike also was covered by twenty-four RAF Spitfires, which claimed an Me-109 damaged. The B-17s striking Tunis fought off twenty-five German fighters without loss and dropped forty 500-pound bombs. Two scored direct hits on a big Italian merchant ship, the 10,000-ton *Argentina*. One bomb was a dud; the other blew off her stern, sending her right to the bottom. The one hit, which sank one of the largest ships destroyed during the whole Tunisian campaign, redeemed an otherwise ill-planned and unlucky operation. Seven B-26s and six B-25s had left Telergma. In a succession of foul-ups, the six escorting P-38s only belatedly rendezvoused with the B-25s. But the latter had gotten separated from the B-26s; the B-25s aborted the mission and returned to base. The P-38s tried to catch up with the B-26s, but failed. With Colonel Charles Phillips, the C.O. of XII Bomber Command, as copilot of the lead plane, the B-26s flew on to El Aouina without escort. Fortunately they did not encounter any enemy planes in the air, but they ran into intense flak from ships as well as shore positions. Dropping 300- and 100-pound bombs from 600 to 1,000 feet, they hit a hangar and six to ten planes. The lead ship was hit by flak and crashed into Tunis harbor; all aboard were lost. After this, there were no more low-level attacks against Tunis and Bizerta; for some weeks, the mediums rarely went there at all.

On December 17, the B-17s hit Tunis and Bizerta, while the mediums tried out a new type of mission, a "sea sweep"—attacks on enemy ships at sea. The term ingeniously gave the impression that they were a sort of random search-and-strike operation rather than being guided by accurate intelligence. (As we shall see, however, it was often very hard to find enemy ships at sea, even with Ultra information.) On this day, five B-26s and six B-25s, escorted by six P-38s from the 1st Fighter Group, searched the area north of the Gulf of Tunis. Despite good visibility, they failed to find any merchantmen at sea and saw only warships and vessels already anchored in Bizerta harbor, which they were not supposed to attack. An unusually important target, the valuable German ship *Ankara* was en route from Naples to Bizerta. Ironically, it may have missed a fatal rendezvous with the U.S. planes because of a British submarine attack. Just as the American planes took off, the British submarine *Splendid* slammed two torpedoes into one of *Ankara*'s escorts, the destroyer *Aviere*. The sinking, and evasive action against another submarine attack may have delayed *Ankara* so that the sea sweep missed her.

She reached Bizerta late that afternoon. The Americans did run into enemy planes; a B-26 turret gunner hit a Ju-88. Smoking, it fell out of control into the sea. Both B-25 and B-26 crews concluded that the two types of plane were not well suited to work together; henceforth, even small forces of each type usually operated separately.

Two more tough missions followed on December 18; thirty-six B-17s, escorted by sixteen P-38s, hit Bizerta harbor, striking an anchored ship but running into violent opposition. Four P-38s were lost. Two B-17s from the 97th Group also went down; they were damaged by flak and then hit by enemy fighters which, unusually, made head-on runs. Both Fortresses managed to crash-land behind the Allied lines, but several men were killed or badly hurt. Only three Me-109s were claimed destroyed. Six B-25s and six B-26s (one turned back), covered by four P-38s, struck Sousse railroad station and railroad yards from a low level. They hit the rail targets, but terrific flak from ground positions and barges in the harbor shot down two B-26s; both crews were killed. Every surviving plane was hit repeatedly. After this there were no more planned low-level bomber missions against land targets in Africa. On December 26, Doolittle ordered that, except for special occasions, medium bombers should bomb from medium altitude (about 10,000 feet), although the available D-8 sights were not well suited for that. The only exceptions would be sea sweeps and shore targets struck as alternates when sea sweeps failed to find enemy ships.

For a week, bad weather, the second spell expected by Doolittle, kept American bombers on the ground or rendered missions abortive. On December 26, the 97th Group struck Bizerta, encountering the heaviest flak yet as well as determined interception. One B-17 blew up when a flak hit set off its bomb load; another crash-landed in the no-man's-land between Allied and Axis lines. Some of the crew got home. Two escorting P-38s were shot down in exchange for two FW-190s. The same day, the 301st Group attacked Sfax; it was escorted by forward-based P-40s of the 33rd Fighter Group, flying from a newly opened field at Thelepte in central Tunisia. The B-17s claimed hits on two large and one small cargo ship in the harbor. Four ships were hit—one blown to bits—the next day in Sousse. The bombers returned to Sousse on December 28 and 29 and to Sfax on the last two days of the year. Joined by B-25s on December 30, they aimed at railroad targets as well as the harbor.[26]

The North African-based air forces' efforts to attack ships at sea en route to Tunisia proved fruitless during 1942; even the Malta-based planes had only modest successes. The Beauforts, so successful earlier in 1942, at first were oddly ineffective on the Tunisian run.

After it became clear that the Italian fleet would not attack the North African invasion forces, most of the Beauforts of the detachment of 39 Squadron that had operated from Malta returned to the Middle East. There they flew against the Libyan route. The Squadron was completing reequipment with the new Beaufort II, with better engines and radar. The Beauforts' mode of attack changed. Instead of large-scale day strikes, with occasional one- or two-plane attacks by night with moonlight, the Beauforts shifted mainly to night operations. Operations requiring moonlight were rather constrained; they were not only limited to certain times of the month but to those hours when the moon was at the right height and it was advisable to attack only relatively near a shoreline. A new technique for attacking on moonless nights was developed. Search planes, after finding and tracking a convoy, guided the strike planes to it by dropping flame floats and finally lit up the target with flares. Given the danger from single-engine Axis interceptors over the Sicilian Strait, it probably would have been unwise to continue the earlier mode of attack, but the RAF unit felt its way slowly for a time.

Until late January 1943, only six Beauforts continued to fly from Malta. They devoted most of their efforts to providing antisubmarine patrols for convoys to and from Malta and mining the approaches to Tunis, Bizerta, and Palermo. They also carried out small-scale attacks with bombs against some Italian island bases. The relatively few offensive sweeps with torpedoes achieved nothing until late January.

The Fleet Air Arm's obsolete Albacore biplanes proved more effective. As noted earlier, they had achieved the first air success against Tunisian traffic by damaging *Giorgio* on December 1. On the night of December 21–22, off of Marettimo island, four Albacores, led by Sub-Lieutenant Maund, who had led the attack on *Giorgio,* fell on a Bizerta-bound convoy consisting of the cargo ship *Etruria* and four German landing craft escorted by a pair of torpedo boats. A full moon had helped *Etruria* evade a submarine torpedo earlier but let British planes follow the convoy without having to use flares. Despite flak that the Italians themselves described as "intense," which seriously damaged one Albacore, one plane put a torpedo into *Etruria*'s starboard side. She sank in just one minute, but the escorts and landing craft got 112 of the 130 people aboard to Trapani. A week later, the cargo ship *Iseo,* loaded with explosives, was en route from Taranto to Tunis in company with a German landing craft, approaching Cape Bon. She had only one escort, the destroyer *Freccia. Freccia* had a new German Metox radar search receiver; it alerted the convoy to the fact that it was being tracked, but it did not save it. A radar Albacore led two torpedo carriers into position down moon of the target. At 3:30 A.M., *Iseo* opened fire with machine guns on an approaching plane, which promptly torpedoed her. *Iseo's* cargo blew up; the British reported that flame and debris shot a thousand feet into the air. *Freccia* was damaged by the blast and reported near misses by bombs, but amazingly she and the German craft saved nearly half of *Iseo's* crew.

Attempts to use Fleet Air Arm torpedo bombers from forward bases in Eisenhower's area did not work well. The Swordfish of 813 Squadron moved up from Gibraltar to Bone and tried to torpedo ships at anchor in Lake Bizerta on December 14 but hit nothing. Their attempts to seek out targets at sea also failed, while an Albacore squadron at Bone was badly hurt by a fighter-bomber attack by Me-109s on December 31.[27]

THE SUBMARINES

As Ben Bryant, one of their most successful commanders, noted, the British submarines hit a "bad patch" after the North African invasion.[28] They had heavy losses and many disappointments. After many failed attacks, they finally sank Tunisian-bound cargoes only a month after the landings. Nevertheless, they were the most effective single weapon the Allies had against the Tunisian supply line in late 1942. And although they could not concentrate all of their efforts on the Tunisian route, they continued to hack away at the enemy's strength at sea and forced him to disperse his defensive efforts all over the Mediterranean. And ships sunk en route to another destination sometimes did more serious harm to the Axis effort in Africa than sinkings on the Tunisian route itself.

For the North African invasion, the Allied submarine force in the Mediterranean—which was overwhelmingly British—had been built up to a temporary peak of thirty-one boats (five more were on their way out); this was a strength that could not be continually maintained. The eastern Mediterranean flotilla, still based at Beirut, was operating in the Aegean. It thus contributed only indirectly to the African campaign. The Tenth Flotilla, based at Malta, and the Eighth, based at Gibraltar, were the main forces operating against the African supply route and accomplished most of the sinkings in the middle sea. After the landing, the Eighth Flotilla gradually moved to a new base at Algiers; submarines newly arrived in the Mediterranean, however, usually stopped at Gibraltar and carried out a full war patrol from there before reaching the Algiers base.

As the Allies landed in North Africa, the submarines were disposed to intercept a sortie by the Italian fleet against the invasion force. The Italians were not foolish enough to give the Royal Navy a fight it would have welcomed, but the submarines did score one success. On November 8, northwest of Trapani, the new light cruiser *Attilio Regolo*, returning from a minelaying mission in the Sicilian Strait, ran into Lt. J. Stevens' P46 (later renamed *Unruffled*), which blew off her bow with a torpedo. The Tenth Flotilla directed Bryant's P211 (later *Safari*) to intercept the cruiser, which was being towed home. Bryant could not catch her, but *Attilio Regolo* was a useful addition to the horde of damaged ships jamming Italy's shipyards.

On November 11, the submarines were redisposed against the Tunisian route; some boats of the Eighth Flotilla, operating north of Sicily, were put under the control of the Tenth Flotilla until the Eighth was fully relocated at Algiers, a move fully completed on January 20. But the Tunisian route proved difficult to attack. It was short and heavily patrolled by planes; the submarines were hampered by darkness on the short late fall and winter days. The Gulf of Tunis was rather shallow for submarine operations and was particularly heavily patrolled. The Tenth Flotilla's own submarines, which were concentrated off of Tunisia's east coast, also had difficulties with shallow water. Although some of its boats had great successes, they scored more against Libyan- than Tunisian-bound traffic. The development of the mine barriers in the Sicilian Strait further hampered the submarines. The older minefields had made it hard just to pass submarines from the central to the western Mediterranean; the British had used a clear channel just three miles south of Cape Granitola on Sicily. The new fields formed a corridor confining any submarine that entered it to a strip one hundred by twenty miles wide (and later even smaller) from which quick escape was almost impossible. To make things worse, as Bryant's *Safari* found, the Sicilian Strait was full of sea turtles, which looked just like bobbing mines. *Utmost*, the first submarine to attack the Tunisian route, worked its way into the corridor by entering the swept channel at the Bizerta end. But she had consistent bad luck; she sank nothing after expending all of her torpedoes, and she was sunk by the Italian torpedo boat *Groppo* as she left the channel. The only submarine success on the Tunisian route in November was on the twenty-first; the destroyer *Velite*, escorting a convoy from Bizerta to Naples, was damaged by a torpedo but survived to be towed home.[29]

Safari had some success off the east coast of Tunisia. Bryant was an unusually determined character, older than most submarine captains. He invariably returned with a bag of several ships, as well as several smaller craft sunk by deck guns. (In Mediterranean conditions, a patrol that sank three ships was very successful.) He was a particularly enthusiastic believer in the deck gun, a weapon most World War II submariners thought obsolete. On the afternoon of November 13, he sank the brigantine *Bice*, which was carrying fuel to Rommel, with gunfire. The next day he hit the steamer *Scillin*, en route from Tripoli to Trapani with a torpedo, and he finished it off with gunfire. But this proved to be one of the less happy sinkings in the Mediterranean; *Scillin* was carrying 800 British prisoners, but only twenty-six survived.[30]

Some submarines operating further afield fared better. The Eighth Flotilla's *Ursula*, commanded by Lt. R. B. Lakin, had an unusual patrol in the Toulon-Genoa region, deep in enemy-controlled seas. Leaving Gibraltar on November 20, she carried two men from the Special Boat Section with a pair of "folbots"—small folding canoes. They were to go ashore to attack trains. *Ursula* hit heavy weather, which delayed her and damaged her high-power periscope and radio; the crew was able to repair the latter. On November 30, Lakin landed the Special Boat men, who blew up a train. Retrieving them, Lakin then boarded and sank *Toga*, a small Italian antisubmarine schooner. (While other navies gave even small craft guns to shoot it out with surfaced submarines, even when they could not be given the elaborate gear needed to hunt submerged ones, the Italians fielded many small craft equipped with hydrophones and depth charges, but which were defenseless against deck guns.) Lakin, another gun enthusiast, shelled trains and olive oil storage tanks but was hampered by a deck gun that jammed, and he had to flee from shore batteries.

On the evening of December 3, *Ursula* came upon a ship. Surfacing, she shelled it, and the crew abandoned ship. Lakin drew up to the lifeboat and learned that he had attacked the 2,000-ton *Marguerite II*, manned by Frenchmen under a German captain and engineer. Taking the Germans prisoner, he left the French free to get to the coast, fifty miles away. The ship was not sinking, and British submariners boarded her (an unusual procedure in World War II). They were disappointed to find that she carried no cargo, but they were pleased to carry off documents and fresh food. They opened the ship's seacocks and left. Lakin decided to hang around to make sure that the French did not try to reman her before she went down. She settled so slowly that Lakin finally had the Special Boat men blow a hole in her side with plastic explosive. After a futile attempt to execute orders to intercept a German-controlled Danish ship, and boarding a Spanish schooner that proved to be carrying a harmless cargo of salt, *Ursula* sailed for Algiers.[31]

Safari returned to the east coast of Tunisia in early December. Along with *Umbra*, she had several successes there and off of the Libyan coast. On a dramatic patrol in which Bryant invaded Ras Ali roadstead to shell German landing craft, *Safari* sank a supply ship, a small tanker, and three schooners hauling gasoline. *Umbra* got three ships. In the Gulf of Hammamet, on the morning of December 9, the German ship *Suellberg*, sailing independently from Trapani to Sousse, became the first ship to go down to submarine attack on the Tunisian run. Another German ship, *Macedonia*, also heading to Sousse, was sunk on December 13. Further north, the British submarines scored heavily in mid-month. On December 14, a convoy consisting of two large Italian freighters, *Honestas* and *Castelverde*, escorted by two torpedo boats, was en route from Naples to Tunis. It was approaching Cape Bon that afternoon when an escorting plane spotted a submerged submarine. In fact, there were two submarines present—P212 (*Sahib*) and P46 (*Unruffled*), one on either side of the luckless convoy. *Honestas* was immediately hit on her port side by a torpedo from *Sahib*; seventeen minutes later, *Unruffled* slammed a torpedo into *Castelverde*'s starboard side. Despite a counterattack, *Unruffled* hit *Castelverde* again, two hours later; then she sank quickly. *Honestas* floated for nearly another hour and a half, but finally blew up; the escorts managed to save 154 of 425 men embarked on the two ships. This was the first Tunisian convoy to be entirely wiped out by submarine attack.[32]

The following afternoon, a 5,000-ton Italian freighter, *Sant' Antioco*, carrying a large cargo of gasoline and over 200 people, also was approaching Cape Bon en route from Naples to Bizerta, in company with the German steamer *Brott* and a pair of torpedo boats. Again, a plane spotted a British submarine, *Splendid*, but just too late. A torpedo sent *Sant' Antioco* down quickly, in rough seas. Despite the efforts of the escorts and motor torpedo boats that had come out of Tunis, only twenty-nine of those aboard were saved. Three days later, *Splendid*, trying to intercept *Ankara*, sank the destroyer *Aviere*.

On Christmas day, P48 had less luck. Trying to intercept a convoy en route from Palermo to Tunis, it was sunk in the Gulf of Tunis by the torpedo boat *Ardente*. The following afternoon, P45 (*Unrivalled*) caught the Italian ship *Margherita*, which was on a short hop from Bizerta to Tunis, and sank her with her deck gun. *Ursula*, back at sea, scored the last success of the month against the Tunisian traffic. In the early hours of December 28, the 4,000-ton German ship *Gran* was near Marettimo island, en route from Naples to Bizerta under escort. After a two-hour chase and approach, Lakin launched three torpedoes (a fourth torpedo tube misfired), and *Gran* went up in a violent explosion; nevertheless, eighteen of the forty men aboard were saved. Escaping a depth charge attack, and later an air attack, *Ursula* shifted to a new patrol area north of Cape San Vito, Sicily. In the early hours of December 30, bright moonlight revealed a convoy. Closing in on the surface, Lakin dived when he realized that he would soon be spotted. Managing the final submerged approach toward the zig-zagging ships proved unexpectedly tricky. The ship Lakin had hoped to torpedo ran into *Ursula* instead, smashing her periscopes. *Ursula* survived, but that was the end of her patrol. She was luckier than some other submarines; November and December had been costly months for Allied submarines in the Mediterranean. In addition to

Utmost and P48, three other submarines had been lost. The Greek *Triton* had been sunk in the Aegean on November 16. On December 4, *Traveller*, sent to the Gulf of Taranto to investigate the possibility of an attack with "Chariot" manned torpedoes on the Italian warships based there, although some thought her too big for that delicate job, apparently hit a mine. On December 12, P222, patrolling off of Naples, was sunk near Capri by the torpedo boat *Fortunale*.[33]

THE RESULTS

By the end of 1942, the Allied effort to stop traffic between Italy and Tunisia had not been very successful, but it had not been negligible either. The Italians calculated that 23 percent of the material dispatched in December was lost en route to Tunisia, while the Twelfth Air Force, in particular, had delayed or destroyed much material after it was unloaded. German records report the loss of 54 tanks, 111 guns, and 964 vehicles at sea (although this may count some material lost on the fading Libyan route). Some thirty-two ships of over 500 tons were sunk at sea or in port in the whole Mediterranean, sixteen of these, according to the Italians, had been sunk at sea on the Tunisian route—six by submarines, four by naval surface attack, four by mines, and two by air torpedo attack.[34] The performance of the air forces, however, had not been satisfactory, and it was worrisome that most sinkings in December were by forces that were a wasting asset or that the enemy could counter to some degree—surface ships and submarines. The submarines did remain an important factor, but only planes could stop the traffic in the Sicilian Strait.

REINFORCEMENTS AND REPLACEMENTS

In the latter half of December, the Allied air forces in North Africa got important reinforcements and replacements for their losses. The distinction between the two was not clear, for the Twelfth Air Force, especially, had to partly cannibalize new units just to keep its old ones going.

On November 26, the British, distressed by the inadequacy of the Bisleys, decided to send two Wellington bomber squadrons to Northwest Africa. After many delays, they arrived at Blida airfield on December 19; it was so muddy that two of the bombers cracked up on landing. After flying antisubmarine patrols and dropping supplies to advanced army units, they began night bombing missions against the dock areas and airfields at Tunis and Bizerta on December 28–29. They not only kept up the pressure on the enemy around the clock and in dreadful weather, but they could drop 4,000-pound blockbusters, a weapon that U.S. planes could not carry, on the docks.[35]

The Twelfth got some welcome new units. The 17th Medium Bomb Group, flying a slightly later model of the B-26B than the 319th, began trickling into Telergma late in December after flying the southern ferry route, and it gradually married up with its ground echelon. Although somewhat understrength at fifty planes, it was better equipped for medium-altitude attacks, having one Norden bombsight for every four planes, and it was in far better shape than the 319th Group. On December 30, it sent six bombers against Gabes airfield in a tough introduction to combat. Every plane was hit by fighters and flak and two had to belly-land at Telergma. The 17th Group returned to the same target the next day. One B-26, already damaged by flak, blew up under fighter attack. Its copilot, Bernard Gillespie, survived and parachuted into enemy captivity, from which he had a most unusual escape.

Other reinforcements flew down from Britain. The 82nd Fighter Group, the Twelfth's third P-38 unit, began to leave Britain on December 23, led by bombers that were belatedly catching up with their units through miserable weather. Four Ju-88s flew out from France to attack the leading contingent. The P-38s downed at least one Ju-88, but the Germans downed an A-20 guide plane and a P-38. The latter's pilot managed to swim ashore and evaded capture with the help of the French Resistance. One P-38 pilot was interned in Portugal, another flew into a mountain at Tafaraoui, and others landed at Morocco or Gibraltar, but the group finally arrived more or less intact. However, it had to part with fifty-one of its eighty-four planes to keep the 1st and 14th Fighter Groups operating. The rest moved up to Telergma, entering combat on January 3.

A less valuable addition to the Twelfth was the P-39 units it had left behind in Britain. The 81st Fighter Group began flying to Morocco on the same day as the 82nd. The small, single-engine fighters had an even rougher time than the P-38s; the 81st alone lost five planes interned in Portugal. The 350th Fighter Group, following in January, did even worse. Ten planes landed in Portugal, one in Spain. Two others were never seen again. Only forty-nine of its planes reached Africa.[36] In view of the losses suffered, and the right addition even the P-39s that arrived made to the effective strength of the Twelfth Air Force, it might have been wiser to send the Airacobras to Africa by ship.

A trickle of replacement B-17s began reaching the 97th and 301st Groups by the southern ferry route. Three crews stumbled into one of the war's odder episodes. On January 3, they were sent from Marrakech to Biskra, which was apparently not told that they were coming. No flight leader was appointed, nor were proper maps provided. Their efforts to make radio contact with Biskra were not answered. Flying over heavy overcast, with a much stronger than expected tailwind, they let down over

Tunisia. Much to their surprise, they saw the sea just to the east and enemy fighters and flak coming up at them. Lieutenant Harry Devers and his crew escaped, but they were still lost. They ran out of gas in the dark and bailed out. Luckily they ran into friendly Arabs, who led them to a French post. Lieutenant Bedford Russell belly-landed his B-17 near Gabes; he and his crew were captured. Lieutenant Jesse Coulter was forced down, but made a good wheels-down landing, also near Gabes. He planned to take off again the next morning, but the enemy quickly captured Coulter, his crew, and the B-17. On January 5, a pair of P-40s of the 33rd Fighter Group saw Coulter's bomber, surrounded by enemy troops, being towed by a truck along the road between Gabes and El Guettar. The enemy soldiers promptly manned the B-17s guns, but the P-40s set it on fire.

Russell and the other three officers of his crew were separated from the other prisoners and sent to Tripoli. There, they, Bernard Gillespie, and several other British and American officers were put aboard the Italian submarine *Narvalo*. The luckier men of this group had one of the scariest escapes of the war.

On January 14, *Narvalo* was running on the surface en route to Italy when a Malta-based Beaufort, on anti-submarine patrol ahead of a convoy outbound from the island, spotted her and attacked. The Beaufort's depth charges knocked out the sub's engines, and she could not submerge; two British destroyers raced up to shell her. The Italians freed the prisoners and let them escape the sinking craft. Russell and some others were lost, but the British ships saved the other men from his B-17, Gillespie, and others, as well as part of the Italian crew.[37]

88mm flak gun being loaded onto freighter at Naples harbor.

Kübelwagen being loaded onto transport freighter at Naples port. In the foreground are local Italian dockside workers. German troops look on from aboard the ship.

A Panzer MkIII crew taking a break.

Supply and transport ships make the crossing from Italy to North Africa

Offloading a Wehrmacht truck at Tripoli's harbor. Local Libyan dockside workers are in the foregound.

An Afrika Korps soldier mans an MG34 in antiaircraft mode. The gun rests on a tripod and is fitted with a special antiaircraft sight. Ammunition cans hang off the tripod.

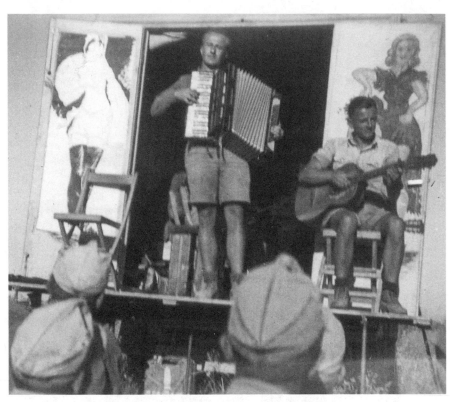

A mobile Afrika Korps entertainment unit gives a show to troops in the field.

A Panzer MkIV with its turret blown off, probably as the result of an internal ammunition explosion.

A Ju52 crew poses beside its aircraft. These men were involved in resupplying the Afrika Korps between Italy and North Africa.

An abandoned Axis train carriage, still loaded with ordnance.

An abandoned Italian M13/40 tank with fuel tanks strapped to sides. Artillery troops from New Zealand inspect it.

An Afrika Korps field bakery.

A semi-sunk transport at Bardia harbor, an important supply depot in Libya.

Afrika Korps troops pose beside their truck convoy in front of the Arco de Felini marble arch near Agedabia, Libya.

Army men posing on the coastline of Libya.

A heavy field howitzer being loaded onto freight in Naples harbor. Italian dock workers and German soldiers are in the foreground.

Bardia harbor, an important supply hub in Libya. In the foreground are ammunition creates. Afrika Korps troops are bathing and resting on the shore.

A pair of soldiers refilling at a water pump.

A Luftwaffe truck parked in front of the Arco de Felini, not far from Agedabia.

Afrika Korps supply trucks. Local Arabs with camels move past.

Afrika Korps troops at a water station refilling jerry cans and water bottles.

An Afrika Korps soldier preparing rissoles on field cooker.

Afrika Korps troops inspecting a knocked-out U.S.-made Lee tank.

Standard-issue AFRIKAKORPS cuff-title as worn by qualified Afrika Korps soldiers.

A burning Axis transport on the Mediterranean during the crossing between Italy and North Africa.

A burning Axis transport on the Mediterranean during a resupply run to the Afrika Korps. A Kübelwagen and motorbike with sidecar are also in view.

A typical palm-tree scene in North Africa, as seen in this German snapshot.

CHAPTER 5

Reorganization, Sea Sweeps, Land Defeats: January–February 1943

It had been clear for some time that the Allied air organization in North-west Africa remained unsatisfactory. Eisenhower's appointment of Spaatz as his deputy for air, which the British had not liked, had improved things, but it was hardly a full solution. The principal air headquarters remained widely dispersed, complicating the job of coordination.

By late December, with the Allies stalled for the foreseeable future before Tunis, Eisenhower's objections to introducing a complex new organization in the middle of a major advance no longer held water. As he explained to General Marshall, he had seriously considered asking that Air Marshal Tedder take command of the air forces in Northwest Africa, but decided to settle for Spaatz instead. A further arrangement would be needed to coordinate his air forces with those on Malta and in the eastern Mediterranean; but a completely unified air command embracing them was not yet desirable. He also wanted Spaatz to retain control of the air forces in Britain as well as in his own theater.

The British, while strongly favoring a single air commander, were not too happy with the choice of Spaatz. But they were willing to accept it as long as an RAF officer became his Chief of Staff and his staff included a senior British officer experienced in maintenance and supply matters. Eisenhower readily accepted these stipulations and largely accepted British proposals to regroup air units of both nationalities along a functional basis. The Twelfth Air Force would conduct "strategic" operations against the enemy rear with heavy and medium bombers and provide tactical air support to U.S. units; Eastern Air Command would control a reconnaissance and striking force to hit ships at sea, defensive fighter forces protecting Allied ports, and support the First Army. On January 5, Spaatz took over as Commander, Allied Air Force. (He still controlled the U.S. air units in Britain as well.) There was still no central command over all of the air units in the Mediterranean and Middle East, nor was there a single air commander able to give orders to all of the tactical air forces in Africa. Still, it was a big advance. A parallel reorganization of the U.S. ground forces at the same time also proved helpful. General Mark Clark's new Fifth Army took control of the ground forces in Morocco watching the Allied rear, with a detachment of XII Air Support Command to control any supporting air units it might need. That freed XII Air Support Command headquarters to manage the U.S. tactical air units in Tunisia without too much distraction.

Eisenhower and his subordinate commanders were none too pleased with the state of the war against enemy supplies. On January 6, he informed the British Chiefs of Staff that "The volume of reinforcements and supply now reaching the enemy through Tunisian ports is a matter for grave concern. Unless this can be materially and immediately reduced, the situation both here and in Eighth Army area will deteriorate without doubt." The enemy was crossing by day and was immune to surface naval action. Only the air forces could stop the enemy. Striking forces required fighter cover, which meant that "even when acting on good information the limitations of endurance renders offensive sweeps abortive unless singularly favored by luck and by weather." His command needed long-range, high-performance reconnaissance planes to cover the lower Tyrrhenian Sea as well as the Sicilian Strait. At least one squadron of Mosquitos (the fast and incredibly versatile but also scarce "wooden wonder") or P-38s was needed for the day reconnaissance task. Radar-equipped torpedo and reconnaissance planes able to cover the Trapani area at night were also required.[1] But no early solution to the problem of finding enemy ships at sea—which was not resolved simply by Ultra intelligence—was available.

CASABLANCA CONFERENCE AND REORGANIZATION

The January 5 reorganization of the Allied air forces was an interim affair, in place for only five weeks. A final arrangement was worked out just two weeks after it went into effect. This was part of a bigger reshuffle of the Mediterranean theater, at the famous conference between President Roosevelt and Prime Minister Churchill and their military leaders at Casablanca, held from January 14 to 24. Many of its decisions would affect the North African struggle.

At that conference, they agreed to impose "unconditional surrender" on the Axis powers, and with the Battle of the Atlantic at a critical point, they gave the fight against the U-boats "first charge" on Allied resources. While planning to invade Western Europe would continue, it was tacitly recognized that such an attack was not likely until 1944. (Trying to hide that from Stalin as long as possible, lest he make a separate peace with the Nazis, occupied the Western leaders for several months.) Supplies to the Soviets would continue at the present level.

The Western powers decided that, after North Africa was cleared, they would invade Sicily; but the Americans refused to agree to invade the Italian mainland. Those decisions proved unwise, as Eisenhower, Admiral Mountbatten, and some British planners foresaw. They realized that if the Allies did wind up invading Italy, as they expected they would, the logical place to strike next was Sardinia, not Sicily. They could take Sardinia earlier and more easily, which would give the Allies air bases that would let them land well north on the Italian peninsula. The decision to take Sicily would lead to the weird result of the world's greatest sea powers crawling up the length of Italy.

The Allied leaders attached increased importance to the bombing of Germany. The Combined Chiefs of Staff stipulated that the aim of the strategic air offensive was to prepare for and support an eventual land invasion— not to provide a substitute for it. In a very confused directive, they ordered a nominally "combined" offensive against Germany, putting General Eaker's Eighth Air Force under the "strategical direction" of the RAF Chief of Staff and setting out targets to be attacked. In practice, the "round the clock" offensive, the British bombing at night and the Americans by day, remained two largely separate national efforts, but the directive registered the detachment of the Eighth Air Force from the Mediterranean campaign.

The Western leaders arranged an awkward "shotgun wedding" between General Giraud, who had taken charge of French North Africa after the assassination of Darlan in December, and de Gaulle's Free French. Theoretically, this unified the French forces fighting the Axis. Actually an unedifying struggle ensued, in which de Gaulle finally ousted Giraud.[2] Eisenhower had to continue to devote much of his time to French affairs, as well as planning an invasion of Sicily, which he did not really favor.

For purely American purposes, Eisenhower became head of a new North African Theater; an AAF general, Frank Andrews, replaced him as commander of the U.S. European theater. Spaatz's domain was now limited to Mediterranean-based AAF units.

Spaatz played a major but subordinate role in the inter-Allied Mediterranean Air Command formed on February 17 under Air Marshal Tedder. For operations in Northwest Africa, Tedder was bound to obey Eisenhower's Allied Force Headquarters. His mission was to support the Tunisian battle, divert the Luftwaffe from the northern fronts, isolate the enemy forces in Tunisia, and interrupt any enemy buildup for the defense of Sicily. Air Marshal Sholto Douglas took over as air commander in the Middle East; Marshal Keith Park remained in command at Malta.

Spaatz would command the newly established Northwest African Air Forces, which included the Twelfth Air Force, the Eastern Air Command

and, after February 21, the Western Desert Air Force, and the U.S. Ninth Air Force. All of these forces would be controlled through three functional subordinate commands. The Northwest African Strategic Air Force (NASAF) under Doolittle would direct the operations of heavy and medium bombers and escort fighters against enemy ports, airfields, and shipping. The Northwest African Tactical Air Force (NATAF) under Air Marshal Coningham would directly support the land battle. Like Spaatz, Doolittle and Coningham had their headquarters at Constantine. The Northwest African Coastal Air Force (NACAF), with headquarters at Algiers, at first under Group Captain G. Barrett and later Air Vice Marshal Hugh Lloyd, who had successfully commanded the air forces on Malta in 1941–42, would defend Allied shipping and ports and provide long-range reconnaissance and sometimes a small anti-shipping striking force of its own. Allied photo-reconnaissance efforts were centralized in a Northwest African Photographic Reconnaissance Wing, commanded by President Roosevelt's son, Elliott.

All of this was part of a bigger reorganization in which Field Marshal Alexander became Eisenhower's deputy and commander of the new 18th Army Group, which would include Montgomery's Eighth Army, advancing from Libya into Tunisia, Anderson's First Army, the U.S. II Corps, and the French forces. Alexander and Coningham, with their long and successful experience in air-ground cooperation, contributed greatly to resolving the serious problems Eisenhower's command had had in managing ground support operations. They had caused more aggravation and attracted more attention at the time (and indeed from later historians) than the long-range operations aimed at isolating Tunisia.[3]

PLANES AND SUPPLIES

Although the reorganization was important, other decisions taken at Casablanca and immediately afterward had more effect on the air war against enemy supplies—notably those straightening out the Allies' own supply and replacement problems. Spaatz reported that by mid-January the Twelfth Air Force's nine groups had just 270 operational planes, just under half of their nominal full strength. The three P-38 groups were especially in a bad way, mustering just ninety planes between them, but other fighter replacements were also scarce. The 14th Fighter Group was exhausted (it had to be removed from combat on January 28), while the new 82nd Group was inexperienced. Both P-38s and B-17s suffered much engine trouble and aborts, and engine changes were frequent at the dusty new inland fields. The poorly trained 47th Light Bomb Group had to retrain and reequip for medium-level operations.

Moving supplies was still hard, and there was a shortage of trucks. At Eisenhower's request, a special convoy was ordered to bring 5,000 trucks to

North Africa; thereafter, the theater was in much better shape. It also was arranged to have the carrier *Ranger*, which was bringing the 325th Fighter Group to Morocco, make another trip to deliver seventy-five P-40s as replacements. General Arnold, conferring with Spaatz at Algiers on January 24, made several important decisions. The 78th Fighter Group, recently arrived in Britain, would send all of its P-38s and all pilots other than squadron and flight leaders to North Africa as replacements for the P-38 groups there. The 78th would be rebuilt as a P-47 group. More P-38s would go to North Africa as deckloads on tankers; fifty more would be flown there over the South Atlantic ferry route. Henceforth, all AAF fighter groups in England would be equipped only with P-47s, freeing all P-38s for the Mediterranean. That delayed the day when fighter escort would be available well inside Germany. The P-47, inherently shorter ranged than the P-38, would not be modified to fly escort missions into Germany for months. Although the Americans would find that the P-38 was not really very suitable as an escort fighter in the peculiar conditions of Northwest Europe, this decision had an important impact on the strategic air offensive.

The Eastern Air Command also was not in great shape, and it was increasingly conscious of the Spitfire V's inferiority to the Me-109 and FW-190. Eisenhower urged Portal, the RAF Chief of Staff, to provide at least two or three squadrons with the much better Spitfire IX. Although Portal tried to put him off, arguing that the Mediterranean should wait for a "tropicalized" version of the Spitfire VII, he finally gave in. It turned out that some Spitfire IXs had been available at Gibraltar for weeks but had been inexplicably held up there.[4]

JANUARY AIR OPERATIONS: TUNISIAN PORTS AND AIRFIELDS

During January, although hampered by bad weather and a shortage of fighter escort, the heavy and medium bombers, in growing numbers, continued to hammer away at the enemy's ports in Africa. Occasionally they also hit airfields and railroad installations, and sometimes inland targets in direct support of the ground forces. Especially when the weather was bad over northern Tunisia, the bombers struck the small east coast ports and airfields. On several occasions, the Twelfth Air Force poached on Libyan targets that were normally the province of the Ninth Air Force and other elements of the Middle East command. The Twelfth's African-based mediums devoted growing efforts to sea sweeps, but due to bad weather and inexperience, it took several weeks before they or the Malta-based Beauforts scored against enemy convoys.

The new year opened with a relatively massive strike in the Tunis area; B-17s and the 310th Group's B-25s were to hit the Tunis docks, while the 17th Group's B-26s hit the railroad marshalling yards. The Fortresses ran a successful mission against the docks, while the 1st Fighter Group snared a pair of Ju-52 transports. Blunders and bad weather, however, led the B-25s and their P-38 escorts to miss their rendezvous. The Mitchells, unescorted, broke through the clouds over Tunis to start their bomb run too late, and never dropped their bombs. The B-26s bombed, but heavy flak hit Lieutenant Frank Marton's Marauder in the tail; it spun into the ground with all aboard. Half a dozen Me-109s pounced on the escorting P-40s from the 33rd Fighter Group and shot one down. The P-40s got an Me-109 and a Ju-88. B-17s bombed Tunis' "suburb" harbor of La Goulette the next day; there was an exceptionally fierce air battle. The 1st Fighter Group got two Me-109s but lost two of the meager escort force of eight Lightnings.

The weather then began to interfere with operations, wrecking a heavy bomber mission to Bizerta on January 4. With solid overcast over northern Tunisia, the 97th Bomb Group sent eleven Fortresses to attack the Sfax power station. The small force of bombers not only wrecked the power plant but hit at least one ship and left the dock area under a blanket of smoke. An engine fire forced one B-17 to land in the desert on the way home. On January 8, the 97th Group went out to hit Bizerta, but the weather forced it to switch to the secondary target of Ferryville, which also was clouded over. The B-17s managed to bomb through holes in the overcast despite powerful opposition; the twenty-six escorting P-38s were able to keep most of the enemy fighters away. The Americans claimed two enemy planes destroyed, while a P-38 was badly damaged. The mission was very successful, sinking five French ships in the harbor, including a submarine, a tug, an aircraft tender, a patrol craft, and a sailing vessel, as well as hitting the docks and oil storage tanks. The Ninth's B-24s hit Tunis that night.

Heavy bomber missions to the "hot" targets were broken by intervals of bad weather and trips to airfields and tactical targets, but the B-17s attacked Sfax and the Sousse dock area on January 14—two escorting P-38s were lost in exchange for one Me-109—and the Tunis marshalling yards on January 19. On January 23, a major mission heavily damaged the Bizerta naval base, sinking a large ship in the channel and damaging two. This attack encountered an exceptionally large number of enemy fighters; the American fighters and bombers claimed twenty. A combined heavy and medium bomber mission struck the Sfax port area and marshalling yards on January 28; after this visit, the east coast harbors were attacked less frequently. Sfax, which could handle only coasters anyway, had been largely blocked by a sunken dredger since December; Sousse, which could handle small seagoing ships, only received eight in January and three the next month. At the end of January and beginning of February, there was a series of blows against the main ports; attacks on Bizerta and Ferryville sank both ships of a convoy that had arrived on January 27. On January 29, the B-17s hit the Bizerta docks; the next day they struck Ferryville. On January 31, an accurate attack hit a large ship Spoleto, in Bizerta harbor; on February 1, this series of missions ended with attacks on Tunis and La Goulette and one of the most fantastic incidents of the war in the air.

After beating off one attack by enemy fighters and dropping its bombs, the 97th Bomb Group was hit by Me-109s coming head on. The crew of Lt. Ken Bragg's *All-American* saw tracers rip into the cockpit of one fighter. Its pilot apparently dead, it crashed into the lead Fortress and tore off a wing. (Three of the B-17's crew managed to bail out; they were taken prisoner.) The German fighter then smashed into the tail of the *All-American* and disintegrated. The collision carried away the whole left stabilizer and nearly tore off the whole tail. Pictures taken from other planes seemed to show a B-17 that had been completely cut in two but was still flying. Just a few spars and a narrow strip of skin kept the tail and the chunks of Messerschmitt embedded in it attached to the bomber. The tail flapped alarmingly, but Bragg had just enough control to fly home. Surprisingly, the crew elected to land rather than bail out, and Bragg eased his plane to a successful landing. The *All-American* finally broke in two after too many men piled in to inspect the unbelievable damage, but it was later rebuilt.

Thereafter, the weather and the priority given to other targets gave the Tunis and Bizerta harbors a respite from daylight attacks until late February.

The Twelfth Air Force's efforts against the ports were supplemented by Wellington night missions and by small dusk or night strikes by the Ninth Air Force. The Ninth's Liberators hit Tunis and Sousse but increasingly concentrated on the European side of the middle sea, hitting Naples and Palermo; the Sicilian port was first attacked on January 7 by ten B-24s. Messina was bombed on January 26, when weather forced a diversion from Naples. Later, planned missions against the Messina train ferry on January 30 and 31 failed to hit it.

SICILY AND SARDINIA

In February, the Twelfth Air Force also finally hit European targets. The air commanders would have liked to strike at Palermo or another "outloading port" for Tunisian supplies, but a strong enemy air attack from Sardinia on an Allied convoy off of Algeria caused them to hit Elmas air base instead. On February 7, both the 1st and 82nd Fighter Groups escorted fifty-one B-17s and B-26s to Sardinia. One Lightning crashed on takeoff—fortunately the pilot escaped unhurt—but the Americans had no combat losses. The bombers claimed twenty-five enemy planes destroyed on the ground, while the P-38s downed three fighters out of the weak defending force. On

February 15, the bombers finally went after Palermo, doing much damage to the dock area and setting a large ship on fire. On February 17, the B-17s hit Elmas airfield again, while B-25s and B-26s struck other Sardinian air bases at Villacidro and Decimomannu. Again, an accident caused the only losses, as two B-26s collided over the target.[5]

The depth of the winter saw a certain crisis of morale in the P-38 units. They had taken heavy losses and were short of planes; the 1st and especially the 14th Fighter Groups were getting tired, while the 82nd Group suffered from its inexperience. On January 28, the exhausted 14th Group was finally pulled out of combat. It turned over its last dozen planes and seventeen replacement pilots over to the 82nd Group and left for rest and reorganization in Morocco, returning to combat only as the Tunisian campaign ended. (A P-40 unit, the 33rd Fighter Group, followed it west in February.) One factor in the pilots' woes, to which the AAF paid insufficient attention, was problems with their planes. The pilots felt that the P-38 was inferior in some ways to the Me-109 and FW-190. One defect at least could and should have been quickly corrected. The P-38 had no cockpit heater. Even in Africa, in the winter it was so cold at 25,000 feet that the pilots' hands and feet became numb. Although Ernie Pyle, who spent some time with P-38 units in early 1943, actually mentioned this in his widely read and justly praised column, no adequate action was taken. In late 1943, pilots flying in even worse conditions in Northwest Europe still had no heater. Some returned from missions with frostbite.

In late January and February, things eased for the escort and other units, partly due to the measure taken at Casablanca, partly to local factors. The last elements of the ground echelons of the 82nd Fighter Group and the 17th Bomb Group finally caught up with their units. The XII Bomber Command/NASAF settled into the bases it would occupy for the rest of the African campaign. The 301st Bomb Group left Biskra for a new base at Ain M' lila in the Constantine area on January 17; the 1st Fighter Group's 71st Squadron followed it there. In March, the B-25s of the newly arrived 321st Medium Bomb Group also would settle in at Ain M'lila. In mid-February, the 97th Bomb Group and the rest of the 1st Fighter Group moved into Chateaudun-du-Rhumel, also near Constantine. Later in February, the 71st Squadron rejoined them there. The new fields were much easier to supply than Biskra and closer to the targets. The Biskra base, however, continued to be used by French pilots flying obsolete Leo 451 bombers in night attacks on forward targets. The Twelfth Air Force also got some welcome reinforcements "on loan" from the Ninth Air Force. Early in February, just as other bomber units were about to leave Biskra, two B-25 squadrons of the 12th Bomb Group flew there from Libya. Assigned to "army cooperation" they played no direct role in the struggle to isolate Tunisia. Finally, the B-25s and Leo 451s also left Biskra for Bertaux.[6]

AIRFIELD ATTACKS

The Twelfth Air Force devoted some of its effort to striking airfields in the Middle East Command's territory. With the Axis forces in Libya fleeing west and demolishing their airfields, the enemy air force in the region had to concentrate on jammed bases around Tripoli, providing profitable targets. The 319th Bomb Group, which was devoting most of its efforts to sea sweeps, started a series of attacks that did the enemy much harm and taught the Allies useful lessons. On January 9, it sent five B-26s carrying a relatively new weapon, "frag clusters," 120-pound clusters of small fragmentation bombs, against Castel Benito airfield near Tripoli. Previously, attacks on airfields had been made with high explosive ("general-purpose") bombs, with spotty results. The B-26s hit hangars and poorly dispersed planes. It was a hazardous mission; the B-26s became separated from their escort of a dozen P-38s and came under determined attack by five enemy fighters. One B-26 was badly hit, but the little formation dived into a timely dust storm and escaped its pursuers.

By January 12, some sixty bombers and transports and fifty fighters and liaison planes were spotted at Castel Benito. The 97th Group sent out a dozen B-17s to try out mixed loads of "frag clusters" and 500- and 1,000-pound bombs on Castel Benito from 10,000 feet. The bombs destroyed a half dozen Macchi 200 fighters and damaged other planes. The B-17s and the sixteen escorting P-38s from the 1st Fighter Group ran into terrific Italian opposition. Intense and accurate flak damaged several planes and killed a B-17 pilot; there was a big air battle against twenty to thirty Macchi 202s. The intensity of the fight was measured by the B-17 gunners' claims of fourteen kills. The escort fighters, normally more accurate, claimed only two damaged. (No Italian planes were actually shot down, but a damaged Mc 202 flipped over on landing and was wrecked.) The Lightnings accomplished the difficult feat of saving a Fortress, which had lost two engines on the same wing from the attacking enemy fighters.

On January 17, reconnaissance showed that nearly 200 planes had gathered at Castel Benito. That night, the Middle East Command sent every available twin-engine bomber to hit the airfield; the next day, the 97th Group returned to Castel Benito with thirteen Fortresses. This time they stayed at 17,000 feet, covered by thirty-three Lightnings, every plane the 1st Fighter Group could put up. For lack of frag clusters, they carried a load consisting solely of high explosive bombs, and they concentrated on barracks and other buildings. Despite the higher altitude and strong escort, the Italians again put up a tough fight. Only a dozen Macchi 202s attacked, but they shot down a B-17 and a P-38; the American fighters destroyed two Mc-202s, while the B-17 gunners made heavy claims. Castel Benito was left to Middle East Command bombers thereafter; they continued attacking it until January 21. On that day, two RAF P-40 squadrons smashed the special "plows" the enemy had been using to tear up airfields that they were abandoning.

Meanwhile, valuable lessons had been learned on how to attack airfields. On January 22, a combined force of forty B-17s and thirty B-25s and B-26s of the 310th and 17th Groups, covered by all three P-38 groups, attacked a concentration of planes at El Aouina. This time, frag clusters were available. The bombers aiming at airfield installations carried a mix of "GP" bombs and frag clusters; planes allotted aircraft parking areas as targets carried fragmentation bombs only. The stunningly successful strike was well timed, catching many planes on the ground. The Americans estimated that they had destroyed a dozen aircraft and damaged nineteen others and set off an ammunition dump; but they actually had destroyed no less than twenty-seven Ju-52s and eighteen Me-109s, as well as several Savoia-Marchettis, and they had killed 200 enemy soldiers.[7]

The medium bombers flew two missions against the Medenine airfield in southern Tunisia, where the enemy air units evacuating Libya were concentrating, on January 19 and 24. The B-17s were supposed to join in the latter attack, but overcast prevented their bombing; the B-25s and B-26s flying under the cloud cover were credited with destroying thirteen planes in a very successful mission; one P-38 and a Spitfire crash-landed upon return. A campaign against airfields, especially on the east coast, followed. An attempt by the 310th Bomb Group to hit El Aouina on January 28 was aborted by bad weather; the next day, the 17th Bomb Group sent eleven Marauders, escorted by 82nd Group Lightnings, to that base. A dozen Me-109s tore into the Americans; they downed two P-38s, while the B-26 gunners claimed four Messerschmitts. One B-26 crash-landed upon return.

Some of the missions to the enemy's southern airfields were extremely tough, as bad as any to the long notorious Tunis or Bizerta areas. American fighter pilots began to describe missions to the Gabes area as "meat runs." (The AAF had come to call relatively easy missions "milk runs.") These missions were exceptionally important, given the fact that the enemy was busy seizing the initiative on the central front.

A January 30 attack on an airfield in the Gabes area ran into furious fighter opposition. The sixteen escorting P-38s from the 82nd Fighter Group claimed six Me-109s, but four P-38s were lost in combat and another was wrecked in a belly-landing at Telegram. (One of the shot down Lightning pilots was captured; another made his way through the lines and got home.) On January 31, ten B-26s from the 17th Bomb Group took off for Gabes, escorted by eight P-38s; but two of the fighters had to abort, and two more somehow strayed from the formation, which was jumped by Me-109s. Once again, the P-38s saved the bombers, but at a heavy cost to themselves. Three were shot down for one Me-109 destroyed, while the B-26s destroyed ten planes on the ground. The 310th Bomb Group lost a B-25 to flak over Sfax on February 2, while three enemy planes were destroyed on the ground. The B-25s were not intercepted, but on February 3 the enemy fighters swarmed over the 17th Group over Gabes, downing a B-26 and three P-38s. Only one Me-109 was shot down, while ten planes were blasted on the ground. On February 4, both heavy bomber groups joined the B-25s and B-26s against Gabes and a nearby landing ground. On this occasion, only the B-17s bombed, amidst a tough battle against enemy fighters. A single B-17 and four P-38s were lost for two enemy fighters claimed by the Lightnings. The weather stopped the mediums from attacking and prevented all attacks for the next two days.

On February 8, while the heavies hit the Sousse railroad yard and shipping, 33 B-25s and B-26s struck the Gabes airfield and rail yard. Four of the eighteen P-38s sent by the 82nd Fighter Group had to abort; they missed one of the most violent battles of the whole Tunisian campaign. Twenty to 30 German fighters attacked, and there was a running fight all the way to the target and back. The P-38s downed eight Me 109s while losing one plane and its pilot, but they were unable to stop the Germans from getting to the bombers. Four B-25s were shot down and two more crash landed upon their return. The bomber gunners claimed no less than ten enemy fighters destroyed. Bad weather again began to interfere with operations; it aborted a B-17 attack on a forward enemy field at Kairouan on February 9 and contributed to the disastrous outcome of an attack on El Aouina by the 319th Bomb Group on February 13, an event which precipitated the withdrawal of that much-tried unit from combat.[8] When the Americans next hit hard the enemy airfields in Tunisia, it would be in the middle of the desperate battle for the Kasserine Pass. The air battles and attacks on air bases in January and early February, though very costly, had at least done something to reduce the Axis' capability before they struck the Allied front.

SEA SWEEPS

Until late January, one feature of Allied air operations was definitely unsatisfactory. Except for some limited successes by the British Fleet Air Arm torpedo units on Malta, the Allies had failed to catch enemy ships while they were still at sea. The prime reason for this was simply bad weather, but flaws in the technique and training of the American units also contributed. The

319th Bomb Group's training for low-level attacks on land targets turned out to be not quite suited to attacking ships. The D-8 sight previously used was replaced by a modified N-6 gunsight installed in front of the copilot, and delay fuses were needed.

The Group's operations officer, Captain J. R. Holzapple, who later became a colonel and commanded the 319th from August 1943 to the end of the war, worked out skip-bombing techniques and tactics. The bombers were sent out in two- or three-plane elements; preferably a pair of three-ship elements, with a squadron formation of a dozen P-38s escorting. Each bomber carried six 500-pound bombs, with four- or five-second delay nose fuses and forty-five-second delay tail fuses. The B-26s searched in a V-formation at 100 feet or so; attacks were made at under 200 feet and speeds of over 220 miles an hour. Upon sighting a ship, or even just a column of smoke, the flight commander would order an attack. The formation then went into an echelon of elements, each element leader picking out a separate target. The element leader then set the course, with each plane solving "rate" (range). The pilot or copilot controlled the bomb release; there were several ways for them to conduct the bomb run. A common method was for the pilot to concentrate on keeping the plane level at the prescribed speed and height while the copilot used the sight and controlled the rudder. Normally three bombs would be dropped "in train" (one after another), saving the rest for a second attack. The attacking plane flew right over the target ship, joining with the rest of the bombers as fast as possible, while rapidly changing altitude to evade flak. There were variations between units, and various refinements were made as experience was gained and more equipment was available. The number of bombers used in low-level attacks increased, up to three six-ship flights, along with the escorts. Later, searches were flown in echelon instead of V-formation, and sometimes at higher altitudes, up to 1,500 feet, depending on visibility. Some experienced crews dispensed with the N-6 sight and bombed by eye. The Americans found that it was preferable to attack from abeam and that tankers were well worth expending a whole bomb load in one run.

Sea sweeps were exciting, tiring, and increasingly dangerous as the enemy antiaircraft fire became thicker. The tedious searches could take up to four strain-filled hours, and they often turned up nothing. Despite Ultra information, actually finding ships that were known to be at sea was not easy. Even when there were no low clouds and rain, haze often severely limited visibility in the Sicilian Strait. The area was too dangerous for day reconnaissance planes to continuously track enemy convoys. The Americans depended on British night reconnaissance planes from Malta for distant warning of their approach. The strike forces based on Malta, flying at night, received news from day reconnaissance of the area farther north while, operating under cover of darkness, radar-equipped Wellingtons could stay in touch with the enemy and guide the night attackers.[9]

During January, a degree of division of effort developed among the units of the XII Bomber Command. The 319th Bomb Group concentrated mainly on sea sweeps, while the larger 310th Bomb Group divided its efforts between sea sweeps and medium-altitude attacks on land targets; the latter were the main task of the newly arrived 17th Bomb Group, which did not go out on a sea sweep until February 28 and flew relatively few thereafter. The 1st Fighter Group specialized in escorting heavy bombers to land targets, while the 14th and 82nd Fighter Groups usually escorted the mediums, both on sea sweeps and land missions.

During the first three weeks of January, many sea sweeps were flown, but few found any ships. The few bombs that were dropped missed their targets. A few sweeps flown by the 310th Group in mid-January offered some recompense. They ran into enemy transport planes that were en route to Tunisia, and the B-25s and their escorting fighters shot down several enemy planes, although not without losses to the Americans. British torpedo bombers were not doing too well either. Determined attacks by Beauforts on a three-ship convoy sailing from Palermo to Tunis on January 17-18 and 19-20 failed. The biggest enemy loss in this period was to another cause. On January 18, the important German ship *Ankara*, carrying a large cargo of vehicles and ammunition to Bizerta, hit a mine laid by the British submarine *Rorqual* near Cani Rocks. Ankara usually hauled tanks, and her loss caused Hitler to decree that tanks must henceforth go to Africa only aboard "ferries."[10]

On the morning of January 20, a convoy, composed of two tankers, the Italian *Saturno* and the German *Sudest*, escorted by two torpedo boats, left Bizerta for Naples. That afternoon, a sea sweep of six B-25s from the 310th Bomb Group, escorted by a dozen P-38s from the 14th Fighter Group, struck while the convoy was still near Bizerta. Only three B-25s, led by Captain Travis Hoover, a veteran of Doolittle's Tokyo raid, went in, but they scored several hits on *Saturno*. (Apparently one hit right at the waterline or below. The Italians thought they had been hit by a torpedo, as well as by bombs.) *Saturno* was badly damaged and stopped. All but a skeleton crew transferred to the German tanker, while the torpedo boat *Ardito* took *Saturno* in tow for Trapani. An additional torpedo boat was sent to reinforce the escort. That night, Wellingtons found the convoy, but the torpedo boats laid a smokescreen that prevented them from attacking. *Ardito*, however, had had to cast off the tow. It was about to resume towing when a pair of Beauforts attacked. One torpedo hit *Saturno* and finally put her under. *Saturno*'s sinking was the first success scored by the Americans at sea—after more than two months in Africa. It also was the first success scored by the Beauforts of 39 Squadron against the Tunisian traffic, at least with torpedoes. The next day, the rest of 39 Squadron finally arrived to reinforce the detachment on Malta.

On January 21, the 319th Bomb Group also scored a success. That morning, a sea sweep of six B-26s went out with a dozen P-38s from the 82nd Fighter Group; two of the Marauders and two Lightnings had to turn back due to mechanical problems. The rest reported finding and attacking a pair of medium-sized freighters and an escort vessel west of Pantellaria. They reported at least one direct hit on one freighter aft of its mid-section and seeing it sink. They believed the other was damaged by near misses. The escorting P-38s claimed destroying a pair of Italian bombers over the convoy. Five to seven enemy fighters tried to get at the B-26s, but they got into a wild engagement with the P-38s. The latter claimed destroying three Me-109s; apparently they actually got one or two Italian Mc 202s, while two P-38s were lost.

The perplexing feature of this engagement is that the Italians reported no ship lost, or even a corresponding attack. Indeed, no convoy to or from Tunisia, other than what was left of the *Saturno* convoy, even seems to have been at sea. A seagoing tug, *Fianona*, sailing with two other tugs from Trapani to Tunis, was sunk by air attack that afternoon, but according to the Italians, long after the B-26s had returned to their base! A sea sweep by the 310th Group that day encountered enemy planes but no ships.[11] A likely explanation is that the B-26s actually mistook the three tugs for a convoy and that the time given by the Italian history for the destruction of *Fianona* was simply mistaken.

There are, however, other discrepancies between Allied and Axis reports in this period that are harder to explain. There is little doubt that American pilots often made mistakes in describing their targets and that they overestimated the number of hits they achieved and even thought they saw ships sink when they did not. There also was a tendency to overestimate the size of the ships they attacked and the escorting warships (e.g., AAF crews often identified escorts as "cruisers," which the Italians did not use on the Tunisian run). All of these problems, it should be noted, occurred often with naval pilots in the Pacific, who had more experience with attacking ships than the AAF pilots in the Mediterranean, and who were certainly better trained at identifying ships. As C. Vann Woodward wrote in 1947, a pilot's "closest look at a target is often at the end of a dive where flak is the thickest and danger greatest, and where he has many things to think about in addition to the bridge structure and the precise number of turrets of the ship under attack. Rain, gun smoke, and clouds often interfere with vision, and photographs do not always settle disputes. Errors in identification and position of targets were notoriously frequent. Only the most experienced A.C.I. (Air Combat Intelligence) and staff officers, who had repeatedly seen 'capsized cruisers' and ships recently reported 'down at the bow' or 'dead in the water' disconcertingly turn up in the enemy's battle line, could feel their way through endless duplications and unintentional error to arrive at accurate evaluations."

Some went further and insisted that only photographs were worthwhile. Pacific observers noted that antiaircraft fire in particular made observation difficult, and pilots often confused bomb hits with the muzzle blast of heavy antiaircraft guns. In high-level attacks on ships, of the sort described later in this chapter, it was nearly impossible for observers to distinguish between hits and near misses. Seeing what was happening in low-level attacks, in the conditions in the Sicilian Strait, probably was even harder than in dive-bombing and torpedo attacks in the Pacific. And, as Harold Buell and others have noted, there was a strong need to believe that attacks made at such danger, in which men often saw friends killed, must have succeeded. Buell notes that deliberate false claims were not unknown in the Pacific; this, however, was not likely to have occurred in the circumstances in the Mediterranean in 1943.[12] There were too few operations, too few targets, and too many witnesses from different organizations.

It is, however, hard to explain Allied accounts of attacks on enemy ships when none were even at sea, according to later Italian accounts, and it is probable that the latter are incomplete. The Italian official history records "return" voyages of some ships from Tunisia whose trips there are not mentioned, and it also seems to overlook some voyages by small ships. It is quite possible that the Allies sank some ships whose losses were never properly recorded, although in all probability the vessels involved were very small, and that some Axis losses that were recorded were attributed to the wrong cause or even the wrong date. Again, similar things are known to have happened in the Pacific. It is worth noting, by the way, that confusion was not one-sided in other respects. Italian seamen often mistakenly identified all twin-engine Allied planes as Lockheed Hudsons (which were not used for offensive purposes in the Mediterranean) and all four-engine bombers as "Liberators." Early in the campaign, German pilots sometimes mistook Flying Fortresses for the very different and far less formidable British Stirlings, and Axis seamen sometimes mistook masthead bombing attacks for torpedo strikes.

On January 22, the 319th Bomb Group sent out another six-plane sea sweep, led by Captain Holzapple. One B-26 returned early; the rest went on, escorted by a dozen P-38s of the 14th Fighter Group. The bombers found

the merchantmen *Chisone* and *Ruhr* and three torpedo boats on their way
from Palermo to Bizerta. Two corvettes attached for antisubmarine defense
had just left the convoy, which was defended by eight German and Italian
fighters. The German Ruhr carried an exceptionally valuable cargo: ten
tanks, other vehicles, and a Giant Wurzburg radar.

There was no overclaiming this day. The B-26s went straight in and hit
both *Ruhr* and *Chisone*. The Americans rated the flak as light. At least some
of the ships were taken completely by surprise and did not fire until the
bombs were already falling, but two planes were hit. A navigator, Richard E.
Miller, another veteran of the Tokyo raid, died from his wounds. The P-38
escort had become separated from the B-26s during the bomb run, and as
the bombers joined and climbed to 300 feet, they came under attack by a
force they estimated at five Me-110s and three or four Me-109s. There was a
fierce running fight. Two B-26s were badly shot up—one actually caught fire,
but the flames went out—and they crash-landed near Bone. Two men were
badly hurt. The Marauder gunners claimed destroying two Me-109s and two
Me-110s; the Italian official history reported the loss of a Ju-88, while other
sources indicated that the Lightnings actually destroyed two Ju-88s. *Ruhr*
sank, while the damaged *Chisone* was towed into Bizerta.[13]

On the afternoon of January 23, five B-26s from the 319th Group and
eleven P-38s from the 82nd Fighter Group went out to search the Gulf
of Hammamet and the area north of Tunis. They spotted two ships in a
cove north of Hergla and strafed and bombed them, but they claimed
no sinkings. Later, while flying between Cape Bon and the Aegades, the
P-38s spotted a plane they identified as an Italian Cant Z1007 and shot it
down. Twenty-five minutes later, the Americans spotted a pair of "barges"
and attacked them. One seemed to blow up; the other was reportedly left in
flames. In fact, they had destroyed a German landing craft heading for Bizerta and forced another to return to Palermo. Lieutenant Charles Meyers'
B-26 was hit hard by 20mm flak and machinegun fire; one shell exploded in
the cockpit and badly injured the copilot. Meyers, also hit, managed to keep
the plane aloft for twenty minutes, although both engines were damaged.
The starboard engine gave only half power; finally, the port engine quit
entirely. Meyers then ditched. The B-26 sank so quickly the crew could not
get the rafts out. After an agonizing half-mile swim, the crew gained the
shore. They then found themselves in a relatively isolated spot, not far from
the front line. Luckily the Arabs they met were friendly, but the Americans
reached a field hospital only after a further unpleasant journey, more than
two days after the crash.[14]

On the night of January 23–24, two Italian cargo ships, *Pistoia* and
Verona, were en route from Naples to Bizerta, escorted by two torpedo boats.

The moon was full, and the Italian commander expected an attack. As soon as the British planes approached, the whole convoy turned toward the moon, while the torpedo boats laid a smokescreen and put up intense flak. But the British also had devised new tactics. A flight of four Beauforts attacked; only two dropped torpedoes, while the others attacked the escorts with bombs. The torpedo boats survived this treatment nicely, but a torpedo hit and stopped *Verona*. *Pistoia* and one torpedo boat sailed on, but Wellingtons caught them three hours later and put a torpedo into *Pistoia*. She went up in flames and sank quickly; *Verona* went down hours later. This was the first enemy convoy to Tunisia that was entirely destroyed by air attack.[15]

On January 27, two sea sweeps went out seeking an especially important target, the big German (ex-Norwegian) tanker *Thorsheimer*, known to be heading for Bizerta from Messina. Another convoy of two merchant ships was also en route to Bizerta from Naples, via Palermo, while four Italian destroyers were carrying 1,200 troops to Tunis. The 310th Group's sweep apparently encountered both the tanker convoy and the troop-carrying destroyers in the same area; an attack aimed at the tanker turned into one on the destroyers. The Mitchells reported leaving one in flames, but none were damaged. A sweep by four 319th Group Marauders found the tanker convoy, but they had lost contact with their fighter escort. The B-26 pilots saw strong enemy fighter cover over the convoy and could not see a way to get at *Thorsheimer* without flying right over one of her escorts. They estimated the latter at being no less than six in number and returned without bombing. Technically, *Thorsheimer* was escorted by just two ships, but it appears, although the Italian accounts do not so state, that the troop-carrying destroyers traveled with the convoy during at least part of the day.

On the same day, the badly depleted 319th Group got an important reinforcement. The 320th Bomb Group, which had just arrived over the South Atlantic ferry route and was only partly trained (it did not enter combat as an organization until late April), turned six crews and eighteen B-26s over to the 319th, enabling that tired unit to continue operations for a time.[16]

A sea sweep on January 28, in bad weather, found no shipping; the B-26s shot down an Me-109. The next day, the 319th Group scored; that morning it sent out six bombers, escorted by twelve P-38s from the 1st Fighter Group. One bomber returned early; the rest came on an unusually large convoy, no less than five cargo ships escorted by four torpedo boats and three motor torpedo boats, with fighter cover. (The Americans counted six freighters and two large "cargo liners" and four destroyers and six smaller escorts.) Concentrating on the "cargo liners," they flew through intense and accurate light flak and inaccurate heavy weapons fire to hit both targets. Later, a second run was made on an escort, and its destruction was claimed. All of this took place amid a violent air battle against an estimated eight or ten fighters covering the convoy and thirty to fifty more that swarmed out from the Tunisian coast. The B-26 crews credited the P-38 pilots with doing a good job, but the enemy was too numerous; some got through. An Me-110 shot down one B-26 in the middle of its bomb run; the B-26s claimed one Me-109 and two twin-engine fighters shot down.

Two bombs had hit and stopped *Vercelli*, which was carrying troops as well as supplies. The Italians removed almost all of her crew and passengers while struggling hard to save her. She was put under tow but sank early the next morning. Another ship, *Lanusei*, was lightly damaged. The convoy's woes were not over; a few hours after *Vercelli* went down, another ship, *Parma*, ran into a magnetic mine at the entrance to the channel to La Goulette. She staggered into shallow water before sinking, and the Axis recovered her deck cargo of vehicles.[17]

Vercelli was the last major loss to air attack at sea for several weeks. Sea sweeps on January 30 made no contact. On January 31, B-26s spotted a convoy heading northeast, but it was covered by a huge number of planes and it was clear that the Americans had been seen; they decided that it would be suicidal to attack. The Italians reported an unsuccessful attack, at about the same time, on the German ship *Lisboa*, which was en route between Trapani and Sousse; later that day, a submarine sank her. The Italians reported an unsuccessful air attack on five troop-carrying destroyers the next day, but this was apparently a B-17 attack while they were in port at La Goulette. On February 3, the 319th Group flew what turned out to be its last sea sweep. A strong force of twelve B-26s (one had to abort) found a convoy of one ship escorted by three or four escorts; apparently this was *Thorsheimer*, returning from Bizerta. Only three B-26s were able to attack, and they claimed only near misses.

The 319th Group went out on only one more combat mission during the Tunisian campaign. On February 13, nine bombers—others were supposed to go but never got off—were sent to drop 120-pound frag clusters on the El Aouina airfield. Four aborted the mission; the last five plowed through bad weather to drop their bombs. A strong force of Me-109s then piled into the Marauders; the bomber crews felt let down by their escorting fighters. One B-26 was destroyed; another, crippled by flak and then badly shot up by fighters, crash-landed behind the Allied lines with a dead tail gunner. With few fit planes left and morale low, Colonel Aring, the 319th Group commander, requested that his unit be relieved for rest and reequipment. That was not a suggestion calculated to make him popular with his superiors, but Doolittle readily agreed. The 319th turned over its remaining planes to the 17th Group and moved to Morocco. Rebuilt, it returned to combat on May 31. Aring remained in command until he was shot down and captured on a mission to Sicily in July.[18]

Sea sweeps went on, but the only success was scored on February 10. On that day, the 310th Group sent out nine planes. General Doolittle was the copilot of the lead plane. North of Cape Bon, the B-25s attacked four Siebel ferries, which put up a lot of flak. Doolittle ordered a second bomb run, something almost never done. The Americans thought that one Siebel ferry definitely went down and that the other three seemed to be sinking. There is no confirmation of this from the Italian side. The Italian official history reported that no landing craft were even at sea at this time, though it is noteworthy that one was reported lost to "maritime hazards" on February 8. Submarines had caused the enemy's losses in the first half of February, although a midget German tanker, *Jaedjoer*, sailing from Palermo to Sousse, was sunk by a mine on February 11.

Then the British planes began to score at night. On the night of February 15–16, they struck a convoy comprised of *Capo Orso* and KT 13 en route to Tunis, escorted by a corvette. Only two of six Beauforts managed to find the convoy; they missed. Then, nine Wellingtons attacked with torpedoes and bombs. A torpedo hit *Capo Orso*, which was carrying gasoline, and set her on fire; she sank in less than half an hour. Luckily for those aboard, a hospital ship was passing nearby and helped KT 13 with rescue work. On February 18, *Col di Lana* returning from Tunis to Palermo and carrying prisoners of war, was repeatedly attacked and finally sunk by a Malta-based torpedo bomber.[19] By the time these successes were scored, a major land battle was taking place.

KASSERINE PASS

While the winter rains kept the front in northern Tunisia locked, there was fighting in the relatively drier center and south. Raff's paratroopers and poorly equipped French forces had formed a weak front in the Eastern Dorsale mountains. The American II Corps, under General Lloyd Fredendall, came up to establish a firm position and possibly to prepare to drive to the coast at Sfax or Gabes to split the Axis forces in Africa. The British finally persuaded Eisenhower that such a move would be reckless; a major offensive must wait until the Eighth Army was in a position to support the Algerian-based forces. The Allies were hampered by a poor command structure—among other things, the French refused to serve under Anderson—and Fredendall proved totally inadequate.

The Axis did not let the Allies build up in peace. From January 18 to 31, a series of local German attacks inflicted heavy losses on the French and took all of the passes in the Eastern Dorsale. They would serve as sally ports for a major offensive when Rommel got behind the Mareth Line.

There was little argument on the Axis side over the basic scheme for a spoiling attack on the First Army–French–American front, and then, while the Allies in the west were crippled, falling on Montgomery's army. How to conduct the western offensive, however, caused a major quarrel. (There was still no Axis army group command in Africa.) Rommel wanted to hit II Corps near Gafsa with all three of the panzer divisions, then in Africa, under his command. Von Arnim disagreed, and a complex compromise was arranged. Von Arnim's Fifth Panzer Army would strike out of Faid Pass against the American forces around Sidi Bou Zid, using 10th and 21st Panzer Divisions. He would then send the 21st Panzer Division south to Rommel to reinforce the latter's attack toward Gafsa.

The Allies fully expected an enemy attack, but Ultra intelligence in this case proved dangerously misleading. On the basis of enemy messages referring to a discarded plan, they expected a main attack at Fondouk, north of Faid, and only subsidiary blows at Faid and Gafsa.

The Allies were thus looking at the wrong place when the Germans burst out of Faid Pass on February 14. The well-planned attack, supported by fighters and Stukas, caught Combat Command A, 1st Armored Division, and two infantry battalions of the 34th Infantry Division, holding a too-widely stretched position. The Germans quickly surrounded the American force. At first the Americans did not realize how strong the Germans really were; the attempts by small American reserves to relieve the trapped units on February 14 and 15 were easily smashed. The Allied high command still expected a main attack farther north; Fredendall, in particular, fumbled things from the start. Finally, Eisenhower ordered a pullback to the Western Dorsale and sent British reinforcements. The advance of Rommel's comparatively weak force was initially unopposed; it took Gafsa on February 15.

But von Arnim would not hand over the 21st Panzer Division. He wished to exploit his victory by attacking north to Sbeitla and rolling up the Allied front. Rommel, in contrast, favored concentrating farther south and attacking northwest toward Tebessa, where II Corps' supply dumps were located, far into the Allied rear. He even hoped to push all the way to Bone on the coast, cutting off most of Eisenhower's forces. The issue was referred to Rome. On February 19, Commando Supremo and Kesselring ruled that the main attack would be under Rommel, but it would go north toward Thala and Le Kef, deep in the Allied flank, instead of northwest to Tebessa. Von Arnim was to give Rommel both the 10th and 21st Panzer Divisions. But he did not fully obey this order and held back part of the force—especially the big Tiger tanks Rommel coveted—for a local offensive he planned to launch against the British in northern Tunisia.

Rommel let the Italian Centauro Armored Division try an advance to Tebessa, but the Americans stopped it without much trouble. The German forces launched a dual drive north toward Thala, via Sbiba and the Kasserine Pass in the Western Dorsale. The Germans soon decided that Sbiba was too heavily defended. The western drive through the Kasserine Pass, which gave its name to the whole battle, became the main attack. After some difficulty and serious delays, the Germans broke through the Americans defending the Kasserine Pass. But then they ran into a small British task force from the 6th Armored Division. It fought heroically until its last tank had been destroyed. On February 21, the Germans resumed the attack. In hard fighting, they pushed toward Thala. But it became clear that the defenders were just too strong and were being reinforced, and rain hampered the Germans' mobility. Rommel decided that there was no point in persisting, and on February 22 he ordered a withdrawal to free forces for the attack on the Eighth Army. He had inflicted heavy losses; 7,000 prisoners had been taken and 200 tanks destroyed. To Rommel's fury, von Arnim then launched his own attack in the north on February 26. Wasting tanks in unsuitable terrain, the attack misfired with heavy losses

Kasserine Pass was the most serious reverse the Allies suffered in Northwest Africa. The Germans won considerable success, due mainly to blunders by Fredendall, but the battle revealed a general slackness in II Corps and some problems with American equipment. But the Germans had thrown victory away through their own quarrels and dispersal of effort. Although far more experienced than the Americans, and far more canny tacticians at all levels, they had made some gross errors after their initial success. Whether because it had become too contemptuous of Americans or had simply forgotten orthodox tactics after such a long time in the desert, the Afrika Korps had tried to bull its way through the passes at Sbiba and Kasserine instead of taking the high ground on either side.

Probably Rommel could not have reached the north coast even if he had completely defeated II Corps. He would have been pushing ever deeper into mountains where the Allies would have found strong defensive positions; his left flank, growing ever longer, would have been difficult and costly to protect, if it could be protected at all. But even a local victory around Tebessa and the capture of the huge supply dumps there would have lamed the American forces and improved the Axis supply situation there. The campaign against the Axis supply line would have had less effect, at least for a time, and the Allies' final offensive in Africa might have been delayed, which also would have delayed the invasions of Sicily and Italy. The Kasserine Pass raised this possibility, only to eliminate it. It produced a general shake-up on the Allied side. Eisenhower replaced Fredendall with George Patton, another old friend, but a far better general, who rapidly improved the performance of II Corps. The formation of the 18th Army Group under Alexander resolved the command muddle. Alexander wanted to replace Anderson, but refrained from doing so because Montgomery did not wish to release one of his corps commanders to take over the First Army. Alexander kept Anderson on a short leash. After the February defeat, Alexander had little faith in the U.S. forces and resolved to depend on them as little as possible. He retained this low opinion of them (which he tactfully hid from the Americans, who greatly respected him) through the Sicilian campaign, although II Corps performance in the later stages of the Tunisian campaign should have changed his mind. (Ironically, Rommel did not consider the Americans all that bad; his view was that, while inexperienced, they learned quickly.) As a result of Kasserine, the American role would be limited; they would merely threaten the rear of the enemy forces facing the Eighth Army and tie down reserves that would otherwise be used against Montgomery, who would launch the main effort.[20]

SEA SWEEPS AND PORT ATTACKS

The Kasserine Pass battle had diverted much of the air effort from "strategic" operations to tactical support of the ground forces when the degree of the crisis was realized. Although for much of the battle the weather was so bad that bombers either stayed on the ground or could not find targets when they flew, the B-17s as well as the medium bombers were sent to hit troop concentrations and forward airfields. P-38s strafed in the battle zone. Still, several successes at sea were scored in the middle of the battle, and late in the month the bombers hit enemy ports hard.

The 310th Bomb Group got off a few sea sweeps, even while the situation was still critical. The Allies were anxious to get an important convoy that had left Naples for Bizerta. It consisted of the large tanker *Thorsheimer*, carrying 13,000 tons of gasoline, and the steamer *Fabriano*, carrying troops as well as supplies and munitions, and three torpedo boats. Ultra gave plenty of warning, and a Baltimore spotted the convoy south of Naples. Wellingtons, Beauforts, and Albacores attacked on the night of February 20–21; a Beaufort finally damaged *Fabriano*, while the convoy broke its journey in the Trapani roadstead. *Fabriano* had to dock at Trapani for repairs. The rest of the convoy went on, covered by ten German fighters and four Italian antisubmarine seaplanes.

On February 21, five B-25s set out, covered by seventeen P-38s from the 82nd Fighter Group. Early in the flight, the P-38s ran into a Ju-52 and shot it down. Over the target, they jumped a force of Ju-88s and claimed no less than seven of them shot down, as well as a German Arado seaplane. (The Italian official history credits the Americans with shooting down only one

Ju-88 and a seaplane; other sources say they downed at least four Ju-88s.) Things were even more confused than usual; some Americans thought a cruiser and a freighter were present, and that heavily armed Siebel ferries were also part of the escort, although that was not so according to the Italian account. The American leader ordered one bomber to attack the Siebel ferries; the rest went for the tanker. Two bombs hit *Thorsheimer*, one was a dud, but the other set her on fire and stopped her. The attack was expensive. One B-25 successfully ditched, another belly-landed near Bone, and a third lost an engine and landed at the British base at Souk el Arba.

The torpedo boat *Orione* was seriously damaged in the attack, but took off *Thorsheimer*'s crew. A tug came out from Trapani to tow *Thorsheimer* to safety. The Americans had ensured that *Thorsheimer* would not reach North Africa and would at least be out of action for the rest of the campaign; the British finished her off. Six Beauforts went out early that evening. They hit her four times; the last two Beaufort pilots decided not to waste their torpedoes as the ship went down in flames. *Thorsheimer* was the largest ship sunk at sea in the Tunisian campaign.[21] Her loss measurably shortened the struggle in North Africa.

A second sea sweep on February 21 found nothing but stumbled on an enemy plane identified as a Heinkel 177—a new type—although none were supposed to be in the Mediterranean at this time. It was a most peculiar plane; the German answer to the B-17 and B-24, it had four engines, but each pair of engines was yoked to drive a single propeller, an arrangement that did not work well. Unfortunately, two Lightnings were lost in the process of shooting down the bomber! The following morning, a six-ship sea sweep from the 310th Group, apparently seeking an inbound convoy, found a large convoy of three German ships, *Gerd, Henry Hestier,* and KT 13, with a destroyer and a pair of torpedo boats, leaving Tunis for Palermo. Six Ju-88s tried to intercept the bombers, but the escorting P-38s parried the attack, shooting down a Ju-88; they also shot down an Italian floatplane at the cost of one American fighter. The B-25s split into attacking elements and went right in. *Gerd*, hit on the stern, sank in just twelve minutes; one B-25 crashed into the sea.

On the afternoon of February 23, another six-plane sweep set out. Near Cape Bon, it spotted seven Siebel ferries and six German motor torpedo boats en route from Marsala to Tunis. (The Americans thought all thirteen craft were Siebels.) The attackers met terrific flak. The entire lead element of three B-25s was shot down. The lead crew managed to ditch. Lashing their two rafts together, they floated around until an Italian floatplane saved them the next day. The 310th Group claimed five ferries sunk and two damaged; in reality, two Siebels went down.

Perhaps fortunately, the 310th Group did not fly any more sea sweeps until March 1. Such fearsome losses cast doubt on the viability of low-level sea sweeps, at least in their present forra.

On the night of February 24–25, the British intercepted another return voyage from Africa by three ships from Bizerta to Naples. Despite a smoke screen, three Beauforts attacked. One was lost, but another torpedoed the ship *Alcamo*. A few hours later, three Beauforts came out. *Alcamo*, dead in the water, was hit again and sunk. One Beaufort crashed into the sea upon its approach; the Italians saved three of the crew as well as the men manning *Alcamo*.[22]

On February 25, the heavy bombers and their escorts were released from direct support of the land battle. For the first time in several weeks, the 97th and 301st Bomb Groups returned to the Bizerta area, which had been left to small-scale British night attacks. This time Spitfires from forward bases in the Bone area joined the Lightnings to provide a heavier escort than ever before, although the trip was a risky one for the short-range British fighters. Unfortunately, the flak also was heavier. The lead bomber was hit in the bomb bay, and an oxygen bottle blew up. When it hastily jettisoned its bombs, other planes "dropped on the leader." Still, some damage was done. Other B-17s were damaged, but none were shot down; one P-38 was, and another crash-landed, in exchange for two Me-109s destroyed.

On February 26, while the 97th Bomb Group attacked Cagliari harbor, the 301st Group's Fortresses tried a new form of attack: a high-level sea sweep by heavy bombers. This was a tricky move. The AAF, like other air forces, had once nursed great hopes for high-altitude attacks on moving ships, even warships. But Pacific War experience, as Walter D. Edmonds wrote, showed that "bombing a moving vessel, even with the Norden bombsight, was a vastly different proposition from hitting a stationary circle on the training grounds at Muroc, California."[23] B-17 attacks on ships at sea had rarely succeeded. At the battle of Midway, the heavy bombers had dropped 314 bombs but did not hit a single Japanese ship. However, it was still hoped that a properly dropped bomb pattern would have a good chance to score against a convoy of relatively slow, unmaneuverable merchant ships. Tactics called for sending a whole group to attack from the rear quarter, with each flight of six aiming at a single ship, dropping 500-pound bombs with a tenth of a second nose fuses and twenty-fifth of a second tail fuses.

On this first mission, the 301st Group sent out twenty bombers; two turned back. The rest struck a heavily escorted convoy en route from Naples to Bizerta, off of the Lipan islands north of Sicily, bombing from 15,000 feet. They believed that they had sunk one ship and damaged three. Me-210s attacked the B-17s, but none were lost, while five of the bombers were damaged by flak. It appears, however, that the only result was to damage an

Italian submarine chaser. Still, the idea was not a bad one, and it worked better later. The relative inflexibility of heavy bomber missions, and the lengthy preparations they needed, however, militated against frequently using B-17s against ships at sea. Once a convoy was located, it took at least four hours to get B-17s over it.

The heavy bombers ended the month with another large, successful attack on Cagliari harbor on February 28. They damaged several ships and sank the 3,800-ton *Paolo*. The Ninth Air Force and RAF Liberators had hit ports on a small scale even more frequently during February; Naples was attacked five times. The Messina ferry terminal was attacked twice, but continued to be a highly resistant target.[24]

SUBMARINE OPERATIONS IN EARLY 1943

British submarines began 1943 with a dramatic special attack on enemy warships. In late 1942, the British had contemplated an attack on Italian battleships based at Taranto with "Chariot" manned torpedoes, launched from submarines. These were copies of similar weapons the Italians had used quite effectively several times against the Allies. Frogmen rode them into an enemy harbor, detached a warhead, and put it under a target ship, then they tried to get away—something Chariot riders rarely managed. While manned torpedo riders usually survived their attacks, they generally were captured. The Taranto attack would have been a sort of reply to the Italian-manned torpedo attack on Alexandria in December 1941, which had knocked two British battleships out of action.

A reconnaissance of Taranto had already cost the British a submarine in December; then the Italian battle fleet had shifted its base. The British now resolved to launch two different attacks, one against Italian cruisers based at La Maddalena on Sardinia, the other against Palermo, on the same day, January 3. The Sardinian attack failed; P311 was apparently sunk in a minefield on January 2 before she could launch her Chariots. *Trooper* and *Thunderbolt* launched five Chariots off Palermo the following day. Three failed to get into the harbor; the other two laid their charges under a new small cruiser, *Ulpo Traiano*, and a passenger-cargo liner, *Viminale*. The cruiser, which might have been a valuable escort on the Tunisian run, was blown in two. *Viminale* was badly damaged and later sunk by air attack while being towed to Naples. Two of the Chariot men got back to the submarines, two were killed, and six were captured. Despite the Palermo success, some British submarine officers doubted that operations of this sort were worth the diversion of submarine effort, much less the losses they cost.[25]

The first half of January was in any case a dry spell for British submarines on the Tunisian route. By January, the combination of mine barriers, shallow waters, and heavy enemy patrols had led the British to largely abandon attacks in the Sicilian Strait. They shifted their efforts to the north shore of Sicily, the western coast of the Italian mainland, and the eastern coast of Tunisia. During January, they sank five medium-sized ships off the latter shore and helped destroy a sixth (shared with the Fleet Air Arm). But all were homebound, and most were on the Libyan, not the Tunisian, run.[26]

Some successes were scored far from the African routes. The Eighth Flotilla's P212 (*Sahib*), patrolling the Gulf of Genoa, had a very successful patrol. After sinking an unescorted merchant ship on January 10, it shelled a seaplane hangar ashore. On January 19, it torpedoed an enemy submarine and picked up a survivor, who reported that they had gotten U-301. *Turbulent*'s guns blasted a train in Calabria on January 11.

On the night of January 16, the British started having more luck against Tunisian traffic. *Splendid* intercepted an important convoy heading for Bizerta, consisting of the German *Ankara* and the Italian *Emma*, escorted by three torpedo boats. The convoy was only few hours out of Naples when *Splendid* halted *Emma*, which was carrying ten tanks, with a torpedo hit. The next morning, *Splendid* attacked again and finished off *Emma* with a pair of torpedoes. *Emma* was the largest ship sunk by submarines on the Tunisian route. (*Ankara*, as noted earlier, never reached its destination either, tangling with a mine.)

On January 17, P45 (*Unrivalled*) caught the tug *Genova* in the Gulf of Hammamet on the east coast of Tunisa and sank her with gunfire. P44 (*United*), which had had a rough patrol—it was one of the few submarines still deployed on the Sicilian Strait route and had survived two enemy attacks, including a rare torpedo attack by an enemy motor torpedo boat—ran into a small convoy bound from Bizerta to Palermo, near Marettimo island. It fired four torpedoes; apparently just one hit, but it sank the destroyer *Bombardiere*. A surviving destroyer laid down a very heavy counterattack and kept P44 down for a long time. Some of her crew suffered carbon dioxide poisoning. The next day, the German cargo ship *Favoer*, on a rare run to Bizerta from Cagliari, escorted only by a subchaser, was blasted off Cape Carbonara by torpedoes and gunfire.

Many submarine successes followed on the east coast of Tunisia against both local and Libyan traffic; the last Axis ships were trying to escape from Tripoli before the Eighth Army reached it. The small *Grondin*, sailing between Sfax and Sousse, was sunk on January 20. On the morning of January 23, another small vessel, *Amabile Crolina*, hauling drummed gasoline from Pantellaria to Sfax without escort, was sunk by *Unruffled*'s deck gun in the Gulf of Hammamet. On January 25, *Unruffled* sank the midget tanker *Teodolinda* with a single torpedo. In the early hours of January 26, a motorized schooner, *Redentore*, trying the same sneak run from Pantellaria as *Ama-*

bile Crolina, this time to Sousse, ran afoul of *Unruffled* at nearly the same spot. On January 31, after a long chase, *Unruffled* caught up with the German ship *Lisboa*, escorted by a single torpedo boat en route from Trapani to Sousse. *Lisboa* had escaped several air attacks earlier that day, but a single torpedo sank her not far from her destination. The Gulf of Hammamet remained quite dangerous for the enemy. Three merchant ships trying to make a run from Tunis to Sousse encountered the submarine *Unison*, which disposed of all three with her deck gun.[27]

Early February saw a series of valuable victories farther afield. Bryant's *Safari*, now transferred from Malta to the Eighth Flotilla at Algiers, sailed up the route from Bizerta to Naples after surviving a mistaken attack by a British Wellington and tangling with a U-boat. *Safari* made several unsuccessful attacks before reaching its station off Naples. This was a rich hunting ground, but also dangerous and difficult. Naples harbor had two exits, which could not be covered at the same time and were heavily patrolled. Contrary to what might be expected, the area proved more dangerous at night than during the day, so the British submariners learned to pull back from the coast during the hours of darkness and close in, submerged, in daylight. On January 30, after further disappointing encounters with a convoy, *Safari* cornered two schooners in the Gulf of Policastro and smashed them with its deck gun. On the afternoon of February 2, *Safari* had some unusual luck. It spotted a tanker, *Val Savoia*, and a coastal steamer, *Salemi* (both larger than Bryant thought) leaving the Bocco Piccolo exit from Naples. Due to some foul-up, they had not yet picked up their escort, and the local air and sea patrols were temporarily away. Out of three individually aimed torpedoes, two slammed into the tanker, and it promptly sank. Bryant then surfaced; in less than three minutes, *Safari*'s gun crew put twenty-six shells into the smaller ship before the sub dived to make its getaway.[28]

On February 1, *Pozzuoli*, hauling salt from Trapani to Palermo, was sunk by *Turbulent*, captained by Bryant's friend, J. W. Linton, off Cape San Vito. On February 3, the ships escorting *Thorsheimer* on her return from Bizerta to Naples had a particularly bad time. The torpedo boat *Uragano* was torpedoed and sank; the destroyer *Saetta*, trying to help her, hit a mine (from the same minefield that sank *Ankara*) and went down too. On February 4, *Unseen* sank *Le Tre Marie* in the Gulf of Taranto. The next day, Linton achieved an important victory off Cape Zaffarano. The tanker *Utilitas*, with three torpedo boats, was en route to Palermo from Taranto with 5,000 tons of fuel for convoy escorts. *Turbulent*, which had tracked the convoy since the previous night, finally closed in and fired four torpedoes, two hit and sent the tanker and her valuable cargo under. Three submarines operating off Italy's southwest and Adriatic coasts sank six ships in a single week. One of these ships,

Petrarca, carrying 1,500 tons of munitions from Taranto to Tunis, had run aground near Croton while trying to evade British torpedo bombers; but she was in water sufficiently deep for *Una* to blow her up with torpedoes.

Late in the afternoon of February 17, two ships, *XXI Aprile* and *Siena*, escorted by two torpedo boats and a corvette, were near Cape San Vito en route to Tunis from Palermo. The merchantmen were very slow, and the convoy was only crawling along when the corvette and one of the torpedo boats picked up a submarine on sonar. They began hunting for it, but *Splendid* nevertheless closed in. Early in the evening, a torpedo streaked into *XXI Aprile*'s stern. She vanished in the resulting blast. On February 21, a convoy of two German ships, *Baalbek* and *Charles le Borgne*, escorted by a corvette and a torpedo boat, tried to reach Tunis from Trapani, with a wide eastern swing via Pantellaria. Delayed by a violent storm, they survived a night attack by bombers and were approaching Cape Bon from the east when a torpedo from *Unruffled* set *Baalbek* afire. That was the last major loss to submarines on the Tunisian run for nearly a month, although February ended with heavy losses elsewhere, as *Torbay* got two ships in the Gulf of Genoa.

January and February 1943 had been good months for Allied submarines, which had inflicted heavy losses at a relatively low cost compared to other periods in the Tunisian campaign. Other than P311, just one submarine, *Tigris*, was apparently lost in this period. Her end was a bit mysterious. She is generally believed to have hit a mine, but some sources estimate that she was sunk on February 27; others state that she went down ten days later.[29]

PROGRESS AND RESULTS

On February 21, Eisenhower for the first time expressed some satisfaction with the war against the enemy's supply lines, telling the Combined Chiefs of Staff that "Action by air, surface, and submarine forces has achieved some measure of success in cutting down [the] arrival of enemy supplies in Tunisia by sea."[30] In fact, there was, as yet, no dramatic rise in the number of enemy ships actually sunk, and the percentage of supplies destroyed en route remained at just 23 percent of that dispatched in both January and February—the same as in December. But less supplies had left Italian ports, so the total that actually landed in Tunisia fell from 69,908 tons in January to 59,016 the following month. Some of the best enemy ships were damaged and under repair, while port facilities on both sides of the Mediterranean were deteriorating under the rain of bombs. The British calculated that some twenty-eight ships of over 500 tons were sunk in port or at sea in January, while only fifteen went down in February—but from a shrinking pool. The Italians (whose breakdown of the causes of losses cannot be fully reconciled with the British analysis) reported that on January 12 ships were sunk at sea on the Tunisian run: four by submarines, five by planes, and three by mines. In February, the total sunk at sea was the same—six to submarines, five to planes, and one to mines. ("Ferries" were not counted by either the Italians or British.) Although the Allies had scored a special success in getting the *Thorsheimer*, they were unfortunate in that their other successes tended to be against ships returning from Tunisia rather than delivering supplies. And they would have done better if the Kasserine battle had not diverted bombers from hitting ports.[31]

By the end of February 1943, the writing was on the wall for the Axis supply effort. Although the heavy losses to the American medium bombers on low-level sea sweeps were worrisome, the difficulties with bad weather, inadequate bases, insufficient supplies, poor organization, and inadequate training and tactics were mostly solved. The pattern of operations established by the end of February, applied by forces that were becoming stronger, would serve for the rest of the Tunisian campaign.

By early 1943, whatever local setbacks the Allies had suffered or would suffer in the future, the tide of war had turned, not only in the Mediterranean region but throughout the world. Stopped in the Caucasus and then smashed at Stalingrad, the Germans, minus their Sixth Army and several allied armies, had lost all of the gains they had made in Russia in 1942 and had been permanently weakened. The Japanese, defeated with ruinous losses at Midway, had been foiled and thrown back in the Southern Pacific at Guadalcanal and New Guinea.

CHAPTER 6

Victory: March–May 1943

With the Axis offensive in February, the battle for Tunisia became more intense; so did the Axis logistic crisis. In March, the Allies stopped the last enemy spoiling attack and took the offensive, compressing the Axis bridgehead as a prelude to a final attack on Tunis and Bizerta. That took until late April. During this period, the Allies won a climactic struggle for air superiority over Africa and the Mediterranean islands and effectively severed the enemy's supply lines. In these last months, they were smashing enemy ports and sinking ships right and left so that by the end hardly anything was getting through to Africa. This made possible a relatively cheap victory on the ground. It must not be forgotten that the struggle in the air and under the sea was not an independent action undertaken for its own sake; it was designed to support the land battle.

Early in March the British contained von Arnim's poorly thought out but stubbornly continued local offensive in northern Tunisia. Rommel, finally taking over Army Group Afrika, prepared a major attack on the Eighth Army. It was to be executed by his old command, now renamed the First Italian Army, commanded by General Messe. All three available panzer divisions, all understrength, were sent south to strike the comparatively weak British advance force at Medenine. Rommel, tired, depressed, and in bad health, let Messe adopt a plan he did not believe in.

Ultra intercepts warned the Allies that the enemy intended to attack well in advance; General Montgomery had plenty of time to bring up reinforcements. When the German tanks started out on March 6, the British were completely ready. They fought a model defensive action. The attack was stopped mainly by well-directed artillery fire and antitank guns, including a heavy new type, the 17-pounder. British losses were very light, and their tanks hardly even engaged. The Germans lost fifty-two of the 160 tanks they committed. Rommel left Tunisia soon afterward; von Arnim took his place.

The Eighth Army, supported by the American II Corps, now began driving the enemy out of south and central Tunisia. It first had to overcome the Mareth Line, built by the French before the war to stop an Italian attack from Libya. Running from the sea, it was protected on its landward end by the rugged Matmata hills and the supposedly impassible sand dunes of the Dahar. Once the enemy was driven from the Mareth Line, the Eighth Army would have to pass through the Gabes gap, a narrow gateway just fifteen miles wide between the sea and a really impassible series of salt lakes. Rommel, von Arnim, and Messe had all wanted to fall back to that very strong position right off. But Kesselring continued to overrule them. He argued, not without reason, that such a move would simply hand the Allies critical airfields in central Tunisia and make the Axis bridgehead untenable. That argument either genuinely convinced Hitler, or he welcomed it as a support for his normal, reflexive opposition to yielding ground. He backed Kesselring. But the Mareth Line had a dangerously open flank. Von Arnim thought that the whole idea of attacking the Mareth Line was a capital mistake on the part of the Allies. In his view, they should have halted before the line, leaving a minimum force of two divisions to contain it. They should then have sent the rest of the Eighth Army on a wide westerly sweep around the end of the line to strike in the Gafsa-Faid area, releasing II Corps to strike farther north at Kairouan. These forces, attacking to the sea, would, he thought, cut off the First Italian Army and greatly shortened the campaign. (Indeed, on other occasions, as we shall see, he even doubted that the Allies needed to attack on land at all.)

The Allies followed a more cautious, orthodox policy.

On March 17, II Corps launched a limited offensive against Gafsa that was designed to threaten Messe's rear and draw off the Axis reserves. The Americans' performance had improved. They quickly gained their initial objectives and repeated the British success at Medenine on a smaller scale. On March 23, the U.S. 1st Infantry Division stopped a major German armored counterattack at El Guettar, although it lost many of the poorly conceived and misemployed "tank destroyers" that the U.S. army had mistakenly hoped were the "answer" to the panzer. Alexander finally let General Patton go further than originally planned and try to push to Gabes on the coast, cutting off the enemy retreat from the Mareth Line. But the Axis defenders proved equally tenacious, and they stopped the Americans.

Meanwhile, the main attack on the Mareth Line by the Eighth Army's XXX Corps, which had started on March 20, was stopped with heavy losses. Although the British Long Range Desert Group had found a way around the southwest end of the Mareth Line, Montgomery had been strangely reluctant to use it on a major scale. He had, however, sent a provisional corps built around the New Zealand Division through the Dakar to threaten the enemy rear. Now reinforced, the New Zealand Corps, and a supporting attack across the Matmata hills, outflanked the Mareth Line. The Axis forces held off the New Zealanders and the Americans just long enough to get back to the Wadi Akarit or Gabes gap position. Fortunately, the 4th Indian Division, unlike most Allied units, was well trained M mountain fighting. On April 5, the Indians attacked through terrain that Messe had thought too rugged for a major force. Although Montgomery did not fully exploit the breakthrough to pass through armor to cut off the enemy, Messe had to retreat far to the north.[1]

The Axis had been squeezed into a narrow slice of northern Tunisia, but the area was highly favorable for defense. In this sort of terrain, even heavily outnumbered but experienced defenders reasonably well equipped with machine guns, mortars, antitank guns, and mines could stop or at least inflict heavy losses on an attacker. That had been shown the previous fall in the race for Tunis, and it was the case again and again in the long struggle for Sicily and Italy—if the defenders could count on an indispensable minimum of supplies. But that was what was lacking in Tunisia.

AXIS LOGISTIC CRISIS

Even in late February von Arnim thought that the Axis supply picture was so bad that the Allies did not really need to launch a major ground offensive in Tunisia. In Eisenhower's place, he declared he would not attack (on land) but concentrate everything on cutting the Axis supply line, attacking ports, the Axis air forces, and ships at sea. If supplies were completely disrupted, Tunisia must fall by July.[2] The very special conditions in Tunisia thus offered, perhaps, the first opportunity in history to achieve a major victory over a land army by air power and submarines alone. Had time been less pressing, and had the Allies not needed to get on to Sicily and Italy while weather conditions were still favorable for amphibious landings, there would have been much to say for exploiting this intriguing possibility. As it was, there had to be a land battle, although the measures von Arnim feared made it far less bloody than it might have been.

On February 26, von Arnim pointed out that the newly formed Army Group Afrika was responsible for maintaining 350,000 personnel (including 120,000 combat troops). The Army Group's Chief of Supply and Transport had estimated its monthly minimum consumption of supplies at 69,000 tons. To stop the Allies however would require an active defense involving major armored movements, which were costly in supplies, and a stockpile of an entire month's supplies in Tunisia. To wage a successful defense and to counter the expected disruption of the supply system by Allied action, no less than 140,000 tons a month had to be landed in Tunisia. Rommel concurred with this estimate.

Kesselring, however, was still more optimistic, while Hitler's response was merely to order that the current rate of supply be doubled or tripled, without disclosing how. For some months Hitler had concentrated his attention on the desperate situation on the Eastern Front; he was only now starting to pay much attention to North Africa. (He was particularly upset by the loss of *Thorsheimer.*) Kesselring promised to deliver 50,000 tons of supplies on the first fortnight in March, in the event that only 32,500 tons were even scheduled to be forwarded. Kesselring did seek out more expedients designed to increase the flow of supplies. The French destroyers being repaired in Mediterranean yards would be switched to troop transport duties. More German antiaircraft ships would strengthen convoy escorts, while a rule against carrying fuel and ammunition in the same ship was rescinded. All escorts would carry deck cargoes. Kesselring got the Italians to shift motor lighters from other areas to Tunisia.

One effective measure, already begun in February, was the greater use of the German KT ships. In March, the Germans began sailing KT ships in groups without escort, depending on speed and their own guns to get through. Usually operating from Sicily—in April they began sailing from Reggio, opposite Messina—they had a fast turnaround. Few were lost until the last days of the Tunisian campaign. But they could not carry enough cargo to make a critical difference. Despite the supply difficulties, the Germans did not reconsider a decision made in January to ship whole new units to Africa. The Herman Goering Panzer Division and the 999th Afrika Division began crossing to the southern continent in March, although only two-thirds of the former and just half of the latter ever arrived. The Italians prudently did not commit new units to Tunisia but sent a steady flow of replacements for those already there.

In mid-March, Hitler conferred with Kesselring (still optimistic despite a visit to Tunisia) and Admiral Doenitz. Still blandly insisting that deliveries to Tunisia be increased to 150,000 to 200,000 tons a month, Hitler did approve some useful steps. Vice Admiral Friedrich Ruge, who had run the German convoy system in the North Sea region, was attached to the Italian naval staff to improve the flow of supplies. More German antisubmarine equipment and personnel were sent to reinforce the Italians. Fortunately the German leaders ignored the air command in Tunisia's intelligent deduction that the courses of Axis convoys were somehow known to the Allies.[3]

ALLIED COMMAND AND INTELLIGENCE ARRANGEMENTS

The organizational pattern set up in February lasted for the rest of the Tunisian campaign, but the Allies continued to improve their intelligence and reconnaissance during March. The staff of specialists long established at Cairo to advise on enemy shipping and supply matters was finally transferred to Algiers. The Northwest African Air Forces' new headquarters at Constantine took several steps on its own. The distribution of Ultra information was improved. Daily meetings on target selection were moved from the Allied

Force Headquarters at Algiers to Constantine, with Group Captain Humphreys or his deputies providing a daily briefing on the enemy's intimate secrets. The communications links between the various subcommands were improved. Doolittle's NASAF was given its own radio intercept station so that it could promptly pick up reports from Malta and the Coastal Air Force. The NACAF had acquired the RAF's 14 Squadron, which flew Martin Marauders equipped as torpedo bombers. Operating from Egypt, 14 Squadron had scored some successes against enemy ships in the Aegean before it was ordered to Eisenhower's area. But it was released from strike work; instead it would provide badly needed long-range reconnaissance over the Tyrrhenian Sea, flying from Telergma and later from Blida. On March 1, the NASAF set up a clear system of priorities for its attacks: (1) Tunisian-bound shipping, (2) shipping outbound from Tunisia, (3) aircraft and aircraft facilities, and (4) critical communications points within Tunisia.

On March 16, this system was modified to stipulate that the heavy bombers would be used only against shipping targets, except when Spaatz's headquarters granted a specific exception. The NASAF was to hold two medium bomber squadrons ready for antishipping strikes at the NACAF's direction. Later this system was made more flexible. If no shipping targets were known by eight o'clock in the evening, the NACAF would release the force for other work the next day. On March 24, tankers underway at sea received overriding priority over all other targets.[4] That was wise; a similar decision, also justified, was taken by the American submarine command in the Pacific, only a good deal later. Ironically, the only Axis tanker, definitely lost at sea on the Tunisian route after this, was sunk by a submarine.

MARCH AIR OPERATIONS

During March, the Allied air forces continued the pattern of sea sweeps, torpedo bomber attacks, and attacks on ports and airfields established in February, with a greater emphasis on the European side of the Mediterranean. The heavy bombers visited not only the major airfields at Tunis and Bizerta and on the east coast but sometimes joined the lighter planes to strike at the widely dispersed landing grounds increasingly used by the enemy's fighters and dive-bombers. The Allies, while still hampered by bad weather, inflicted increasingly heavy losses of ships at sea and in port and began taking a growing toll of the escort vessels.

They began March with a double blow at the enemy's main "outloading" ports. The Ninth Air Force's B-24s hit Naples harbor, where they sank the Italian torpedo boat *Monsone*. The Twelfth Air Force/NASAF's B-17s hit Palermo harbor for the second time, forty-one P-38s from the 1st Fighter Group escorting the 97th Bomb Group's Fortresses in an effective strike that sank the destroyer *Genere*. The next day the B-17s hit the Tunis dock area. One plane was badly hit by flak, but the German fighters did not get at the bombers. On March 3, the effort shifted to airfields. The 1st Fighter Group escorted the 97th Group to a landing ground near Gabes and conducted the 301st Bomb Group to El Aouina. There, a dozen Me-109s came up to fight. Two P-38s and two Me-109s went down in the melee, while another P-38 pilot had to bail out because of a mechanical failure on the way to the target. The bombs destroyed an Italian transport plane on the ground and damaged three other planes.

A 97th Group mission to Bizerta on March 4 misfired due to heavy over-cast; the B-17s returned without dropping their bombs. The German fighters nevertheless intercepted; the Americans claimed only "probable" and "dam-aged" enemy planes in the resulting fight. The 301st Group seemed to have better luck. It sent out seventeen B-17s on the second heavy bomber sea sweep, with strong P-38 escort. Two bombers returned early; the rest spotted the target convoy, three cargo ships and four escorts en route from Naples to Bizerta, off Porto Farina, Sicily. Bombing from 15,000 feet, they reported sinking four out of six ships. Apparently, however, not one ship was hit.[5]

The weather, bad enough to keep planes on the ground some days, seri-ously hampered the conventional sea sweeps by B-25s and B-26s. Those that were flown turned up nothing until March 7.

That morning, the 310th Bomb Group sent out a sweep of six B-25s with eighteen P-38s from the 82nd Fighter Group. They were after an impor-tant convoy—the German steamer *Henri Estier*, and two big diesel-powered freighters, the German *Balzac* and the Italian *Ines Corrado*, with a heavy escort of six torpedo boats and air cover en route from Naples to Tunis. *Ines Corrado* towed barrage balloons to discourage low-level attacks. Despite some trouble with fog, the Americans finally spotted the convoy southwest of Marettimo island. The B-25 crews estimated the escort, which was fearsome enough, at no less than eight ships, including a cruiser, but they rocketed in at 200 feet. Some of the P-38s climbed to go after the Axis air cover, but others stayed with the bombers and strafed the escorts to reduce the terrific flak. Even the Italian account conceded that this convoy enjoyed strong antiaircraft defenses. Concentrating on *Ines Corrado*, the largest ship, the B-25s hit her several times. All the bombers were badly shot up by flak and Me-109s, and several men were seriously hurt. One turret gunner lost his sight in one eye. One B-25 staggered back to base for a belly-landing with over 150 holes in it. The P-38s suffered no losses and got a pair of Ju-88s, a Macchi 200, and a large seaplane.

They left *Ines Corrado* a flaming wreck. She had been carrying tanks, vehicles, artillery, and gasoline in drums. With her fire-fighting equipment knocked out, fires raged out of control. It was soon obvious that she could not be saved; three of the Italian torpedo boats rescued the 200 men aboard with their usual efficiency. The hulk of *Ines Corrado*, one of the largest ships lost on the Tunisian run, continued to burn, and sank the next day.

Meanwhile, the rest of the convoy sailed on, but its problems were not over. Early in the afternoon, *Henri Estier* hit a mine and started to sink. Shortly thereafter, more trouble arrived from the sky. The 97th Group had sent out nineteen B-17s on a sea sweep, escorted by twenty P-38s of the 1st Fighter Group; they spotted the remnants of the convoy and attacked. Several bombs hit and sank *Balzac*. To complete the disaster, the torpedo boat *Ciclone*, trying to save the men on the *Estier*, hit a mine and sank.[6]

The convoy attack of March 7 was the first definite success scored by a heavy bomber sea sweep, but the results of this form of attack remained spotty. On March 8, the 97th Group went out again on a sea sweep, attacking the tanker *Labor*, which was sailing from Palermo to Bizerta, escorted by only two antisubmarine patrol boats but with good air protection. The Americans ran into a big air battle. The Fortress gunners claimed eleven German fighters, while the 1st Fighter Group reported downing five Me-109s and two FW-190s. Apparently the P-38s actually shot down a Me-110 and three Me-109s; one Lightning lost an engine, but no Americans were hurt. However, the B-17s missed their target. The heavy bombers did better on their next mission.

On March 10, both heavy groups combined to strike El Aouina and La Marsa airfields. The escort fighters were handicapped by many aborts—no less than fifteen of the thirty-six dispatched by the 1st Fighter Group had to turn back—but did a good job, claiming two Me-109s. One P-38 pilot had to bail out. The B-17s claimed eleven enemy fighters destroyed, while their bombs smashed two Savoia-Marchetti 82s on the ground.[7]

IMPROVED SEA SWEEPS

It was becoming clear that low-level sea sweeps by medium bombers were getting too costly. The Americans experimented with medium-altitude (8,000 to 10,000 feet) attacks using Norden sights to drop instantaneously fused bombs, and combined medium- and low-altitude strikes. Medium-altitude attacks were usually executed by three three-ship elements. Upon spotting the enemy, the bombers climbed to attack altitude, approaching the targets from astern. The two wing or outer elements turned forty-five degrees away from the lead element, then back to converge with the lead element on the target. The elements were staggered at levels of 500 feet. Such medium-altitude attacks, by themselves, were not too promising, so attention was focused on combined medium and low attacks. In this case, the "high" flight carried out an attack of the sort described above, while a "low flight" of two three-ship elements came in at low level. Alerted by the leader of the high flight calling "bombs away" over the radio; the low flight would strike thirty to forty seconds later. Hopefully it would hit an enemy watching the high flight and distracted by bomb blasts. But executing such attacks was tricky. Attaining complete surprise was hard, because the high flight was likely to be picked up on radar, and the flights could easily lose contact or attack either too far apart or too close together. Later in March, the high and low flights searched together, flying at 5,000 to 6,000 feet, splitting up to attack. The high flight would turn away from the enemy convoy before turning again to approach from behind, while the low flight broke away in a diving turn, letting down to 2,000 feet, then making another turn and descending again to come in from abeam. But as Colonel Howard Engler ruefully commented, such combined medium and low strikes "were never entirely successful."[8]

On March 4, the 17th Bomb Group, which had flown its first sea sweep just a few days earlier, tried out the new tactics, going out at 8,000 feet and "on the deck" against a heavily escorted convoy of three ships en route from Naples to Bizerta. But only the high flight attacked, and it missed.

On the afternoon of March 11, the 17th Group tried again, attacking a group of Siebel ferries. (Ferry traffic across the Sicilian Strait was unusually heavy at this time.) Twelve B-26s took off, escorted by twenty P-38s of the 82nd Fighter Group. One B-26 returned early. The rest plowed through rain and, despite the haze, spotted a convoy of eight Siebels and two motor torpedo boats en route from Trapani to Tunis; the Americans counted seven Siebels and four "possible destroyers." Things did not go well. The low flight did not attack; the high flight, comprised of just six planes, bombing from the relatively low altitude of 5,500 feet, thought it had hit at least one Siebel ferry. The Lightning pilots, more optimistic, thought the bombers had damaged three. According to the Italian records, however, they hit nothing. The flak was quite inaccurate, but four twin-engine German fighters made a determined attack. Two Me-210s got past the escorts and shot down Lieutenant Daniel Logan's B-26. The victory was a costly one for the Germans; the P-38s promptly got both Me-210s. The circling B-26s spotted six men swimming in the water and dropped life rafts for them. An unusual attempt at a sea sweep by P-40 fighter-bombers also failed; it found nothing.

The next day the 310th Bomb Group tried the new tactics again. The mission was led by the group commander. General Doolittle's Chief of Staff, General Hoyt Vandenberg, who commanded the Ninth Air Force later in the war and was U.S. Air Force Chief of Staff during the Korean War, and two British officers, went along as observers. Fifteen B-25s escorted by thirty-two

P-38s from the 82nd Fighter Group went out just before noon. Two of the fighters had to abort.

Visibility was good. The Americans reported sighting eleven Siebel ferries. Nine planes bombed from 8,000 feet, while six swept in on the deck. The Germans, however, had enough time to bring some guns to bear, and the low flight ran into a lot of flak. One man was hit by a 20mm shell and later died of his wounds. Lieutenant Richard Schrupp's starboard engine was blown right off the plane, and a wing tank burst into flames. Schrupp managed to ditch. Though one man was badly injured, all five crewmen got into a raft. After considerable suffering, they reached an enemy-held part of the Tunisian shore. French collaborators turned them over to the Germans.

The Americans were sure that they had sunk at least three Siebel ferries and at least damaged, if not destroyed, three more. The P-38s definitely shot down two Cant Z1007s close to the convoy. Yet according to the Italian account, the only ferry group at sea at this time, five Siebels and seven motor torpedo boats running from Tunis to Marsala, reached port intact; in fact, no attack was recorded at all![9] But whatever the real results, the Americans thought that this time the new tactics had been vindicated. However, targets could not always be found; on the same day, March 12, a B-17 sea sweep, unable to find ships, went to a secondary target, the railroad yards at Sousse.

That night, the Malta-based torpedo bombers, which had achieved little for some weeks, attacked an important Tunisian-bound convoy off Sicily. It included the German ships *Caraibe* and *Esterel* and the Italian tanker *Sterope*, heavily escorted by no less than six torpedo boats, three corvettes, and five German subchasers. Repeated attacks were to wreck it. The Beauforts caught up with it near Palermo. Stanley Muller-Rowland, the ace Beaufort pilot of the Tunisian campaign, hit *Sterope*. The tanker survived and staggered into Palermo, but she would never reach Tunisia. The success was costly; the escort vessels shot down two Beauforts and badly damaged another. The enemy rescued three of the downed airmen. An hour after *Sterope* was hit, a torpedo from the submarine *Thunderbolt* damaged *Esterel*, but it was another expensive hit. The Italian torpedo boat *Libra* sank *Thunderbolt*. Tugs got *Esterel* into Trapani. Because of a report that British destroyers had left Bone, heading northeast at high speed, the rest of the convoy also beat into Trapani. *Caraibe* and her escort left Trapani the next evening. In the early hours of March 14, the British torpedo planes found *Caraibe*. One hit started to set off the ammunition she carried. The Italians were lucky to save sixty-three of the one hundred men aboard. Once again, albeit at a high cost, a whole convoy had been wrecked.[10]

The much-tried 310th Bomb Group now had a well-deserved time off. After the March 12 mission, most crews went to a rest camp, and the group did not fly any more missions until March 26. The heavy bombers and the 17th Bomb Group's mediums continued the NASAF's war against shipping. They were joined by the newly arrived 321st Medium Bomb Group, whose Mitchells had arrived by the southern route. They included fifteen new B-25Cs modified for low-level strikes, with greatly improved armament. The nearly worthless belly turret had been removed, and tail guns and large side windows carrying waist guns had been installed.

Sea sweeps continued to have spotty results. A high-level attack by the 97th Bomb Group on March 15 apparently missed the target completely. The next day, the 301st Group sent out twenty B-17s, escorted by twenty-three P-38s. The sixteen bomber crews that reached the target could not agree on exactly what they saw, but according to the Italians their bombs sank a pair of Siebel ferries heading for Tunis. One P-38 pilot was missing.

On March 17, the British Malta force tried a rare day attack comparable to those of 1942, far from the usual hunting grounds. Nine Beauforts, escorted by as many Beaufighters, struck a convoy bound from Taranto to Bizerta, off the southern tip of Calabria. It turned out to be a bad idea. The two freighters had a slightly heavier than usual surface escort, but a heavy air cover, which shot down a Beaufighter and a Beaufort; the torpedo bomber crew was rescued by the Italians. The Beauforts pressed home their attacks but, in another example of the fallibility of observation, their claims of hits proved erroneous. Their torpedoes had exploded, after hitting reefs rather than the target ships.

After several stops in Sicily and a reinforcement of its surface escort, the convoy was in the Sicilian Strait on March 20 when the 321st Bomb Group came after it. The new group had completed one mission against the Mezzouna landing ground in Tunisia; bad weather had aborted another attack on a railroad target. This was its first sea sweep. Fifteen B-25s, escorted by twenty-nine P-38s from the 82nd Fighter Group, flew out, searching at low level. Two P-38s had to abort. The Americans had passed up a group of Siebel ferries to seek the big targets, when a half dozen Heinkel-115 seaplanes jumped a P-38 squadron. The He-115 was an excellent torpedo bomber, but not exactly a fighter plane. Nevertheless, the daring attack worked well, diverting part of the American force. Nine P-38s chased the He-115s toward Tunis; they soon ran into a flight of FW-190s. Losing sight of both the enemy bombers and their own, the Lightnings went home. The rest of the force spotted the convoy, estimating it at four freighters and two escort ships. The high flight climbed to 7,500 feet, but circled for over half an hour before attacking. Intense flak damaged two B-25s. The fighter and bomber pilots agreed that at least one freighter had been hit and left burning; some B-25s reported hits on another and near misses on a destroyer.

But the time consumed in setting up the attack had allowed a big force of enemy single-engine and twin-engine fighters, estimated to number as many as fifty, to arrive. There was a terrific air battle. One flak-damaged B-25 was shot down. Another crash-landed at Bone with more than 500 holes in it. The P-38s alone claimed eight Me-109s, two Ju-88s, and an unidentified Italian plane. The bomber crews had good reason to be thankful for the new waist and tail guns. One P-38 also crash-landed at Bone; two more were damaged. Despite the American claims, the convoy apparently reached Bizerta intact.[11]

If the Axis congratulated themselves on a success, albeit at a high cost in planes, the mood did not last long. March 22 proved to be a very long and unpleasant day for the Germans and Italians. The Italian cargo ships *Mario Roselli* and *Manzoni* had left Naples for Bizerta escorted by three torpedo boats. *Manzoni* had fallen behind the convoy due to an engine failure; near Capri, a torpedo bomber hit her on the stern and she sank. (The very next night the British scored again, although not in the way they wanted. Beauforts spotted the small German ship, *Bernadette*, which was damaged at Tunis, being towed to Sicily. But their torpedoes sank the tug rather than the freighter.)

During the day, another convoy on the Naples-Bizerta route ran afoul of the 17th Bomb Group. *Ombrina* and *Monti*, carrying ammunition and fuel, escorted by three torpedo boats and strong forces of German and Italian motor torpedo boats in distant support, and covered by a dozen German fighters, were approaching Bizerta when *Ombrina* apparently hit a magnetic mine, and the convoy was attacked from the sky.

Fifteen B-26s, escorted by thirty-eight P-38s from the 82nd Fighter Group, had taken off, but no less than two bombers and five Lightnings had to return early. Some Me-109s jumped the P-38s early in the flight and shot one down. The mission was conducted in an unusual way; the "high flight" flew at 7,500 feet, while the "low flight" was up at 3,500 feet instead of being down on the deck. Visibility was bad. As the strike force approached the convoy, it ran into fierce fighter opposition, soon joined by more enemy fighters flying out of Tunisia. A wild, confused battle ensued. The low flight did not attack at all, but the eight Marauders up top did quite well. *Monti* was badly hit. Her cargo caught fire and exploded, while the *Ombrina* may have sustained additional damage. The Americans believed that they had sunk a big troop ship and had seen no less than three merchant ships and six escorts, one of them a light cruiser which had been hit by two bombs. One B-26 had its left wing shot off by an enemy fighter; three of the crew managed to bail out before it plunged into the sea. Another crash-landed at Bone. Bomber gunners claimed three Me-109s, the P-38s five; two more P-38s were lost in addition to the one shot down earlier. (The Italian official history reported that just one Me-109 actually went down.) *Ombrina* just managed to reach harbor, but her cargo was never fully unloaded.[12]

That same day, twenty-four B-17s from the 301st Bomb Group, escorted by twenty-five P-38s from the 1st Fighter Group, carried out the Twelfth Air Force's/NASAF's third daylight attack on Palermo. It was by far the most spectacular. Dropping 500-pound bombs from 24,000 feet, they exploded an ammunition ship. The blast must have been equivalent to that of a tactical nuclear weapon. Even the B-17 crews were shaken up as a huge mushroom cloud soared over the port. When the smoke cleared, the ammunition ship was gone, three other ships had been sunk, and two 120-foot coasters had been blown right out of the water onto a pier. Thirty acres of waterfront were reduced to ruins, and the seaplane station was damaged. One B-17 was lost to fighters or flak; the P-38s claimed a Macchi 202 destroyed. Palermo harbor was almost unusable for several weeks.[13] It was a serious blow to the enemy's supply system, and it was especially well timed. Due to the Palermo mission and the sinkings at sea on March 22, no cargo at all was unloaded in Africa from March 23 to March 30, despite bad weather that would have provided good cover for convoys.

On March 24, two Italian destroyers, *Malocello* and *Ascanti*, tried to run troops to Tunisia; they hit mines and sank. Over 600 Germans were killed. Several ships used the foul weather to return from Tunisia to Italy; sea sweeps that tried to catch them not only failed but cost the 82nd Fighter Group one pilot killed and another badly injured in crashes. On March 23 and 24, the B-17 units pounded the offloading ports at Bizerta and Ferryville. The Ferryville attack set off another huge blast, destroying the still loaded *Ombrina* and another merchant ship; the attack also sank a minesweeper and a tug. A mission to Sousse on March 25 hit a ship there. Bad weather then disrupted operations completely for some days.

During this period, a third B-17 group, the 99th, prepared for combat. As the weather cleared, on March 31, it went with the other Fortress units on a big mission to Sardinia. They attacked Cagliari harbor and the Monserrato and Decimomannu airfields, following up a night strike by Wellingtons on the air bases. The B-17s' bombs sank two ships, *Capo Mele* and *Albisola*, and four motor torpedo boats, and destroyed five planes and damaged forty-two. Sea sweeps were finally able to hunt successfully, and several convoys were at sea. A morning sea sweep nevertheless failed to find anything. That afternoon, the 321st Bomb Group dispatched fifteen B-25s and the 82nd Fighter Group twenty-five P-38s. One B-25 and three P-38s returned early. The rest found a convoy of three cargo ships escorted by three torpedo boats, a corvette, and three German subchasers. There was another combined medium- and low-level attack amid a tough air battle; two B-25s were shot down from the low flight, but the bombers sank the Italian ship *Nuoro*. The Mitchells' gunners claimed four German fighters downed; the P-38s definitely got a Ju-88 and an Me-109, while losing two of their own. The convoy went on, but not for long. In the early hours of April 1, British motor torpedo boats attacked. They sank the freighter *Crema* and damaged the *Benevento*, which ran ashore on Cape Zebib; they also sank a Siebel ferry. *Benevento* did not remain there alone. Later on April 1, two more ships, part of a convoy that had escaped attack but not the bad weather, ran aground. *Aquila* beached near Cape Zebib and *Charles le Borgne* near Cape Bon. Although the beached ships became favorite targets for U.S. fighter-bombers, the Italians salvaged part of their cargo. To complete a disastrous two days, KT13 hit a mine off of Cape Bon and sank that afternoon.[14]

THE NINTH AIR FORCE

The NASAF's and Malta's operations continued to be supplemented by the Ninth Air Force's operations deep in the enemy rear. The 93rd Bomb Group had returned to the Eighth Air Force on February 21, but in mid- and late-March, the Ninth received significant reinforcements of lighter planes—a B-25 unit, the 340th Medium Bomb Group, and two more P-40 groups, the 79th and 324th. The fighter groups had actually reached Egypt in late 1942, but the 79th had been used as a reserve of pilots for the 57th Fighter Group (which it finally relieved), while the 324th Group had only completed training in February. The P-40 units concentrated on supporting the land battle in Africa, but in April they would have an important role in the final disruption of the enemy air transport system. The two remaining B-24 groups, tired and having difficulties absorbing replacement crews, had to stand down for rest and retraining from March 5 to March 12. They and the RAF Liberators of 178 Squadron concentrated on attacking Naples and Messina, the RAF unit bombing at night and the Americans—unescorted—near dusk. Messina was sometimes hit only because the weather over Naples was impossible—it was usually bad there during March—and when neither could be seen, the B-24s unloaded on an important chemical plant at Crotone in the "foot" of Italy.

After the successful mission flown on March 1, Naples proved to be a frustrating target; of seven strikes flown, at least two were complete failures. Apart from the bad weather, the flak defenses became tougher. On March 18, the Americans started coming over at higher altitudes; with squadrons staggered from 28,000 to 30,000 feet, which proved much safer. Surprisingly, bombing accuracy did not suffer. On that mission the enemy introduced a new tactic, one used against the Eighth Air Force the previous month—air-to-air bombing. Fortunately, it rarely worked.

Messina was also frustrating. On March 24, the B-24s managed to hit one end of the ferry terminal and damaged a ferry and the naval base, setting oil storage tanks on fire; but even this modest success was unusual. IX Bomber Command now tried a new tactic—a low-level B-24 strike. On March 28, three Liberators from the 376th Bomb Group flew from the Libyan bases to Malta. Refueling there, they took off at midnight and flew all the way around Sicily to hit the ferry terminal at dawn from the west. But one bomber became separated from the rest and returned to Africa. The other two ran into thick morning mists and had to attack secondary targets. One hit an airfield, the other attacked a train, and then bombed and strafed the Crotone chemical plant. The accurate, low-level attack did considerable damage. The basic idea seemed good, so the mission was run again, with some variations, on April 1. This time the attack came at dusk to avoid the mist, and the RAF Liberators hit Messina first from high altitude to distract the defenders. Only two of the American B-24s reached Messina. They lobbed their bombs right into the ferry terminal, however, there were not enough of them to smash such a large target. Flying home, they ran into a huge formation of Ju52s and shot one down. The Messina bottleneck continued to resist attack. The low-level B-24 missions against it helped inspire the Ninth Air Force's great attack on the Ploesti oil refineries in August 1943.[15]

THE BATTLE FOR AIR SUPERIORITY

Between what were called "strategic operations" against shipping and ports and airfields far in the enemy's rear and the "tactical operations" in Tunisia (all would be "tactical operations" by later classification), the Allied air forces were wearing down the enemy air opposition in the Mediterranean. Much of this was accomplished not by the attacks on the main Tunisian and Mediterranean bases by the NASAF's bombers and escort fighters but by the short-ranged planes that covered and supported the Allied armies in Africa. Spitfires and P-40s flew sweeps and escorted light, medium, and fighter-bombers against enemy airfields and ground targets. Often flying from poor forward airstrips—which, especially early in the campaign, were subject to enemy attack, they frequently encountered enemy fighters and sometimes bombers over the front line. Spitfires particularly suffered from a lack of dust filters and wear and tear on their engines, while the living conditions and frequent bombings were so unpleasant that the RAF concluded that they reduced effective tours of duty far below the 200 combat hours accepted at the start of the campaign. In contrast to the fighting over Western Europe from 1941 to 1944, the Allied single-engine fighters generally fought a battle of squadrons rather than large forces. Individual combats were common. The Allied pilots, usually in P-40s and older-model Spitfires, enjoyed no advantage in performance. Those flying the new Spitfire IX were better off. They even found that they could sometimes overtake the Me-109s in a prolonged dive—previously a sure way for German pilots to escape from a tight situation, for the great defect of the Spitfire had been its poor performance in a dive. The British Commonwealth pilots were impressed by the enemy's use of the sun, his careful use of camouflage and strong top cover for his strafing attacks on ground targets, and reluctance to engage, except when at an advantage. They found that the Germans did not willingly initiate combat without a height advantage. On the other hand, the Germans' evasive action when they were attacked seemed unimaginative.

Between the combined Allied forces, the enemy was gradually worn out and worn down. The AAF's retrospective appreciation, in July 1943, was that enemy fighter opposition had built up to a peak in March before quickly starting to subside. The quality of enemy pilots seemed to drop off. This formed a curious parallel with the defeat the whole Luftwaffe fighter force would suffer exactly a year later in the great air battle over Germany, but seems to have reflected a combination of heavy local losses and the exhaustion of the men on the spot. Already, at the beginning of March, the Axis could not move vehicles by day in Tunisia. It was increasingly hard for the old Stukas to operate in Tunisia; by mid-month, the Germans felt forced to divert their medium bombers to support ground troops for which they were not suited. That was stopped in the last week of March. Their offensive forces were just worn out; by the end of March, not one German torpedo bomber was operational. A growing proportion of enemy fighter operations was devoted to defending convoys; on March 22, Fliegerkorps Tunis complained that it did not have enough fighters to do the job. In early April, the Germans had spectacular failures when they tried to escort their bombers in daylight attacks. On April 3, the American 52nd Fighter Group shot down fourteen Stukas for only one Spitfire lost. Six days later, it shot down eight Ju88s, again losing just a single Spitfire.[16]

SUPPLY CRISIS

During March, an already critical Axis supply situation lurched into collapse. The Germans had increased air transport efforts, flying 12,000 men and 8,000 tons of supplies into Tunisia, but that did not compensate for their losses at sea and in port. Due to the ferries, some types of supplies and equipment did surprisingly well—all twenty German tanks dispatched in

March 1943 arrived—but 41.5 percent of all the tonnage leaving Italy was lost; unloadings in Tunisia fell to 43,125 tons. The Axis in the Mediterranean lost thirty-six ships of over 500 tons at sea or in port in March, eighteen to aircraft and sixteen to submarines. Another calculation, counting smaller craft but also a few Italian losses outside of the Mediterranean, shows that the Italians alone lost sixty-four ships, thirty-six to air attack. The Italians themselves listed thirteen Axis merchant ships lost at sea on the Tunisian route, six to air attack, six to submarines, and one to mines.[17]

Bad weather kept Allied planes in North Africa mostly on the ground for the first three days of April, save for desultory fighter sweeps and some bomber operations in central Tunisia. Oddly, this had little effect on the struggle against the enemy sea supply lines. The mighty effort at the end of March seemed to have temporarily exhausted the Axis. For the first four days of April, not a single ship left for Tunisia. A few ships made return voyages to Italy; on April 4, a sea sweep by the 310th Bomb Group failed to catch them. A strike on a two-ship convoy suffered repeated attacks by twenty enemy fighters; one shot-up fighter slammed into a B-25, and both planes crashed into the sea. The bombers scored no hits. That day the NASAF tried something new—using P-38s as fighter-bombers. The 1st Fighter Group experimented with both low-level bombing and dive-bombing. That afternoon six P-38s, carrying bombs, escorted by eight others, dive-bombed the beached ships at Cape Zebib, which became a favorite target for such attacks. Techniques were developed for sea sweeps by P-38s alone. Twelve to twenty-four P-38s, one-third to one-half carrying bombs, would search from 8,000 to 9,000 feet, and they approached targets in the same way as the mediums. They would finally peel off and attack individually, entering a glide and finally steepening it into a dive at an angle of sixty degrees, dropping their bombs from 2,000 to 3,000 feet. The P-38 fighter-bombers also were employed in conjunction with the medium bombers; on occasion, one-fourth of the escorts carried bombs. They would either drop their own bombs when the high flight of a combined medium- and low-altitude strike let go, or dive down in pairs to attack on their own. Such attacks were an increasing feature of sea sweeps and contributed to their success.[18]

In the biggest blow against the enemy on April 4, the NASAF and the Ninth Air Force combined to bomb Naples. All three B-17 groups joined in the first Twelfth Air Force attack on the European mainland, striking Naples harbor and marshalling yards and the Capodicino airfield. The B-17s sank *Sicilia*, the largest enemy ship sunk that month (she was, unfortunately, a hospital ship), and destroyed four and damaged thirty-two Axis planes on the ground. Serious damage was done to the supply center at Naples.[19]

THE *LADY BE GOOD*

The Ninth Air Force's Libyan-based B-24s, which followed the B-17s with a dusk attack, had less success and suffered a notable tragedy. The 376th Bomb Group suffered from taking off in a sand storm. Of its first section of twelve planes, only one aborted. The rest reached Naples harbor and attacked successfully. But none of "Section B"s thirteen planes reached the target. One after another, planes fell out with engine trouble. The last few planes, realizing that they had been too delayed to bomb while there was still light, turned back at Sorrento. The formation split up at sunset. One B-24, *Lady Be Good*—she was named after a popular 1941 movie musical— vanished, only to reappear in the late 1950s, when the fate of those aboard became an intriguing mystery.

Apparently *Lady Be Good* was hit by an enemy fighter right at dusk. One engine was knocked out, but the crew survived and flew on.

It would have been better for them if they had died then.

The Liberator struggled along on three engines. Shortly after midnight, the pilot called a radio direction finder station at Benina in Libya, requesting an inbound emergency course. The B-24 crew and the RDF station fatally assumed (although a single direction finder could not actually determine this) that *Lady Be Good* was still over the Mediterranean and hampered by a strong head wind. In reality, she had a strong tail wind. Her crew had evidently missed seeing the break between the sea and the shore. They did not realize that they had long since crossed the coast and were already deep into the Sahara. Unfortunately, they also had failed to use their own Automatic Direction Finder, which should have picked up the low-powered radio beacon stationed at Benina. Picking up and then losing the beacon would have warned them that they had flown past it.

When two of the remaining engines ran out of gas, the crew jumped, still thinking that they were over the sea. A routine air-sea rescue search, based on the same assumption, naturally failed to find anything.

Lady Be Good flew on before gently crashing into the desert, 385 miles south of Tobruk, where an oil-exploration plane found her in November 1958, still nearly intact.

When land parties reached her in 1959 and began searching the region, they were puzzled to find no sign of her crew. *Lady Be Good* became a minor sensation of the period, inspiring several television shows (both documentary and fiction). Finally, in February 1960, the discovery of several bodies and a diary made it possible to reconstruct what had happened.

Eight of the nine crewmen had joined up quickly (they never met the other man) and tried to walk out of the furnace-like desert. Had they had the precious emergency supplies aboard *Lady Be Good*, or even if they had just had better maps, they might have made it. As it was, they lasted far longer than the one or two days most survival experts would have forecast for men without water in such terrific heat, so their bodies were found much farther from the plane than the initial searchers had expected. After terrible suffering, five men collapsed on April 9 after covering an incredible sixty-five miles. Even then, three men went on. The entire crew died on April 11 and 12.[20]

OPERATION FLAX

For months the Allies had pondered a major attack on the enemy air transport effort, whose scale and importance had risen as Axis losses at sea mounted. The Eastern Air Command had devised a plan for such an attack as far back as early February; the Kasserine Pass battle had caused the Allied command to postpone it and give the job to Doolittle's NASAF. The Allied leaders then decided to delay further to accumulate more intelligence and let the enemy effort continue to build up. Then they would cut it off when it was most needed, and the greatest amount of destruction would result.

The operation, called "Flax," depended heavily on excellent intelligence. The Allies wanted to know the size of the transport formations, their departure, refuelling and arrival points, the route, times of arrival and departure, the extent of fighter escort, fighter cover flying from Tunisia, and the antiaircraft defenses at the terminal airfields. The data was supplied partly by Ultra but mostly by "Y Service" eavesdropping on enemy tactical signals—the latter gave the timing, normal routes, and escort strength. In its final form, the NASAF planned to start with a morning P-38 sweep over the Sicilian Strait—cunningly synchronized with a B-25 sea sweep over the Strait, which would bring still more P-38s to the vicinity in a way that would not alert the enemy to the fact that something unusual was going on. A Spitfire sweep over the Gulf of Tunis would catch enemy planes that got past the long-range fighters. The B-17s would strike the destination airfields, El Aouina and Sidi Ahmed, while further missions by B-17s and B-25s would depart for the western Sicilian airfields, timed to catch the arrival there of the day's second flight. Further fighter sweeps would try to catch enemy planes crossing the Strait from those fields late in the afternoon. The Ninth Air Force was asked to hit Naples with B-24s in a dusk or night attack to follow up the NASAF operation. On April 2, Tedder and Spaatz decided to launch "Operation Flax" on the next day the weather was good.[21] "Flax" was executed as exactly as any military plan in history. An apparent late alteration was made to begin it with an attack on the night of April 4–5 by the AAF and the RAF Liberators on Bocca di Falco airfield near Palermo.

The main action began the next morning, on April 5. The 1st Fighter Group sent twenty-six P-38s over the Sicilian Strait at 6:30 A.M. Eighteen

B-25s of the 321st Bomb Group, escorted by thirty-two P-38s of the 82nd Fighter Group, set out on a shipping sweep at about the same time; six of the P-38s had to turn back. The B-25s found and attacked a convoy, claiming hits on two Siebel ferries and blowing up a destroyer. One B-25 was shot down.

At eight o'clock, the 1st Group's Lightnings ran into a huge force off Cape Bon. They estimated it at fifty to seventy Ju-52s, twenty Me-109s, four FW-190s, six Stukas, and a Focke-Wulf 187. Some of the enemy fighters were thought to be covering the nearby surface convoy rather than escorting the transport planes. Actually, the enemy force consisted of thirty-one Ju-52s, escorted by ten Me-109s, six Me-110s, four Stukas, one Me-110, and a single FW-190. A huge air battle began; one squadron of Lightnings flying top cover, while the other pounced on the transports. The all but helpless Stukas boldly sailed into the Americans amid the confused combat. The 82nd Group planes that had been escorting the shipping sweep joined in against another part of the formation. The 1st Group claimed shooting down eleven Ju-52s, two Stukas, two Me-109s, and a FW-187; it lost two P-38s. The 82nd Group claimed seven Ju-52s, three Stukas, an Me-110, one Me-210, and three Me-109s, losing four Lightnings. There were a lot of duplications; it seems that fourteen or fifteen Ju-52s and two or three German fighters actually went down. The second phase in the day's action was then set into motion; the 97th Bomb Group sent eighteen B-17s, escorted by Spitfires, to cover El Aouina with frag clusters. A pair of Me-323s, two Ju-52s, and five Italian transports were destroyed. Later, the 97th flew a second mission with twenty-three bombers to Sid Ahmed, also under Spitfire protection. A few German fighters intercepted both missions, but without success; the bombers claimed one fighter destroyed.

One hour after the B-17s set out for El Aouina, bombers began leaving for the attack on the Sicilian airfields. The 310th Bomb Group dispatched thirty-five B-25s to the Borizzo airfield, escorted by eighteen P-38s from the 82nd Group. The B-25 crews counted eighty to ninety twin-engine and three-engine planes on the field, poorly dispersed. They had finished dropping their frag clusters, with excellent results, when fifteen Me-109s attacked. They claimed downing three of the enemy fighters (the Lightnings got two), but two B-25s were shot down, ditching near the Aegades island group. The 301st Bomb Group sent twenty-eight B-17s to the Milo airfield near Trapani, escorted by sixteen planes from the 1st Fighter Group; they found seventy to eighty planes on the ground, and it was estimated that they destroyed fifty-two of them. Probably they actually smashed thirteen German and eight Italian planes, damaging eleven German and thirty Italian craft. The 99th Group sent twenty-two B-17s to Bocca di Falco, where they saw

100–150 planes. The bombers claimed two Me-109s and one Macchi 200 destroyed in the air; it seems that they smashed four German planes on the ground and damaged several. Spitfires sweeping the Tunis area claimed two Me-109s, but one Spitfire was shot down and another had to crash-land, while an afternoon P-38 sweep of the Sicilian Strait found nothing. The afternoon "pulk" never even got started.

The NASAF estimated that it had destroyed no less than 201 planes, only forty in the air, for only nine Allied planes lost. These claims were an overestimate, although it is hard to say by how much. The Germans admitted only fourteen Ju-52s shot down, and eleven Me-323s and Ju-52s destroyed on the ground, but about sixty-seven transports had been damaged. The British official historians later concluded that apart from combat planes, at least twenty-seven German and three Italian transports had been destroyed on April 5; other sources give a higher figure.[22]

The "Flax" attacks had been the first daylight blows against the Sicilian airfields; such strikes continued, merging into the preparatory phase of the Sicilian campaign, while "Flax" continued on a smaller scale, with the emphasis on fighter operations. On the morning of April 10, "Flax" was renewed. The 1st Fighter Group sent twenty-five planes to the Sicilian Strait; four returned early. Eight Lightnings cruised at 1,000 feet; the rest flew just above the water. They spotted the regular shuttle coming into Tunisia, estimating the enemy formation at fifty Ju-52s covered by fifteen Macchi 200s and FW-190s. (Actually, the planes were all Italian; twenty Savoia-Marchettis escorted by six or more Macchi 200s.) The top cover engaged the Axis fighters, claiming seven Mc200s and FW-190s, while the low flight claimed a score of Ju-52s as they scattered and dived. In fact, ten transports were shot down and another crash-landed; two escorting Macchi 200s were downed. Later that morning, a sea sweep of eighteen B-25s from the 310th Group, escorted by twenty-seven P-38s from the 82nd Fighter Group, sighted about thirty transports, escorted by just a pair of Me-110s, a pair of Stukas, and three Ju-88s, a few miles north of Cape Bon. Most of the Lightnings pulled away and went right for the German formation. Eleven stayed with the bombers, which also engaged the transports, flying past them so their gunners could get in some bursts. Fifteen Me-109s flew out from Tunisia to join the battle but arrived only after most of the transports were done for. One P-38 pilot closing in on an Me-110 ran into his target; he was the only American lost that day, though some of the B-25s were badly shot up. The Americans claimed twenty-five enemy aircraft—twenty-one Ju-52s—but actually got ten Ju-52s, a Ju-88, an Me-110, and an Me-109. One or two of the luckier Ju-52 crews managed to ditch in a controlled manner and survived. A Spitfire sweep later caught four Ju52s.

The next day, the 82nd Fighter Group took over the sweep duty, sending out two squadrons. The first patrol, at eight o'clock, spotted an estimated twenty transports north of Tunis, covered by four Me-110s, at least four Ju-88s, and seven or more Me-109s. The Americans claimed that the transports were totally wiped out, along with seven of the escorts. One Lightning collided with an enemy plane in the melee, and two more were shot down. Their pilots were lost. Another P-38 crashed at Bone, but the pilot got out. The twenty P-38s conducting the second phase of the sweep, at 10:30 A.M., largely missed their targets. But one flight ran into another convoy of twenty-five to thirty Ju-52s on a return flight to Sicily—without fighter cover. One P-38 and its pilot were lost, apparently to fire from the Ju-52s' dorsal guns, but the Americans downed five Ju-52s. The actual total for the day was apparently seventeen Ju-52s, an Italian SM-82, and two Me-110s.[23]

Not surprisingly, an afternoon sweep by the 1st Fighter Group found nothing. On April 12, however, the enemy resumed flying.

By mid-April, the Desert Air Force, now based on airfields in the Sousse area, was able to take over the "Flax" operation, releasing the NASAF P-38s for shipping sweeps and long-range escort. The new operations were supported by seaward-looking radar, but it is not clear that they were of great value, given the German practice of flying very low. Even with the new airfields, patrolling the northern approach to Tunisia stretched the short-range P-40s and Spitfires to the limit. The British at first spread their patrols thinly, maintaining continuous coverage by small groups of planes. On April 16, however, thirteen Spitfires trying to get at transport planes ran into a bigger force of escort fighters. Two Spitfires were lost for seven SM 82s and an Me-109—a creditable feat but also a near disaster. After this, the Desert Air Force and the Ninth Air Force fighter units operating with it stuck to big sweeps. At least three P-40 squadrons covered by a Spitfire squadron went out at a time.

The patrols failed to catch a large air convoy coming into Tunisia on the afternoon of April 18. Late that afternoon, the Ninth Air Force's 57th Fighter Group sent out all three of its squadrons, along with the 314th Squadron of the 324th Group. The 57th Group had already flown an unproductive sweep earlier in the afternoon. One plane turned back with engine trouble, but forty-seven P-40s arrived in the sweep area with a dozen Spitfires from the RAF's 92 Squadron. The Spitfires flew top cover at 15,000 feet; the P-40s were stacked down to 4,000. The fighters flew back and forth. They were six miles off Cape Bon, with just enough fuel for fifteen minutes, or one more run, when the lead, low squadron spotted German fighters at 1,000 feet and then three huge "V" formations estimated at thirty or more Ju-52s each, flying northeast on their return flight, a few hundred feet above the water. The for-

mation actually consisted of sixty-five Ju-52s, sixteen German and Italian single-engine fighters, and five Me-110s. The Spitfires and one squadron of the
57th Group took on the escort, estimated to be twenty-five to thirty fighters;
the rest of the 57th Group and the 314th Squadron fell on the transports.
The big formations began to fray apart, some Ju-52s putting on maximum
power, others falling out as stragglers. Finally they all turned and began running for the coast. Desperate passengers fired submachine guns out of the
windows, but the sea was soon full of flaming and crashing transports. Some
ditched, while others force-landed on a nearby beach. The Americans were
not impressed with the escort pilots, who seemed confused, but the Allies did
lose six P-40s and a Spitfire. The Americans alone submitted initial claims for
146 planes destroyed! But they later settled on perhaps fifty-eight or fifty-nine
Ju-52s, fourteen Mc 202s and Me-109s, and two to four Me-110s. Three Americans became the AAF's first "aces in a day." Two were credited with destroying five Ju-52s each, the third with four Ju-52s and an Me-109. The Germans
actually lost twenty-four Ju-52s over the water, while thirty-five crashed on the
coast, and at least ten fighters; it is possible that some Italian planes were
downed.

The Axis suffered another disaster the next morning. The South African
Air Force's No. 7 Wing sent out thirty-six P-40s. They and their Spitfire cover
ran into a well-escorted Italian transport formation. The Allies claimed
twelve Ju-52s, two SM 79s, a Stuka towing a glider, an Italian Re-2001, two
Me-109s, and a Ju-88 for the loss of five Spitfires and three P-40s. A dozen
Savoia-Marchettis and an Mc 202 had in fact gone down; the RAF Spitfires
based on Malta shot down two more Italian transports.

On April 22, the Germans sent in twenty-one of the huge Me-323s, each
carrying ten tons of fuel to Tunisia. Although the clumsy transports were
strongly escorted, this move marked the passage of the Axis daylight transport effort, already irresponsible after April 5, to the stage of insanity. The
South Africans sent out thirty-eight P-40s, covered by a South African Spitfire squadron and additional flights of British- and Polish-manned Spitfires.
They downed sixteen (or possibly seventeen) Me-323s, an Mc 202, and an
Re-2001, and perhaps three or more German fighters. Curiously, Allied
losses also are uncertain; at the most they lost four P-40s and a Spitfire,
which had to belly-land.

Goering, angry or panicky or both, forbade all transport flights to Africa
for a time. Finally, after Kesselring objected, he relented and allowed night
flights. These used a new western route via Sardinia, but no more than sixty
to seventy sorties could be flown in one night; up to 250 had been mounted
daily before "Flax." The night flights had to run a gauntlet of radar-equipped
RAF Beaufighters, but these rarely intercepted successfully. On April 27, the

Allies terminated "Flax." The Desert and Ninth Air Force fighters shifted to intercepting the enemy's last efforts to run ships to Tunisia. "Flax" seems to have destroyed at least 157 German transport planes, not counting Italian losses. It is possible that the real overall total was as many as 432 planes. The German air transport fleet was crippled for the rest of the war. Some thirty-five Allied planes had been lost in all phases of the campaign against Axis air transport.[24]

CONVOY ATTACKS

On April 5, a convoy left Naples for Bizerta with an unusually heavy escort. One cargo ship fell out with a rudder defect. The two remaining ships, *Rovereto* and *San Diego*, both carried ammunition; the latter ship also carried gasoline. Protected by five torpedo boats, they were passing Zembra Island on the morning of April 6 when the Americans attacked for the first time. An eighteen-plane sea sweep from the 310th Bomb Group, encountering intense flak, bombed from 7,000 feet, without hitting anything. Later in the morning, eighteen Fortresses from the 97th Group struck. But twenty-five to thirty Me-109s and FW-190s attacked the bombers, which were unescorted, and there was a violent air battle that made the bomb run difficult. The B-17s missed. They claimed four German fighters, while two men were wounded aboard a B-17. By late afternoon, *Rovereto* and *San Diego* were in sight of the coast when a second heavy bomber sweep caught them; twenty-two B-17s from the 301st Group flew through heavy flak to bomb from 10,500 feet. *Rovereto* blew up so violently that it damaged several bombers. *San Diego*, also hit, caught fire. An attempt to take her in tow had to be given up when flaming gasoline threatened to set off ammunition. The abandoned ship finally exploded a little over two hours later. Of 242 men aboard the two ships, only ninety-nine survived. *Rovereto* was the second largest ship destroyed at sea on the Tunisian run. Twenty to thirty fighters attacked the bombers after the bomb run; there was another violent fight, in which several B-17s were damaged and nine men were wounded. The bombers claimed eight enemy fighters. The April 6 attack cost the Axis a huge amount of ammunition; they must have been heartily tired of ammunition ships blowing up.[25]

THE KLESSHEIM CONFERENCE

The "Flax" operation and other disasters had surprisingly little impact on the top Axis leaders, who met at Klessheim Castle in Austria from April 7 to 10. Even some Germans indicated to the Italian delegates that they hoped Mussolini could persuade Hitler to make a separate peace with Stalin. Instead, the Nazis rebuffed suggestions for an approach to the Soviets or a defensive strategy in the east, and a "European Charter" to compete with Allied propaganda to the occupied countries and the Axis satellites. They even criticized the Italians for making use of the Chetniks (the anti-Communist Serb resistance force) as allies against the Communist Partisans in Yugoslavia. The Italians described their desperate shipping and food situation and requested that the Germans provide more forces for the air defense of Italy. Hitler vaguely promised more planes and antiaircraft guns for Italy, but he would not be dissuaded from a new summer offensive against the Soviets. He and Mussolini agreed that Tunisia must be held at any cost, at least until the fall, to prevent the Allies from invading southern Europe. But they did not take serious, specific steps to implement this resolution. They willed the end, but not the means.

Even from the warped viewpoint of the Axis leaders, it should have been clear that attacking in Russia would render any hope of holding Tunisia null. By then, in fact, even immediate peace with the Soviets would not have enabled the Axis to seriously prolong the battle for Tunisia. But a change in strategy would have made an immense difference in meeting an Allied invasion of southern Europe. Hitler and Mussolini obstinately continued to rule out evacuating the Axis forces from Africa. Although von Arnim, on March 30, had urged that only material be sent, they continued to pour fresh men across the Mediterranean. Had maximum use been made of the available ships and planes to get men out of Tunisia instead of throwing them in, they might still have rescued a substantial fraction of Army Group Afrika. Admiral Ruge later estimated that, right up to mid-April, destroyers and transport planes could have saved the men of two or three divisions.

Strangely, the unsatisfactory Klessheim agreement pepped up Mussolini for a while, although the other Italian leaders certainly were not pleased. En route home, however, the Italian dictator became sick. When the doctors could not diagnose his problem, he glumly joked, "My illness has a name—'convoys.'"[26]

PORT AND AIRFIELD ATTACKS

On April 6, B-17s had bombed the Trapani docks even as other Fortresses went after *Rovereto* and *San Diego*. The NASAF was then kept on the ground by bad weather from April 7 to April 10, but the Libyan-based Liberators kept up small-scale attacks on Palermo. Then the Algerian-based forces returned to the battle with growing effectiveness. They received considerable reinforcements in the last stage of the North African campaign. On April 17, the P-40s of the 325th Fighter Group, transferred from the NATAF, finally went into action. They were joined by the B-26s of the 320th Bomb Group, which had also been in the theater for months, on April 22. A new

B-17 unit, the 2nd Bomb Group, entered combat on April 28. Just as the fighting in Tunisia ended, the rebuilt 14th Fighter Group, filled out with replacement pilots and planes from the States, a complete squadron transferred from the 55th Fighter Group in England, and pilots transferred from the 1st Fighter Group, returned to battle. Even before the new units were operational, the Allies were launching several attacks daily on distant targets; only the most important missions can be described.

By now, the Axis air forces were being swamped by superior numbers. By mid-April, 3,241 Allied aircraft under Tedder's command in the Mediterranean and the Middle East faced 900 Axis combat planes; only 270 were still based in Africa. While the Allies had attained a daily serviceability of 80 percent, the Germans could only keep about 58 percent of their planes operational; the Italians could keep only half of their planes flyable on any given day.

Both heavy and medium bombers, and fighter-bombers, went out on sea sweeps, but in other respects there was a fairly clear division of labor in the NASAF bomber operations, especially after the air preparation for the final land offensive began on April 18. On that day, Spaatz's entire command began intense attacks on the enemy airfields in Tunisia. The NASAF carried out a few missions in direct support of this effort. But its part of "Phase II" of the air plan for the final offensive emphasized continuing attacks on Sicilian airfields; heavy bombers also were to hit Bari in Italy.

The NASAF heavy bombers carried out a few missions to the familiar targets at Tunis and Bizerta and their airfields but mainly operated against the other side of the Mediterranean, concentrating on the "outloading ports" on Sicily—Palermo, Trapani, and Messina—and on the airfields on Sicily and Sardinia, but they hit other targets as well. The two Wellington squadrons that bombed at night shared some of the B-17s' targets; they continued to strike Tunis, El Aouina airfield, and Bizerta and attacked Trapani on Sicily and the Sardinian airfields. The Ninth Air Force B-24s continued to bomb Naples, Palermo, and Messina. Increasing opposition over Naples was countered by making use of the strong high-altitude winds, up to 125 miles an hour, prevailing over the city. Bomb runs were made downwind. The Ninth hit some new targets; the air base at Bari in the heel of Italy, Reggio, on the mainland opposite Messina and the departure point for the Sicilian ferries and KT ships, and Catania harbor on Sicily. Aside from sea sweeps, AAF mediums mostly hit land targets in Tunisia, striking the smaller landing grounds to ensure control of the air and supporting the advance of the 18th Army Group. The B-25s and and B-26s flew only a few missions to targets on Sicily and Sardinia.[27]

The B-17s hit Tunis harbor on April 11, 19, and 20, and again on May 5; Bizerta on April 12 and 17 and May 3; El Aouina airfield on April 14; and Sidi Ahmed and La Marsa on April 20. During April, small forces of German fighters still intercepted some missions to Tunis and Bizerta but generally without much harm, except to themselves.

On April 10, the three B-17 groups carried out a major mission against the Italian fleet. Two of its last three heavy cruisers, *Trieste* and *Gorizia*, were based at La Maddalena in Sardinia, anchored in coves behind torpedo nets in apparent security. The B-17s came over at 19,000 feet, dropping 1,000-pound bombs; they pattern-bombed on element leaders. The 97th Group sent thirty-six planes against *Gorizia*, while twenty-four planes from the 301st Group went after *Trieste*; another twenty-four from the 99th Group attacked the harbor installations and the submarine base. *Trieste* was sunk; the more heavily armored *Gorizia* survived, but it was heavily damaged. Three seaplanes were destroyed on the water. It was a striking success against anchored warships in a defended base, targets of a sort that had proved resistant to high-level attack by heavy bombers earlier in the war.

On April 13, the 1st Fighter Group tried to finish off *Gorizia* with a skip-bombing attack by five Lightnings. They scored a direct hit that inflicted more serious damage, although the Italians were able to get *Gorizia* to their main base at La Spezia on the mainland. Lt. Colonel Weltman, leading the fighter-bomber attack, overshot the target and attacked merchant ships at nearby Porto Torres instead. His bomb crashed right through one ship without exploding, before hitting and blowing up another. There were more sequels to the La Maddalena strike. When *Gorizia* reached La Spezia, the RAF Bomber Command launched a pair of its rare operations across the Alps. On the night of April 13–14, 211 British-based heavy bombers attacked La Spezia. On April 18–19, 178 bombers returned there, sinking the destroyer *Alpino* and some smaller craft, and damaging the battleship *Littorio*. On April 18, in a follow-up to the April 13 strike, the 310th Bomb Group dispatched one of the infrequent medium bomber missions to European targets, sending thirty-six B-25s to Sardinia. Half smothered the airfield at Alghero-Fertilia with frag clusters. The rest blasted freighters at Porto Torres, a minor harbor the Italians had been forced to use because of damage and congestion in other ports.[28]

The 310th Group's mission to Sardinia came amidst a whole series of heavy bomber missions to the Mediterranean islands, mainly to Sicily. The B-17s attacked Trapani harbor twice, on April 11 and 12, also hitting Marsala the second day. On April 13, they struck the Sicilian airfields of Milo and Castelvetrano, doing particular damage at the latter base; forty-four planes were destroyed or damaged on the ground. On April 14, the B-17s attacked the Elmas and Monserrato airfields on Sardinia. On April 16, the Fortresses started a three-day assault on Palermo, already hit by the Ninth on April 7 and 12. The B-17s sank the *Giacomo C*, a fairly large ship for what was left of the Italian merchant marine, which had just been damaged by the British submarine *Unbroken*. On April 18, the bombers switched from attacks on Palermo's harbor to the marshalling yard and Bocca di Falco airfield. The Ninth Air Force carried out a concurrent series of attacks on Catania harbor; on April 16, the B-24s sank the torpedo boat *Medici* and damaged a tanker. The NASAF then shifted its attacks mostly back to the Tunisian end of the supply line to the Sidi Ahmed airfield, and to shipping sweeps as the Allied ground force got ready for the final breakthrough and the last enemy ships reached African ports. On April 26, the NASAF and the IX Bomber Command struck major blows against the airfields on the Italian mainland. The B-17s hit Grosseto, while B-24s bombed Bari. Bari was not just a transport base, but was full of replacement German fighters, when seventy Liberators dropped 500-pound bombs on its hangars and frag bombs on parking areas. The AAF thought that they had destroyed twenty-seven planes, but for once this was a grave underestimate. This remarkable attack actually destroyed 107 German and five Italian planes, and damaged forty-five other German aircraft. The Bari strike was the most successful single bombing attack against an enemy air base during the entire campaign, and perhaps during the whole European war.[29]

CLIMAX OF THE SUBMARINE WAR

After the sinking of *Baalbek* in February, there was another gap of several weeks before Allied submarines again scored directly against Tunisian traffic. They continued to strike effectively elsewhere in the enemy rear. As before, the British submarines, twenty-four of the thirty-six Allied craft available in the Mediterranean, scored a disproportionate number of sinkings, although the one Dutch submarine, *Dolfijn*, had some success. The last months of the submarine campaign, however, proved the most costly. The relative reprieve of the first two months of 1943, in which just two boats were lost, was now followed by an exceptionally bad period in which no less than five, including some of the very best in the fleet, were sunk. Although the submarines continued to be a useful supplement to the planes, which were doing most of the killing of enemy ships, it is even arguable that, in the last stages of the Tunisian campaign, the balance had turned against the submarine effort and that it now cost more lives than it was worth in terms of damage done to the enemy and lives saved in Tunisia. But that could not be clear at the time, and the submariners carried on bravely.

In March, the submarines found their best hunting ground off northern Sicily. The Malta-based submarines increasingly crossed into the northern area to operate in the Tyrrhenian Sea. On March 10, a large, heavily defended convoy from Naples was heading for several destinations in Sicily. Northeast of Cape Milazzo, *Trooper* maneuvered between two columns of ships and fired four torpedoes at a tanker 1,500 yards away. Two hit, sinking *Rosario*. But *Turbulent*, one of the most successful British submarines, was lost with all hands off Sardinia on March 12. She probably was sunk by an Italian antisubmarine craft, but she may have been mined.[30]

On the night of March 13–14, the first submarine success on the Tunisian route in almost a month was scored by *Thunderbolt* when it damaged the German ship *Esterel* east of Cape San Vito, but it was a costly success, for *Thunderbolt* was sunk right afterward. Also on March 14, *Pegli*, dashing from Trapani to Palermo with a pair of corvettes, was sunk off Cape Gallo. Farther afield, off eastern Calabria, *Unbending* sank two ships, *Citta di Bergamo* and *Cosenza*, on the same day. Off Cape San Vito, on the morning of March 17, *Splendid* fell on a large convoy en route from Taranto to Bizerta and slammed a torpedo into the bow of the tanker *Devoli*, which had been accompanying the convoy only between Palermo and Trapani. *Devoli* sank that afternoon. On the same day, the submarines finally scored a sinking against the Tunisian traffic proper, albeit on a homebound ship. A large convoy of ships from both Bizerta and Tunis, with a final destination at Naples—several ships dropped off at other ports along the way—was south of Capri when it ran into *Trooper*, which had been shifted to patrolling the Naples area. Lieutenant J. S. Wraith fired two torpedoes at the leading ship and two more at the second ship in the column from the long range of 5,000 yards. Wraith thought he had hit both, but he had done well enough, sinking the 1,519-ton ship *Forli*.

A few days later, on March 21, a submarine completed some unfinished business. The tanker *Giorgio*, damaged by torpedo planes and run aground the previous December, had been recovered and was being brought from Palermo to Genoa for repairs when she was sunk off Cape Cefalu. On the afternoon of March 23, yet another tanker, *Zeila*, en route from Palermo to Messina, apparently to join a Tunisian convoy forming there, was sunk off Cape Spartiveno by *Unison*.[31] Submarines seem to have been peculiarly successful in sinking tankers, the most valuable targets of all, more so than aircraft.

In April, the hunting ground shifted again. The submarines scored most heavily around Sardinia and, on several occasions in the very last weeks of the campaign (which will be treated later in a separate section), on the Tunisian route proper. Some successes were scored farther afield. On April

14, *Unbroken* attacked the big tanker *Regina* and forced her to beach herself in Italy. Unfortunately, *Unbroken* had expended her last torpedo and could not finish the enemy ship off.

Safari, *Saracen*, and *Taurus* were particularly successful off Sardinia.[32] Ben Bryant, in *Safari*, had a particularly spectacular patrol. (It was his last.) Sailing from Algiers on March 27, he reached his patrol area off southern Sardinia on March 30. The following day, he passed up a convoy of two schooners and a coaster, heavily escorted by planes as well as a minesweeper; the chances of hitting such shallow-draft targets with a torpedo were not good enough to balance the risks. On the afternoon of April 3, he surfaced and sank a 350-ton minesweeping trawler in the Gulf of Orosei, attacking from behind where the enemy ship's gun could not be brought to bear. He then chased and sank a 150-ton schooner. Off Cavoli, on April 6, he found a convoy of ships worth a torpedo attack. Launching three torpedoes at short range, he was disappointed to see only one hit a 2,000-ton ship, which apparently limped into port. On April 9 he spotted one of the strange auxiliary craft the Italians equipped to fight submerged but not surfaced submarines. This one was a 300-ton square-rigged sailing ship. He surfaced, and *Safari*'s deck gun set her on fire.

Gambling that the enemy would not expect a *sane* submarine skipper to hang around in a dangerous area where his presence was well known, Bryant continued to patrol by the channel through the minefield off Cagliari. On the afternoon of April 10, he spotted a convoy of three fairly large ships, including a 5,000-ton tanker and a cargo liner, heavily escorted by two Cant seaplanes, two large escort vessels, a minesweeper, and a motorized antisubmarine boat.

Safari was approaching the convoy when its hydraulic system failed; emergency gear allowed only very slow operation. The submarine drifted through the enemy escort screen with its propeller spinning just fast enough to maintain control, as Bryant occasionally peeped through the attack periscope. He fired two torpedoes at the liner, swung to get away from his torpedo tracks, then aimed two torpedoes at the tanker. *Safari* then hastily put on speed while diving deeper, passing close by cliffs that were supposed to overlook deep water. The charts proved wrong. *Safari* grounded at 210 feet less than a mile from shore amid an enemy counterattack. She could not get off without blowing tanks and rocketing right to the surface, or at least releasing bubbles that would lead the enemy to her. There was a panicky moment when one of the ships that it had sunk seemed to be drifting down on the helpless submarine, and anxious hours followed, since there seemed to be no chance of the crew escaping if *Safari* could not get unstuck. The "escape sets" carried by British submarines (similar to the American Momsen lung) were thought to be useless at that depth after a long dive. (In fact, although it was not realized at the time, men stood some chance of escaping from sunken submarines, even without such devices.) Finally, after six hours, Bryant calculated that the enemy was gone. He managed to get off the bottom without much trouble. Then depth charges began raining down again; one of the escorts had stayed around after all. *Safari* evaded the attack and passed out through the minefield. Bryant discovered that the surviving ship of the convoy, a tramp steamer, had run aground. He put two torpedoes into her then escaped yet another counterattack in which the enemy seemed to be using a new and bigger type of depth charge. Corsica remained a good place to find targets; *Saracen* got a pair of large ships there, *Francesco Crispi* and *Tagliamento*, in one attack on April 19.[33]

Such spectacular successes by old hands were not, of course, typical. Often it was hard to find targets; a "normal" patrol spotted only a few small ships and was lucky to sink one or two. New submarines were still coming out. *Unruly*, setting out from Gibraltar on April 5, patrolled the western basin north of 42 degrees, 15 minutes north. While off Cape Bear, it was told to intercept a Vichy French ship, but it could not find it. The captain did spot a small ship "painted in Spanish colors" and sent two torpedoes at this "neutral"—but missed. On April 12, he found the German-controlled 1,300-ton *St. Lucien*. Two torpedoes fired from 2,000 yards destroyed her. A motor launch attacked with depth charges, but none came close. *Unruly* saw just one more ship before reaching Algiers, but it was too shallow draft to torpedo and too well protected to attack with the deck gun.

April proved to be a costly month. In addition to *Sahib*, which was lost while attacking one of the last Tunisian convoys, the very effective *Splendid* was sunk by the German-manned (ex-Greek) destroyer *Hermes* off Capri on April 18. Fortunately, thirty of the forty-nine men aboard survived. *Regent*, the last submarine lost during the Tunisian campaign, apparently hit a mine in the Strait of Otranto on or before May 1. None of her crew survived.[34]

THE AIR BLOCKADE

Even as enemy ships were being sunk right and left by air attack in ports, those at sea faced a virtual air blockade of the approaches to Tunisia. By late April, the NASAF alone flew four or more sea sweeps a day (the 1st Fighter Group alone sometimes sent out two antishipping missions a day); by the end of the month, the tactical air forces had joined in. So many planes were chasing so few targets that it is sometimes hard to determine who sank what. The main new features of the last stages of the campaign against enemy ships at sea were the greater roles of the heavy bombers and fighter-bombers. They tended to eclipse the "conventional" sweeps by AAF medium bombers—themselves assisted by dive-bombing by accompanying P-38s—and the British torpedo bombers. Sea sweeps remained tough. On April 16 the 82nd Fighter Group attacked what were believed to be two freighters and a Siebel ferry. The Lightning pilots claimed hits on the ships and blew up the ferry, but three pilots fell victim to the flak. (This is one of the attacks that cannot be correlated with the Italian accounts.) And the German fighters also fought furiously to defend convoys. On April 29, the 82nd Group lost six P-38s while shooting down eight German planes in the course of escorting a morning B-25 sweep and carrying out an independent fighter-bomber mission later in the day. The air attacks were supplemented by a greater, although still subsidiary, effort by British surface forces. Few large ships now set out for Tunisia. Fewer still arrived there, or returned—perhaps "escaped" would be a better way to put it—from Africa.

After the *Rovereto-San Diego* disaster, no Axis ship reached Tunisia for four days. On April 10, a single ship, *Tommaseo*, escorted by one torpedo boat, slipped through to Tunis. Only four other cargo ships would reach Tunisia for the rest of April. On April 11, a convoy of three ships and three escorts left Naples for Tunis. Late on the night of April 11, one ship, *Fabriano*, fell out due to damage to her pumps and steered for Palermo accompanied by the corvette *Driade*. Shortly thereafter, the Italian naval command, having received a report that British destroyers were in the Sicilian Strait, ordered the rest of the convoy to take refuge in Palermo. Four Beauforts and three Wellingtons were hunting the broken convoy. A Wellington caught *Fabriano* off Cape Gallo and sank her and her cargo of fuel. The convoy left Palermo with just one cargo ship (another broke down) on April 13. At 10:30 that night it was attacked again off Trapani. The torpedo boat Aretusa was hit by a bomb; it and the cargo ship *Caserta* ran aground. Both ships were saved. Meanwhile, the German ship *Aalborg*, en route from Naples to Tunis, simply vanished without a trace (according to the Italians) on April 12; she may have fallen victim to a sea sweep by the 301st Group Fortresses that morning. On April 15, a single ship, *Foscarini*, with a heavy escort, sailing from Naples via Trapani, fought its way through to Bizerta, surviving six air attacks.[35] *Belluno* repeated this performance the next day, reaching Tunis. *Belluno* convoy survived a British surface attack, although not without cost. Except for the success scored by motor torpedo boats on April 1, British surface forces had accomplished little for months. Indeed, Force Q had lost a destroyer to enemy motor torpedo boats on the night of March 12–13.

Early on April 16, the destroyers *Pakenham* and *Paladin*, part of the Malta-based Force K, brushed with two of Belluno's escorts, sailing ahead of the convoy. The torpedo boat *Cigno* was sunk and *Cassiopeia* damaged; but *Pakenham* was hit in the engine room. *Paladin* took her in tow, but after enemy planes attacked Malta ordered her sunk, lest both destroyers be lost.[36] *Caserta*, along with a pair of KT ships and two torpedo boats, dashed from Trapani to Tunis on April 17. Two days later, a German merchant ship, *P. Claude*, reached Tunis. She was the last regular cargo ship to reach Tunisia that month. Two Italian destroyers, still bringing in fresh troops, arrived in Tunis on April 17 and 23. Two more, and the German destroyer *Hermes*, landed reinforcements there on April 26; one of the Italian destroyers, *Pigafetta*, was lightly damaged by air attack that afternoon off of Cape Bon on its return run. Other than the destroyers, only the KT ships and landing craft managed to reach Africa.

Returning from Africa was no picnic either; indeed, for a brief period the Allies enjoyed more success against return voyages. The Italian freighter *Foggia*, fleeing Sousse for Italy on April 8 as the Allies closed in on that port, ran into submarine *Unshaken*. In a night surface attack, the submarine fired three torpedoes from 2,000 yards; one hit *Foggia* aft of her funnel, and she went down. A two-ship convoy returning from Bizerta to Italy ran into British motor torpedo boats. With assistance from Albacores of 826 Squadron, which had been transferred from Malta to the NACAF at Bone, they sank *Mongineovo* off Zembra Island on April 16–17. The German ship *Mostagamen*, en route from Bizerta to Palermo, was sunk by an aircraft torpedo in the early hours of April 19.

On April 18 the tanker *Bivona* had left Palermo for Bizerta with a heavy escort of small antisubmarine craft. Despite this, the British sub *Unseen* sank the German subchaser 2205. The convoy took refuge in Palermo and sailed again on April 19. That afternoon, another British submarine, *Unrivalled*, sank *Bivona* off Trapani. Early on April 21, the Allies finally snared a KT ship. The KT 5 and KT 7, returning from Tunis to Trapani, were intercepted by the destroyers *Laforey*, *Loyal*, and *Lookout* of Force Q from Bone. They sank the KT 7. That afternoon, the submarine *Unison* hit *Foscarini*, returning from Bizerta to Naples, with two torpedoes off Sicily. The fast cargo ship *Aquino*, trying to make Tunis from Livorno with a very light escort of just one torpedo boat, was blasted by 97th Group B-17s off of Marettimo Island late on the afternoon of April 23. Three bomb hits sent her cargo of fuel up in flames. Unable to control the fires, the Italians abandoned her. Rather unnecessarily, Beauforts came out from Malta to finish off the burning hulk.

That was the last success for torpedo planes in the North African campaign. Beaufighters, which could haul torpedoes, began replacing the Beauforts soon after. But with the European enemy shoved back largely to continental positions, with far less important maritime communications, the torpedo bombers no longer played a critical role; even in attacks on shipping, the aerial rocket tended to eclipse the torpedo.

The next morning, on April 24, *Galiola*, a single ship with a relatively heavy escort (two torpedo boats and two corvettes) sailing from Reggio to Tunis ran afoul of *Sahib* off Cape Milazzo. The escorts, however, sank *Sahib*. Depth charges forced her to surface and scuttle; the Italians rescued all but one man. Submarines scored one more victory on the Tunisian route. On April 27, the torpedo boat *Climene*, escorting the KT 5 and KT 14 back to Trapani, was sunk by the submarine *Unshaken*.[37]

THE FINAL OFFENSIVE

The southern Axis forces had, improbably, escaped being trapped in central Tunisia, but they had fled into a cui de sac. Army Group Afrika now held a front only one hundred miles long in front of Tunis and Bizerta. Nineteen fully equipped and supplied Allied divisions faced fifteen skeletal Axis divisions. The Allies nearly 1,000 tanks against, at the most, 150 Axis tanks. On April 20, the Germans began transferring their last air units out of Tunisia.

Alexander's Army Group began its final offensive on April 22. The British First Army's V Corps launched the main effort; it was to take Tunis, while the American II Corps, which had been switched to the north, attacked toward Bizerta in a semi-independent action. French forces and Montgomery's Eighth Army, now facing extremely rugged terrain around Enfidaville, launched supporting attacks designed to divert the enemy. Despite the shortage of equipment and supplies, von Arnim and his subordinates directed the defense with great skill, committing what was left of their mobile forces where they were most needed. The Axis forces were pushed back, but they did not crack, and the Eighth Army's attack proved to be a costly failure. By April 26, the 18th Army Group had largely ground to a halt. Only the U.S. II Corps continued to gain ground, slowly and with considerable losses. Alexander hastily changed his plans. The Eighth Army hurried its best units—the 7th Armored Division, the 4th Indian Division, and the 201st Guards Brigade—over to the First Army, which prepared a concentrated blow of overwhelming power in the Medjez el Bab sector. The renewed Allied attack on May 6 broke right through; the enemy's power of resistance had been used up in meeting the first attack. Losses of equipment could no longer be replaced—the Germans in Tunisia had received only three new tanks, seventeen guns, and twenty-one vehicles during the whole month of April. Fuel to run what was left no longer existed. By April 29, the Germans could no longer find fuel to run radar sets or move repaired tanks from workshops. As May began, only sixty-nine German tanks were operational. On May 4, von Arnim's headquarters gave notice that it could no longer assure the delivery of ammunition, or even water and food, to units. The trickle of supplies still arriving aboard ferries could not replace what was used up. Lack of fuel alone would have vitiated resistance to the attack on May 6. Von Arnim's intelligence had tracked the British troop movements, and he deduced the Allied plan of attack, but he could no longer complete planned movements of units to counter them. On May 7, the First Army took Tunis, and II Corps entered Bizerta. The fuel shortage prevented many enemy troops from retreating into the Cape Bon peninsula for a prolonged, Bataan-type defense there. On May 13, the last enemy troops in Africa surrendered.[38]

Observers noted that Tunis was a remarkable example of precision bombing. The dock area was a shambles, and the harbor was full of sunken ships, but the city proper was hardly touched. Bizerta, however, had sometimes been protected by smokescreens, so the bombing there had been far less accurate. Ernie Pyle pronounced it the most completely wrecked place he had ever seen, and many others agreed.[39]

Kesselring, who had repeatedly turned down his subordinates' pleas to begin an evacuation, had finally relented on May 7. The Luftwaffe, having lost many of its bases during April, had been forced to withdraw many planes from Africa; on April 26, *Hermes* had removed the ground personnel of Jagdgeschwader 53. By the time Kesselring finally acted, General Karl Korchy, the air commander in Tunisia, had already ordered the last German planes, mostly from Jagdgeschwader 77, out. A pair of ground crewmen were jammed into the back of each fighter as it left for Sicily. They were almost the only Germans to get out.

In early May the medium bombers continued to support the land offensive. The heavies struck Bizerta on May 3 and Tunis on May 5, but the NASAF increasingly shifted its efforts from Africa to prepare for the Sicilian invasion. On May 6, the B-17s attacked Marsala and Trapani. On May 9, the four B-17 groups sent 122 planes to Palermo, followed by eighty-nine B-26s; they devastated the port and industrial area. On May 10, the Fortresses bombed the Milo and Borizzo airfields. They returned to Marsala, with B-25s and B-26s, on May 11. The heavies and mediums again combined to bomb Cagliari harbor on May 13. The Ninth had added a new target, hitting Reggio on April 28, May 1, and May 4, while also bombing Catania, Taranto, and Messina, where it flew an unusually successful mission on May 9.

Even amid the chaos of the final offensive, the Axis had tried to run supplies and even troops to Tunisia. The KT ships ran in pairs from Trapani and Reggio, reaching Tunis on April 24, 27, and 29. Siebel ferries and other landing craft continued to struggle across the Strait of Sicily daily through May 5. Their exact losses are unknown, but they must have been heavy. In a typical attack, on April 26, the 1st Fighter Group sent a dozen P-38s on the second dive-bombing mission of the day to the Strait. They caught seven

Siebels, reporting that one blew up, while two more were left burning and another was left listing badly. A small escort craft seemed to have capsized. (Siebels often were escorted by motor torpedo boats.) On April 29, the 1st Fighter Group sent fourteen P-38s to Marettimo Island, where they found two Siebels and three small boats. Despite an attack by a half dozen Me-109s and Macchi 202s, the Lightnings went into dive-bomb runs, seven dropping 500-pound bombs, four more releasing 1,000-pounders. They claimed the destruction of one Siebel and claimed to have shot down an Me-109. Medium-bomber sweeps also hunted the Siebels; in one of the last such missions, on May 5, nineteen B-26s from the 17th Bomb Group and sixteen P-38s of the 82nd Fighter Group—eight of the latter carried bombs— spotted seven Siebels and seven small boats heading for Sicily. The P-38s sank three of the Siebels and four boats, while the mediums attacked yet another ferry group, claiming to have destroyed three out of four Siebels. A few hours later, fifteen B-25s from the 321st Bomb Group and thirty-six P-38s from the newly operational 14th Fighter Group reported blasting yet another Siebel ferry.[40]

Several merchant ships dared the trip to Tunisia. *Teramo*, escorted by the torpedo boat *Sagittario*, left Pozzuoli in Sicily for Tunis, carrying gasoline barrels on its deck. On April 28, the convoy began crossing the Strait to Africa. That afternoon, fighter-bombers attacked, concentrating on *Sagittario*. It survived, though many crewmen were wounded. The Italians then fended off an attack by British motor torpedo boats, sinking one. In mid-afternoon, the South African 7th Wing's P-40s struck. Two squadrons dive-bombed, while a third provided cover; the Spitfires of the RAF's 601st Squadron flew top cover above the South Africans. Teramo was hit and "burned like a torch," according to the Italian description. She did not sink but finally drifted aground, still flaming, south of Cape Bon. One P-40 was lost, apparently to engine failure.

The next day, the Italians lost a small minesweeper, *Luigi Razza*, to air attack off Tunisia. The ubiquitous Allied planes also caught vessels not engaged in the African traffic, such as a motorized sailing craft engaged in supplying Pantellaria. On April 30, much against the advice of the Italian leaders, three destroyers made a last, fatal trip to Tunisia, carrying 900 men. U.S. and South African fighter-bombers swarmed over them. *Pancaldo* and *Hermes* survived several attacks before dive-bombing P-40s of the 79th Fighter Group severely damaged *Pancaldo* off Cape Bon, losing three P-40s to collisions in a frantic melee when they were jumped by Me-109s. Other fighter-bombers finished off Pancaldo and the severely damaged *Hermes*, which ran aground.

Later that day, the fighter-bombers caught the destroyer *Lampo*, which was carrying ammunition, and they attacked her repeatedly. The 79th Fighter Group apparently delivered the fatal blow, claiming three bomb hits, while the P-40s flying top cover claimed two Me-109s (apparently they actually got a Macchi 205, a new Italian plane that was just as good as the latest-model German fighters). The destroyer caught fire and finally blew up and sank. To complete the disaster for the Axis, two motor torpedo boats carrying Pancaldo's survivors home to Italy were caught by Allied planes off Zembra Island. One sank, and the other ran aground on Zembra, a hopeless wreck. A South African squadron commander was shot down while setting one of the enemy vessels on fire. The South Africans' performance in these attacks was particularly good considering their planes were suffering serious problems with their engines. They finally had to be grounded on May 1.

Despite these disasters, the Italians sent still more ships. *Belluno*, a fast ship, escorted by the torpedo boat *Tifone*, dashed successfully from Trapani to Tunis, delivering 2,000 tons of supplies on May 4. The British, for once, had not received any signals intelligence about this trip. But they did know of the voyage of *Campobasso*, which had reached Pantelleria from Naples with a large cargo of ammunition, artillery, and vehicles. Escorted by the torpedo boat *Perseo*, she started across the Sicilian Strait. Three destroyers from Force K caught both ships near their destination and sank them. A large German ship, *San Antonio*, left Naples for Tunis, escorted by two torpedo boats. On the afternoon of May 5, a B-17 sweep struck the convoy northwest of Cape San Vito, Sicily. *San Antonio* promptly exploded and sank.

No large ships tried the route after that, but in another incredible folly, three KT ships left Trapani late on May 7 in the hope that they could land supplies on Cape Bon. They ran into a whirlwind of attacking planes and surface sweeps. That day, U.S. P-40s had already sunk *Belluno* (loaded with Allied prisoners) and *Tifone* as they tried to flee Tunis. They also claimed sinking Hermes, which had been towed into Tunis. Apparently they did hit her, but she was finally sent to the bottom by deliberate scuttling. Within the harbor, bombers did sink a merchant ship, *Arlesiana*. Precisely how the KT ships met their end is uncertain. They evidently cruised up and down Cape Bon seeking a place to unload. The British reported that KT 5 and KT 21 were sunk by their destroyers, *Laforey*, *Tartar*, and *Loyal*, off the Cape, and that KT 9 was sunk by British and U.S. planes north of Bizerta, all on May 9. The Italians flatly insisted that Allied planes destroyed all three off Cape Bon on May 8.[41]

In April, the Allies had destroyed 41.5 percent of all the supplies dispatched from Italy by sea, the same percentage as in March—but of a far smaller tonnage leaving the country. Only 29,233 tons were landed in Africa. Thanks to "Flax," the tonnage landed by air had fallen from 7,651 to 4,327 tons. Some 77 percent of the tonnage sent by sea in May was lost. The usual variety of figures can be found for Axis shipping losses. The British concluded that the Axis lost thirty-three ships of over 500 tons throughout the Mediterranean in April (fifteen to planes and ten to submarines). In May, mostly after the African campaign was over, they lost thirty-nine ships (thirty to planes and four to submarines). In April, the Italians alone had lost 104 ships, counting those under 500 tons; in May, that figure was 144.

In all, the Germans and Italians had lost 506 ships, of which 170 were over 500 tons, in the Tunisian campaign. The smaller vessels, it should be noted, were mostly sunk by air attacks on Italian and Tunisian harbors. The Italian official history counted only seventy-nine merchant ships sunk at sea on the Tunisian route, but the well-informed naval officer and historian Marc'antonio Bragadin estimated that the Tunisian effort directly cost 243 ships sunk, counting merchant ships and warships of all sizes. Of these, 151 were cargo ships of over 500 tons. Moreover, another 242 ships had been damaged.

These losses had taken place during a period of almost exactly a half year. In contrast, in the three years and eight months of the Pacific War, the Allies sank 2,257 ships of over 500 tons. (They never bothered to total the smaller ones.)[42] The struggle in the Mediterranean during the Tunisian campaign, while smaller in scale and briefer than the Pacific fighting, was thus just as intense and destructive while it lasted. As we have seen, the campaign was not a walkover, and in some ways it was slow to achieve major results. Nor was the opposition feeble. The fact that it was fought in large part against the despised Italians may have caused many to discount its intensity. But although the Italian armed forces in general may have performed poorly during World War II, there were many exceptions to the rule; and it is a dangerous error to assume that the Mediterranean campaigns after the Germans arrived in 1941 can be treated as though the Italians were not present, or were merely a negative asset for the Germans. Some army and air units fought well, while the bad reputation of the Italian armed forces is entirely irrelevant to the Italian navy. Its escort craft fought hard and well; it is hard to see how the Germans, or anyone else, could have done better with what they had.

The war against the Axis supply line to Tunisia had contributed greatly to ensuring an early and a relatively cheap victory there. The efforts of their planes and submarines enabled the Allies to exploit the enemy's fatal decision to fight at the end of a tenuous, vulnerable supply line on the wrong side of the Mediterranean. The Axis suffered enormous, one-sided losses that could not be replaced. In May 1943, the Allies destroyed an entire enemy army group and took approximately 240,000 prisoners (perhaps 130,000 Germans). The German element of Army Group Afrika 155,000 casualties during the entire Tunisian campaign. (All of the Allies together totaled 70,000 casualties.) The Luftwaffe alone had lost 2,422 planes—888 single-engine fighters, 117 twin-engine fighters, 128 dive-bombers, 734 bombers, and 371 transports—with heavy losses of pilots. The Tunisian campaign led to the end of Italian fascism, and the German and Italian losses left southern Europe weakly defended against the next Allied attack. Although Allied strategy in the Mediterranean, after the Tunisian victory, was not of a high order, Allied attacks forced the Nazis to commit strong forces to hold part of Italy and replace the Italian forces in the Balkans and southern France. If the forces committed, and lost, in Tunisia had been held back to defend Sicily, the enemy would have had a good chance of throwing back the Allied attack on the island.[43]

Victory in Tunisia thus began the unraveling of the defense of "Fortress Europe." The efforts of the Allied air forces and submarines had contributed greatly to that victory.

Notes

CHAPTER 1

1. Raymond de Belot, *The Struggle for the Mediterranean* (Princeton, N.J.: Princeton University Press, 1951), 35–39, 111; Donald Macintyre, *The Battle for the Mediterranean* (New York: Norton, 1965), 1–19; John Ellis, *Brute Force* (New York: Viking, 1990), 229–34; Charles Jellison, *Besieged* (Hanover, N.H.: University Press of New England, 1984), 31–42; James J. Sadkovich, *The Italian Navy in World War II* (Westport, Conn.: Greenwood Press, 1994), 1–41. (The Sadkovich book should be used with caution; the older work of Bragadin, cited below, and the Italian official history are generally more reliable.)

2. R. J. Overy, *The Air War* (New York: Stein and Day, 1981), 52–53; Jellison, *Besieged*, 35; Walter Boyne, *Clash of Wings* (New York: Simon and Schuster, 1994), 89, 169–77; Bill Olmsted, *Blue Skies* (Toronto: Stoddart, 1987), 122.

3. C. E. Lucas Phillips, *Alamein* (Boston: Little, Brown, 1962), 38; F. W. von Mellenthin, *Panzer Battles* (New York: Ballantine, 1971), 178–79; Paul Carell (Paul K. Schmidt), *Foxes of the Desert* (New York: Bantam, 1967), 226–27; Ian Cameron (Donald Payne), *Red Duster*, White Ensign (New York: Bantam, 1983), 11–12.

4. Marc Antonio Bragadin, *The Italian Navy in World War II* (Annapolis, Md.: United States Naval Institute, 1957), 129–36; Sadkovich, *The Italian Navy in World War II*, 19–20, 103–9, 150, 174–78, 210–11, 227–28, 232–34, 268; Macintyre, *Battle for the Mediterranean*, 96; Arthur Hezlet, *The Submarine and Seapower* (New York: Stein and Day, 1967), 142. Some authors, most notably Martin Van Creveld, *Supplying War* (London: Cambridge University Press, 1977), 182–202 and John Ellis in *Brute Force* (cited above) have suggested that the Axis supply situation in Libya was inherently so difficult because of the lack of port capacity and the amount of fuel consumed between the ports and the front, that the attacks on shipping made little difference, and that the importance usually attributed to them is grossly exaggerated. Even Van Creveld admits that the period of November–December 1941 may be an exception to this generalization, and he conceded that the bombing of Benghazi and Tobruk kept those ports from being used to capacity (*Supplying War*, 187–88, 195–96, 199). *The Rommel Papers*, edited by B. H. Liddell-Hart (New York: Harcourt, Brace, 1953), 266, 296–97, and the evidence adduced by the historians of British intelligence, F. H. Hinsley and Ralph Bennett, strongly suggest a different conclusion. The failure of supplies to arrive forced Rommel to delay his planned attack on Tobruk from September to November 1941, when it was aborted by a British offensive, whose success was enormously aided by his supply shortages. The arrival of replacement tanks (not detected by the British) enabled Rommel to launch a counterattack in January 1942, and the suppression of Malta permit-

ted the Axis to take the offensive in May–June 1942. Later losses of fuel forced Rommel to limit his attack at Alam Haifa in August–September 1942 and seriously impaired the defense of El Alamein (F. H. Hinsley et al., *British Intelligence in the Second World War*, 3 vols. [New York: Cambridge University Press, 1979–1988]), Vol. II, 416–24; F. H. Hinsley, *British Intelligence in the Second World War*, abr. ed. [New York: Cambridge University Press, 1993], 182, 195–98, 235, 243; Ralph Bennett, *Ultra and Mediterranean Strategy* [New York: William Morrow, 1989], 79–80, 137–38, 159–60).

5. Cameron, *Red Duster, White Ensign*, passim; Jellison, *Besieged*, 12–19, 22, 34–35, 51–52.

6. Hezlet, *The Submarine and Seapower*, 156–64, 275; Macintyre, *The Battle for the Mediterranean*, 16, 23, 27–28, 33, 36–38, 95.

7. Hinsley et al., *British Intelligence in the Second World War*, Vol. I, 109, 144; Gordon Welchman, *Hut Six Ultra* (New York: McGraw-Hill, 1982), 11–12, 35–52, 77–82, 88–89, 96–102, 119, 125, 130–32, 167–69; Ronald Lewin, *Ultra Goes to War* (New York: Pocket Books, 1980), especially 1–59, 113–42; Peter Calvocoressi, *Top Secret Ultra* (New York: Ballantine, 1981).

8. Hinsley et al., *British Intelligence in the Second World War*, Vol. I, 206–14, 375–76, 386, 389, 409; Vol. II, 282–87, 319–24; SRH-037 Reports received by the U.S War Department on the use of Ultra in the European theater, World War II: The Use of "U" in the Mediterranean and Northwest African Theatres of War, by Group Captain R. H. Humphreys, National Archives and Records Administration, 17–18; Bennett, *Ultra and Mediterranean Strategy*, 24, 30–34, 50–62; Lewin, *Ultra Goes to War*, 142–43, 147–81, 187–93, 196–98; Sadkovich, *The Italian Navy in World War II*, 125–26. Sadkovich claims that c38m was broken as early as September 1940, though there were many gaps and delays in reading it until April 1941. This is hard to square with Hinsley.

9. Welchman, *Hut Six Ultra*, 163–69; Calvocoressi, *Top Secret Ultra*, 39.

10. Calvocoressi, *Top Secret Ultra*, 33; Lewin, *Ultra Goes to War*, 58–59; Bragadin, *The Italian Navy in World War II*, 100–101; Hinsley et al., *British Intelligence in the Second World War*, Vol. I, 145; Vol. II, 290.

11. Ben Bryant, *Submarine Commander* (New York: Ballantine, 1960), 35–37, 44, 52–63, 69, 75, 107, 127–29, 149; Hezlet, *The Submarine and Seapower*, 113–20, 137–42, 155; Alistair Mars, *British Submarines at War, 1939–1945* (Annapolis, Md.: Naval Institute Press, 1971), 45, 81–82, 84, 86, 104, 131–32, 197; F. W. Lipscomb, *The British Submarine* (London: Adam and Charles, 1954), 112–17, 151, 162–75.

12. Hugh Lloyd, *Briefed to Attack* (London: Hodder and Stoughton, 1949), 28–46, 50, 206; Charles Lamb, *To War in a Stringbag* (New York: Bantam, 1980), 43–49, 83–84.

13. Hezlet, *The Submarine and Seapower*, 142–43; S. W. Roskill, *The War at Sea*, 3 vols. (London: Her Majesty's Stationery Office, 1954–1961), Vol. I, 524–30; Lloyd, *Briefed to Attack*, 28–52, 60, 64–68, 71–74, 76, 80–82, 87–88; Macintyre, *The Battle for the Mediterranean*, 83–109; Hinsley, *British Intelligence in the Second World War*, abr. ed., 79–80, 182–83, 195–96; Bennett, *Ultra and Mediterranean Strategy*, 71–80; Sadkovich, *The Italian Navy in World War II*, 204; Bragadin, *The Italian Navy in World War II*, 115, 129–46.

14. Lloyd, *Briefed to Attack*, 94–103; Hinsley, *British Intelligence in the Second World War*, abr. ed., 201–06; Jellison, *Besieged*, 51–219; Bennett, *Ultra and Mediterranean*

Strategy, 112–13; Hezlet, *The Submarine and Seapower*, 146–48; Lipscomb, *The British Submarine*, 190–95; Macintyre, *The Battle for the Mediterranean*, 140–63; Bragadin, *The Italian Navy in World War II*, 152–54, 157–98.

15. Peter C. Smith, *Operation Pedestal*, 2nd rev. ed. (London: William Kimber, 1987); Jellison, *Besieged*, 219–58; Macintyre, *The Battle for the Mediterranean*, 164–84; Roskill, *The War at Sea*, Vol. I, 301–8; Sadkovich, *The Italian Navy in World War II*, 285–99.

16. Ralph Barker, *The Ship Busters* (London: Pan, 1959), 33–34, 71–72, 158–237; Bragadin, *The Italian Navy in World War II*, 200; Peter C. Smith, *The Story of the Torpedo Bomber* (London: Almark, 1974), 32–34, 38–41.

17. Wesley F. Craven and James Lea Cate, *The Army Air Forces in World War II* (Chicago: University of Chicago Press, 1948–1958), Vol. II, 32; Bennett, *Ultra and Mediterranean Strategy*, 136; Macintyre, *The Battle for the Mediterranean*, 165, 192; Hinsley et al., *British Intelligence in the Second World War*, Vol. II, 424, 734.

18. Giuseppe Fioravanzo, *La Difesa Del Traffico con L'Africa Settentrionale, dal 1 Ottobre 1942 alla Caduta Della Tunisia*, Vol. VIII, La Marina Italiana Nella Seconda Guerra Mondiale (Rome: Marina Militare, 1964), 94–96, 282–83; Barker, *The Ship Busters*, 205–37; Hinsley et al., *British Intelligence in the Second World War*, Vol. II, 416–24, 427, 435–36, 442–43, 734–36; Bennett, *Ultra and Mediterranean Strategy*, 149–51; Macintyre, *The Battle for the Mediterranean*, 188–96; Hezlet, *The Submarine and Seapower*, 149–50; Sadkovich, *The Italian Navy in World War II*, 304–10.

19. Craven and Cate, *The Army Air Forces in World War II*, Vol. I, 329, 341–42; Vol. II, 10–40; U.S. Army Air Force, *Ultra and the History of the United States Strategic Air Force in Europe vs. the German Air Force* (Frederick, Md.: University Publications of America, 1980), 4; Maurice Matloff and Edwin Snell, *Strategic Planning for Coalition Warfare, 1941–1942* (Washington, D.C.: Department of the Army, 1953), 139, 246–51; Kenn C. Rust, *The Ninth Air Force in World War II*. 2nd ed. (Fallbrook, Calif.: Aero, 1970), 11–21; James Dugan and Carroll Stewart, *Ploesti* (New York: Ballantine, 1973), 3–20, 33.

CHAPTER 2

1. Dwight D. Eisenhower, *Crusade in Europe* (New York: Avon, 1968), 45–48, 72; Matloff and Snell, *Strategic Planning for Coalition Warfare, 1941–1942*, 102, 111–14, 175–77, 179–97, 200–203, 234–56, 272, 278–80; Keith Sainsbury, *The North African Landings* (Newark: University of Delaware Press, 1979), 9, 76–80, 90–119; Omar Bradley, *A Soldier's Story* (New York: Popular Library, 1970), 193.

2. Walter Scott Dunn, *Second Front Now 1943* (Tuscaloosa: University of Alabama Press, 1980); John Grigg, *1943: The Victory That Never Was* (New York: Hill and Wang, 1980); Trumbull Higgins, *Winston Churchill and the Second Front* (New York: Oxford University Press, 1957); Albert Wedemeyer, *Wedemeyer Reports* (New York: Henry Holt, 1958), 168–70, 175–76, 212–13.

3. George F. Howe, *Northwest Africa: Seizing the Initiative* (Washington, D.C.: Department of the Army, 1957), especially 677; Eisenhower, *Crusade in Europe*, 72; Sainsbury, *The North African Landings*, 9, 171–73; Bennett, *Ultra and Mediterranean Strategy*, 372; David Fraser, *Alan Brooke* (New York: Atheneum, 1982), 314, 331–32, 342; Russell Weigley, *Eisenhower's Lieutenants* (Bloomington: Indiana University Press, 1981); George E. Mowrey, *Landing Craft and the War Production Board*, WPB Special Study No. 11, rev. ed. (Washington, D.C., 1946).

4. I. S. O. Playfair, *The Mediterranean and Middle East*, Vol. IV (London: Her Majesty's Stationery Office, 1966), 115, 124, 152; Hinsley et al., *British Intelli-*

gence in the Second World War, Vol. II, 464–74, 487–88; Bennett, *Ultra and Mediterranean Strategy*, 188.

5. Samuel Eliot Morison, *Operations in North African Waters—Volume II of History of United States Naval Operations in World War II*, rev. ed. (Boston: Little, Brown, 1961), 182–84; Mark Clark, *Calculated Risk* (New York: Harper, 1950), 57–58; Eisenhower, *Crusade in Europe*, 82; Howe, *Northwest Africa: Seizing the Initiative*, 16.

6. Sainsbury, *The North African Landings*, 124–43; Eisenhower, *Crusade in Europe*, 77–84; Howe, *Northwest Africa: Seizing the Initiative*, 53–57; Morison, *Operations in North African Waters*, 28, 31–33, 182–83; Matloff and Snell, *Strategic Planning for Coalition Warfare, 1941–1942*, 282–317; Hinsley et al., *British Intelligence in the Second World War*, Vol. II, 464–75; Playfair, *The Mediterranean and Middle East*, Vol. IV, 115–30.

7. Alfred D. Chandler et al., *The Papers of Dwight David Eisenhower, The War Years*, 4 vols. (Baltimore: Johns Hopkins University Press, 1970, Vol. I, 410–11, 461, 469–72, 493 (hereafter cited as *Eisenhower Papers*); Howe, *Northwest Africa: Seizing the Initiative*, 29; Eisenhower, *Crusade in Europe*, 84.

8. Hinsley et al., *British Intelligence in the Second World War*, Vol. II, 474; Bennett, *Ultra and Mediterranean Strategy*, 188.

9. Christopher Shores, Hans Ring, and William N. Hess, *Fighters over Tunisia* (London: Neville Spearman, 1975), 2–4; Craven and Cate, *The Army Air Forces in World War II*, Vol. II, 53–56; Playfair, *The Mediterranean and Middle East*, Vol. IV, 120, Richard G. Davis, *Carl Spaatz and the Air War in Europe* (Washington, D.C.: Smithsonian Institution Press, 1992), 123–24, 136; Howe, *Northwest Africa: Seizing the Initiative*, 53–59.

10. Davis, *Carl Spaatz and the Air War in Europe*, 108, 125; Craven and Cate, *The Army Air Forces in World War II*, Vol. II, 51–53.

11. Roger Freeman, *The Mighty Eighth* (Garden City, N.Y.: Doubleday, 1970), 4–13, 17, 24–25; Craven and Cate, *The Army Air Forces in World War II*, Vol. I, 314–15, 342, 634, 650–51, 657; Vol. II, 61, 209, 231–33, 295, 311; Paul Tibbets, *Mission Hiroshima* (New York: Stein and Day, 1985), 74–87; Thomas F. Gulley et al., *The Hour Has Come: The 97th Bomb Group in World War II* (Dallas: Taylor, 1993), 14–15, 18–48; Alan J. Levine, *The Strategic Bombing of Germany, 1940–1945* (Westport, Conn.: Praeger, 1992), 74–76, 78–79.

12. Freeman, *The Mighty Eighth*, 14–17, 24–25, 249, 264–65; Kenn C. Rust, *The Twelfth Air Force Story in World War II* (Temple City, Calif.: Historical Air Album, 1975), 5–6; Craven and Cate, *The Army Air Forces in World War II*, Vol. II, 52–60, 65, 128, 138, 235; Davis, *Carl Spaatz and the Air War in Europe*, 108; Roger Freeman, *B-26 Marauder at War* (London: Arms and Armour Press, 1991), 31–33; Harold Oyster and Esther M. Oyster, *The 319th In Action* (privately published, 1987), 5–21, 281–90. (This work reprints Lieutenant Hodge's diary.)

The air echelons of the 81st Fighter Group, the 310th Bomb Group, and half of that of the 68th Observation Group were established in England and flew from there to North Africa. The ground echelons of all three groups went to Africa directly from the United States, as did half of the 68th Group's planes. The 47th Light Bomb Group's planes, and part of its ground echelon, reached England; the rest of the ground echelon traveled directly to Africa. The ground echelon of the 320th Bomb Group, and part of that of the 17th Bomb Group, went to Britain, but the B-26s of those units flew the South Atlantic ferry route. The rest of the 17th Group's ground echelon sailed directly from the United States to Africa.

13. Martin Caidin, *Flying Forts* (New York: Ballantine, 1969), 4–5, 48–117, 121–22, 143–59; Roger Freeman, *B-17 Fortress at War* (New York: Scribner's, 1979), 1–33, 38, 54, 83–84, 86, 94; Craven and Cate, *The Army Air Forces in World War II*, Vol. VI, 205–7; Freeman, *The Mighty Eighth*, 72–73; Jack Sun, "Fighter Armament of World War II," *Aerospace Historian*, Summer 1981, 74–81; Col. John Driscoll, "Impact of Weapons Technology on Air Warfare, 1941–1945," *Air Power Historian*, January 1959, 28–38.

14. Craven and Cate, *The Army Air Forces in World War II*, Vol. VI, 199–200; Lloyd Jones, *US Bombers* (Fallbrook, Calif.: Aero, 1980), 84–87; Ray Wagner, *American Combat Planes*, 3rd ed. (Garden City, N.Y.: Doubleday, 1982), 219–24; Carroll Glines, *The Doolittle Raid* (New York: Orion Books, 1988), 18–19, 33; John Sherlock, "Pacific Marauder," *American Aviation Historical Society Journal*, Fall 1966, 190–96; Devon Francis, *Flak Bait* (New York: Duell, Sloane, and Pearce, 1948), 13–45, 69, 102, 124; J. K. Havener, *The Martin B-26 Marauder* (Blue Ridge Summit, Pa.: Tab, 1988), 5, 46, 79–99, 248; Command Informational Intelligence Series, June 22, 1943, 7; Special Informational Intelligence Report 43–10, June 16, 1943, "The B-26 in the Southwest Pacific Area," File 142.034-3, Center for Air Force History; Miscellaneous Documents on Operation Torch, 650.01, Center for Air Force History; Report of Col. Stuart Towle, April 1943, 650.03-2, Center for Air Force History.

15. Craven and Cate, *The Army Air Forces in World War II*, Vol. II, 29, 141; Vol. VI, 212–215; Command Informational Intelligence Series, June 22, 1943, 2–4; Report of Col. Stuart Towle, 5–8; A. J. Liebling, *Mollie and Other War Pieces* (New York: Schocken Books, 1989), 37.

16. Craven and Cate, *The Army Air Forces in World War II*, Vol. VI, 227; Martin Caidin, *The Fork-Tailed Devil* (New York: Ballantine, 1971); Freeman, *The Mighty Eighth*, 11; Hubert Zemke and Roger Freeman, *Zemke's Wolfpack* (New York: Pocket Books, 1991), 229–30; Joe Christy and Jeffrey Ethell, *P-38 Lightning at War* (New York: Scribner's, 1979).

CHAPTER 3

1. Sainsbury, *The North African Landings*, 139–41, 143, 199; Playfair, *The Mediterranean and Middle East*, Vol. IV, 135–36; Eisenhower, *Crusade in Europe*, 103–6; Howe, *Northwest Africa: Seizing the Initiative*, 74, 185–87: Bragadin, *The Italian Navy in World War II*, 221–24.

2. Morison, *Operations in North African Waters*, 71.

3. Playfair, *The Mediterranean and Middle East*, Vol. IV, 130–51, 158–61; *Eisenhower Papers*, Vol. II, 680, 693, 735; Sainsbury, *The North African Landings*, 141, 145–51; Morison, *Operations in North African Waters*, passim; William Breuer, *Geronimo* (New York: St. Martin's Press, 1988), 35; Robert O. Paxton, *Vichy France* (New York: Norton, 1974), 282–84, 306.

4. Playfair, *The Mediterranean and Middle East*, Vol. IV, 157, 172; British Air Ministry, *The Rise and Fall of the German Air Force* (New York: St. Martin's Press, 1983), 144–48; Hinsley et al., *British Intelligence in the Second World War*, Vol. II, 488; U.S. Army Air Force, *Ultra and the History of the United States Strategic Air Force*, 12–13.

5. F. W. Deakin, *The Brutal Friendship*, 2nd rev. ed. (New York: Doubleday/Anchor, 1968), 68–76; Playfair, *The Mediterranean and Middle East*, Vol. IV, 161–63, 170–72; Howe, *Northwest Africa: Seizing the Initiative*, 254–60, 263–65, 283, 286–87; Albert Kesselring, *A Soldier's Record* (New York: William Morrow, 1954), 168–69.

6. Playfair, *The Mediterranean and Middle East*, Vol. IV, 152, 170–72; Howe, *Northwest Africa: Seizing the Initiative*, 255–61; Carell, *Foxes of the Desert*, 310–12; Shores, Ring, and Hess, *Fighters over Tunisia*, 41; Hinsley et al., *British Intelligence in the Second World War*, Vol. II, 488–491; Matthew Cooper, *The German Air Force* (New York: Jane's, 1981), 213–15.

7. Fioravanzo, *La Difesa Del Traffico con L'Africa Settentrionale*, 292; Bragadin, *The Italian Navy in World War II*, 226–30; Howe, *Northwest Africa: Seizing the Initiative*, 258; Hinsley et al., *British Intelligence in the Second World War*, Vol. II, 491. (There are noteworthy discrepancies between the British and American official histories.)

8. Playfair, *The Mediterranean and Middle East*, Vol. IV, 171–72; Howe, *Northwest Africa: Seizing the Initiative*, 294–95; Hinsley et al., *British Intelligence in the Second World War*, Vol. II, 488–91.

9. Ernest Harmon, *Combat Commander* (Englewood Cliffs, N.J.: Prentice Hall, 1970), 128; Carlo D'Este, *Bitter Victory* (New York: Dutton, 1988), 59, 74, 345. For friendlier estimates of Anderson, see Eisenhower, *Crusade in Europe*, 87–88; Playfair, *The Mediterranean and Middle East*, Vol. IV, 157; Kenneth Macksey, *Crucible of Power* (London: Hutchinson, 1969), 90–91, 189.

10. *Eisenhower Papers*, Vol. II, 751, 761.

11. Howe, *Northwest Africa: Seizing the Initiative*, 277–95, 321; Playfair, *The Mediterranean and Middle East*, Vol. IV, 153–55, 165–70, 173–75, 177; Edson D. Raff, *We Jumped to Fight* (New York: Eagle, 1944); Breuer, *Geronimo*, 45–47; Craven and Cate, *The Army Air Forces in World War II*, Vol. II, 78–84, 89; Hinsley et al., *British Intelligence in the Second World War*, Vol. II, 492–93, 496–502; *Eisenhower Papers*, Vol. II, 730, 737, 759, 770; Morison, *Operations in North African Waters*, 220; Davis, *Carl Spaatz and the Air War in Europe*, 139–40, 143; Shores, Ring, and Hess, *Fighters over Tunisia*, 79–80. There are many small discrepancies between the official British and American accounts of the advance into Tunisia during the period November–December 1942.

12. Craven and Cate, *The Army Air Forces in World War II*, Vol. II, 85–91; Davis, *Carl Spaatz and the Air War in Europe*, 142; W. G. F. Jackson, *The Battle for North Africa* (New York: Mason Charter, 1975), 397–400; Howe, *Northwest Africa: Seizing the Initiative*, 295–310; Playfair, *The Mediterranean and Middle East*, Vol. IV, 176–79.

13. Howe, *Northwest Africa: Seizing the Initiative*, 310–18, 326–47; Playfair, *The Mediterranean and Middle East*, Vol. IV, 180–88; *Eisenhower Papers*, Vol. II, 791–93; Jackson, *The Battle for North Africa*, 399–408.

14. Sainsbury, *The North African Landings*, 158–61; Bennett, *Ultra and Mediterranean Strategy*, 188.

15. Bennett, *Ultra and Mediterranean Strategy*, 188; *Eisenhower Papers*, Vol. II, 791–93, 801–2, 11, 822, 853–54, 873–74; Hinsley et al., *British Intelligence in the Second World War*, Vol. II, 474, 487–88; Eisenhower, *Crusade in Europe*, 119–20; Jackson, *The Battle for North Africa*, 394, 397–99.

CHAPTER 4

1. *Eisenhower Papers*, Vol. II, 867, 871, 873–74.

2. Howe, *Northwest Africa: Seizing the Initiative*, 260–62, 321; Eduard Mark, *Aerial Interdiction in Three Wars* (Washington, D.C.: Center for Air Force History, 1994), 25–26; Deakin, *The Brutal Friendship*, 26–27, 65, 83, 89–92, 95–96, 98, 139, 161–62, 318; Trumbull Higgins, *Soft Underbelly* (New York: Macmillan, 1968), 36–37.

3. Howe, *Northwest Africa: Seizing the Initiative*, 260, 321–26, 368; *Rommel Papers*, 360–64; Ronald Lewin, *Rommel as Military Commander* (New York: Ballantine, 1970); Samuel Mitcham, Jr., "Arnim," in *Hitler's Generals*, ed. Correlli Barnett (New York: Weidenfeld, 1989), 335–56; Shores, Ring, and Hess, *Fighters over Tunisia*, 79–82; *Rise and Fall of the German Air Force*, 250; Jackson, *The Battle for North Africa*, 404, 412–13.

4. Maj. Gen. Conrad Seibt, "Railroad, Sea, and Air Transport Situation for Supply of Africa through Italy (Jan.–May 1943)," Ms D-093, Historical Division, HQ U.S. Army, Europe (1947), Records Group 338, National Archives and Records Administration, 1–7; Bragadin, *The Italian Navy in World War II*, 231, 237–338; Howe, *Northwest Africa: Seizing the Initiative*, 258, 325, 365–68; Playfair, *The Mediterranean and Middle East*, Vol. IV, 203, 209–10, 240–41, 243, 245–47, 409–10; Mark, *Aerial Interdiction in Three Wars*, 35–37; Cooper, *The German Air Force*, 216. Sadkovich, *The Italian Navy in World War II*, 313–14, 317–18, provides somewhat different figures for Axis shipping.

5. Playfair, *The Mediterranean and Middle East*, Vol. IV, 240–41, 245–46, 409–10; Roy Nesbit, *The Armed Rovers* (Shrewsbury, U.K.: Airlife, 1995), 122–23; Seibt, "Railroad, Sea, and Air Transport Situation for Supply of Africa through Italy," 3–5; D'Este, *Bitter Victory*, 500–501; Samuel Eliot Morison, *Sicily, Salerno, Anzio— Volume IX of History of United States Naval Operations in World War II* (Boston: Little, Brown, 1954), 210, n.12. Sadkovich, *The Italian Navy in World War II*, 212, terms the Siebel ferries "extremely vulnerable," one of his many inexplicable statements.

6. Williamson Murray, *Strategy for Defeat* (Maxwell Air Force Base, Ala.: Airpower Research Institute, 1983), 160–63; Playfair, *The Mediterranean and Middle East*, Vol. IV, 203n, 208–9, 246, 249; Howe, *Northwest Africa: Seizing the Initiative*, 366–67; Mark, *Aerial Interdiction in Three Wars*, 36; Craven and Cate, *The Army Air Forces in World War II*, Vol. II, 189; Seibt, "Railroad, Sea, and Air Transport Situation for Supply of Africa through Italy," 7–8.

7. Howe, *Northwest Africa: Seizing the Initiative*, 363–65, 513, 682; Bragadin, *The Italian Navy in World War II*, 248; Playfair, *The Mediterranean and Middle East*, Vol. IV, 274, 407–8; Mark, *Aerial Interdiction in Three Wars*, 38–39; Sadkovich, *The Italian Navy in World War II*, 283. There are serious discrepancies in Axis totals for deliveries to Tunisia. The Italians give higher tonnages, apparently due to their practice of counting the weight of tanks, vehicles, and guns, while the German records of troop transports contain "irreconcilable differences," apparently due to typographical errors when they were first compiled (Howe, *Northwest Africa: Seizing the Initiative*, 683).

8. Roskill, *The War at Sea*, Vol. II, 341–42; Playfair, *The Mediterranean and Middle East*, Vol. IV, 198–99, 202–5; Hinsley, *British Intelligence in the Second World War*, Vol. II, 493–94.

9. Nesbit, *The Armed Rovers*, 106–21; Martin Bowman, *Wellington: The Geodetic Giant* (Washington, D.C.: Smithsonian Institution Press, 1990), 121–26; Playfair, *The Mediterranean and Middle East*, Vol. IV, 185, 188–89, 203, 207–8.

10. Playfair, *The Mediterranean and Middle East*, Vol. IV, 205–8; Roskill, *The War at Sea*, Vol. II, 343; Bragadin, *The Italian Navy in World War II*, 238–39, 241–44, 247–48; Fioravanzo, *La Difesa Del Traffico con L'Africa Settentrionale*, 145–70, 310; Kenneth Poolman, *Night Strike from Malta* (London: Jane's, 1980), 180–81; Hinsley et al., *British Intelligence in the Second World War*, Vol. II, 494–95. The usually accurate

Hinsley, however, mistakenly credits Force K with destroying an additional Tunisian-bound convoy.

11. John Mullins, *An Escort of P-38s* (St. Paul, Minn.: Phalanx, 1995), 30–35; Gulley, *The Hour Has Come*, 50–53; Oyster and Oyster, *The 319th in Action*, 14, 21–24, 175; The 319th Bomb Group, Medium, Special Historical Account, 22 August 1944, Roll BO 240, Center for Air Force History.

12. Liebling, *Mollie and Other War Pieces*, 28.

13. Alfred Beck, Abe Bartz, Charles Lynch, and Lida Mayo, *The Corps of Engineers: The War against Germany* (Washington, D.C.: Center for Military History, 1985), 85–87; Craven and Cate, *The Army Air Forces in World War II*, Vol. II, 116–18; Liebling, *Mollie and Other War Pieces*, 28–31; Ernie Pyle, *Here Is Your War* (Cleveland: World, 1945), 26, 32, 138: Mullins, *An Escort of P-38s*, 34–35; Caidin, *The Fork-Tailed Devil*, 98; Gulley et al., *The Hour Has Come*, 50–55; Oyster and Oyster, *The 319th in Action*, 23–25.

14. Craven and Cate, *The Army Air Forces in World War II,* Vol. II, 82; Gulley et al., *The Hour Has Come*, 51–53; War Diary, 97th Bombardment Group, Roll BO 196, Center for Air Force History (like many microfilmed AAF materials, this source is unpaginated); Tibbets, *Mission Hiroshima*, 115–17.

15. Playfair, *The Mediterranean and Middle East*, Vol. IV, 174; Craven and Cate, *The Army Air Forces in World War II*, Vol. II, 83–87; Gulley et al., *The Hour Has Come*, 53–56; Mullins, *An Escort of P-38s*, 35; Shores, Ring, and Hess, *Fighters over Tunisia*, 61–72; Christy and Ethell, *P-38 Lightning at War*, 48–50; Rust, *The Twelfth Air Force Story in World War II*, 10; entry of November 21–22, 1942, War Diary, 97th Bombardment Group; entry of November 24, 1942, War Diary, 1st Fighter Group, Roll BO 040, Center for Air Force History.

16. Oyster and Oyster, *The 319th in Action*, 25–26, 163–64; The 319th Bomb Group, Medium, Special Historical Account, 27–28; Playfair, *The Mediterranean and Middle East*, Vol. IV, 172; Craven and Cate, *The Army Air Forces in World War II*, Vol. II, 88; Rust, *The Twelfth Air Force Story in World War II*, 10.

17. *Eisenhower Papers*, Vol. II, 778; Gulley et al., *The Hour Has Come*, 55–56; entry of November 30, 1942; War Diary, 1st Fighter Group; Mullins, *An Escort of P-38s*, 35–37; Eric Hamel, *Aces Against Germany* (New York: Pocket Books, 1995), 25–31.

18. Craven and Cate, *The Army Air Forces in World War II*, Vol. II, 121–22.

19. Mullins, *An Escort of P-38s*, 42–43, 84; Operations Bulletin No. 1, A-3 Section Headquarters NW African Air Forces, 30 April 1943, 14, 650.01-1 Center for Air Force History; Headquarters 12th Air Force, 4 February 1943, "Fighter Tactics Applied by U.S. Army Air Corps (African Campaign)," RG 331 AFHQ Microfilm R-50H, National Archives; Tactical Bulletin, No. 22, 1 July 1943, "Bomber Escort Tactics and Techniques in Northwest Africa," RG 331 AFHQ Microfilm R-50H, National Archives; U.S. Army Air Force, *Ultra and the History of the United States Strategic Air Force in Europe*, 14.

20. Oyster and Oyster, *The 319th in Action*, 26–27, 50, 166; Intelligence Narrative No. 3, Day Operations, 2 December 1942, Intelligence Narrative No. 4, Day Operations, 4 December 1942, 319th Bomb Group Medium, Roll BO 239, Center for Air Force History; Group History, 310th Bomb Group, Roll BO 229, Center for Air Force History; Entries of December 1–7 1942, War Diary, 1st Fighter Group; Craven and Cate, *The Army Air Forces in World War II*, Vol. II, 88, 90–91, 108; Mullins, *An Escort of P-38s*, 40–49; Gulley, *The Hour Has Come*, 55–56; Rust, *The*

Twelfth Air Force Story in World War II, 11; Howe, *Northwest Africa: Seizing the Initiative*, 310; Shores, Ring, and Hess, *Fighters over Tunisia*, 82, 84, 88, 92. There are many discrepancies in contemporary accounts of these operations, especially those on December 3 and 4.

21. HQ XII AF, "Twelfth Air Force Official History through February 1943," File 650.01-01, Center for Air Force History.

22. R. H. Humphreys, "The Use of 'U' in the Mediterranean and Northwest African Theatres of War," 22–23, 25–26; Howe, *Northwest Africa: Seizing the Initiative*, 310; Hinsley et al., *British Intelligence in the Second World War*, Vol. II, 492–94; Bennett, *Ultra and Mediterranean Strategy*, 192, 194; Davis, *Carl Spaatz and the Air War in Europe*, 114–15, 140–46; Craven and Cate, *The Army Air Forces in World War II*, Vol. II, 83–84, 90, 105–8; 110–11, 116–18; David Syrett, "Northwest Africa, 1942–1943," in *Case Studies in the Achievement of Air Superiority*, ed. Benjamin Franklin Cooling (Washington, D.C.: Center for Air Force History, 1994), 231, 233–36.

23. Steve Blake and John Stannaway, *"Adorimini": A History of the 82nd Fighter Group* (Boise, Idaho: 82nd Fighter Group History, 1992), 25.

24. Oyster and Oyster, *The 319th in Action*, 28–29; Craven and Cate, *The Army Air Forces in World War II*, Vol. II, 116–19, 122–23, 127, 131–33; Gulley, *The Hour Has Come*, 56–59, 67, 73; Mullins, *An Escort of P-38s*, 44–46; The 319th Bomb Group, Medium, Special Historical Account, 28–29; Shores, Ring, and Hess, *Fighters over Tunisia*, 131.

25. Craven and Cate, *The Army Air Forces in World War II*, Vol. II, 98–105, 119–20; Bragadin, *The Italian Navy in World War II*, 240; Rust, *The Ninth Air Force in World War II*, 22–24; Dugan and Stewart, *Ploesti*, 33; Freeman, *The Mighty Eighth*, 34–35.

26. Craven and Cate, *The Army Air Forces in World War II*, Vol. II, 120–24; Oyster and Oyster, *The 319th in Action*, 28–29, 159–60: Wilford G. Corey, *Bombs on the Target* (privately published, 1946), 28; Shores, Ring, and Hess, *Fighters over Tunisia*, 101–3, 106, 113; Operations Bulletin No. 2, Northwest African Air Forces, May 31, 1943, 43, File 650.01-1; Gulley, *The Hour Has Come*, 57, 68; Fioravanzo, *La Difesa Del Traffico con L'Africa Settentrionale*, 178–79, 319–20; Intelligence Narrative, Number 7, Day Operation, 14 December 1942; Intelligence Narrative, Number 8, Day Operation, 15 December 1942; Intelligence Narrative, Number 9, Day Operation, 17 December 1942; 319th Bomb Group Medium. The Army Air Force official history and other sources erroneously identify the large ship sunk on December 15 as *Arlesiana*, a considerably smaller ship that was actually destroyed in May 1943. (Cf. Operations Bulletin No. 2, cited above, and Playfair, *The Mediterranean and Middle East*, Vol. IV, 423).

27. Poolman, *Night Strike from Malta*, 181; Fioravanzo, *La Difesa Del Traffico con L'Africa Settentrionale*, 179–81, 321, 323; Shores, Ring, and Hess, *Fighters over Tunisia*, 117; Ken Delves, *The Winged Bomb* (Leicester, U.K.: Midland Counties Publishers, 1985), 81–82, 85–88.

28. Bryant, *Submarine Commander*, 182.

29. Bryant, *Submarine Commander*, 176; Hezlet, *The Submarine and Seapower*, 152–53; Playfair, *The Mediterranean and Middle East*, Vol. IV, 202–3, 212; Mars, *British Submarines at War, 1939–1945* (Annapolis, Md.: Naval Institute Press, 1971), 165–70; George W. Simpson, *Periscope View* (London: Macmillan, 1972), 266, 268–70; Fioravanzo, *La Difesa Del Traffico con L'Africa Settentrionale*, 301.

30. Fioravanzo, *La Difesa Del Traffico con L'Africa Settentrionale*, 292, 294; Playfair, *The Mediterranean and Middle East*, Vol. IV, 202–3; Simpson, *Periscope View*, 270; John

Wingate, *The Fighting Tenth* (London: Leo Cooper, 1991); Bryant, *Submarine Commander*, 179–80, conflates several events.

31. Patrol Report, HMS *Ursula*, RG 331 AFHQ Microfilm R-6-A, National Archives.

32. Fioravanzo, *La Difesa Del Traffico con L'Africa Settentrionale*, 176–77, 296, 314, 316; Playfair, *The Mediterranean and Middle East*, Vol. IV, 207; Patrol Report, HMS P219, RG 331 AFHQ Microfilm R-6-A, National Archives.

33. Fioravanzo, *La Difesa Del Traffico con L'Africa Settentrionale*, 177–79, 181, 317, 319, 323–24, 325; Playfair, *The Mediterranean and Middle East*, Vol. IV, 212; Patrol Report, HMS *Ursula*; Wingate, *The Fighting Tenth*, 257; Simpson, *Periscope View*, 270–72.

34. Playfair, *The Mediterranean and Middle East*, Vol. IV, 210; Bragadin, *The Italian Navy in World War II*, 248; Howe, *Northwest Africa: Seizing the Initiative*, 683; Fioravanzo, *La Difesa Del Traffico con L'Africa Settentrionale*, 439; Roskill, *The War at Sea*, Vol. II, 344, gives considerably different figures from Playfair but counts craft below 500 tons and Italian ships lost outside of the Mediterranean. Playfair's breakdown of enemy losses by cause or agent contains errors.

35. Bowman, Wellington, 127–31; Playfair, *The Mediterranean and Middle East*, Vol. IV, 189.

36. "Twelfth Air Force Official History through February 1943"; Freeman, *The Mighty Eighth*, 265; Craven and Cate, *The Army Air Forces in World War II*, Vol. II, 60; Blake and Stannaway, *"Adorimini,"* 19–25; Freeman, *B-26 Marauder at War*, 36; Oyster and Oyster, *The 319th in Action*, 29, 159.

37. Richard Thruelsen and Elliott Arnold, *Mediterranean Sweep* (New York: Duell, Sloan, and Pearce, 1944), 42–47, 62; Pyle, *Here Is Your War*, 119; Gulley, *The Hour Has Come*, 61–67; Nesbit, *The Armed Rovers*, 125; Raff, *We Jumped to Fight*, 179; *New York Times*, January 19, 1943, 1, 7, February 1, 1943, 4. As usual, there are significant differences between accounts, especially in the number and nationalities of the Allied prisoners aboard Narvalo.

CHAPTER 5

1. *Eisenhower Papers*, Vol. II, 873–74, 878–79, 892 n.1, 897–98; Davis, *Carl Spaatz and the Air War in Europe*, 140–46, 152–53; Craven and Cate, *The Army Air Forces in World War II*, Vol. II, 108–10, 112; Syrett, "Northwest Africa, 1942–1943," 236–38.

2. Playfair, *The Mediterranean and Middle East*, Vol. IV, 261–63; Herbert Feis, *Churchill, Roosevelt, and Stalin* (Princeton, N.J.: Princeton University Press, 1957), 105–13; Levine, *The Strategic Bombing of Germany, 1940–1945*, 77–78; Winston Churchill, *The Second World War*, Vol. IV (New York: Bantam, 1962), 587–603.

3. Davis, *Carl Spaatz and the Air War in Europe*, 156–57, 181–82; Craven and Cate, *The Army Air Forces in World War II*, Vol. II, 113–15, 161, 301–6; Playfair, *The Mediterranean and Middle East*, Vol. IV, 271.

4. Craven and Cate, *The Army Air Forces in World War II*, Vol. II, 126, 130–31, 138, 268; Davis, *Carl Spaatz and the Air War in Europe*, 171, 174; *Eisenhower Papers*, Vol. II, 912, 920; Playfair, *The Mediterranean and Middle East*, Vol. IV, 283.

5. Craven and Cate, *The Army Air Forces in World War II*, Vol. II, 98, 102, 103, 123, 125, 151–53; Shores, Ring, and Hess, *Fighters over Tunisia*, 126, 137, 139, 152; Gulley et al., The Hour Has Come, 57, 72–74, 77–81; Playfair, *The Mediterranean and Middle East*, Vol. IV, 242, 248; Blake and Stannaway, *"Adorimini,"* 37; Mullins, *An Escort of P-38s*, 45; Charles Hair, *The Saga of 54 and More* (Anaheim, Calif.:

Robinson Typographics, 1987), 55–86; Rust, *The Ninth Air Force in World War II*, 24; Rust, *The Twelfth Air Force Story in World War II*, 12.

6. Craven and Cate, *The Army Air Forces in World War II*, Vol. II, 133, 151–53, 168; Mullins, *An Escort of P-38s*, 45–50; Pyle, *Here Is Your War*, 35–39; Blake and Stannaway, *"Adorimini,"* 35–39; Levine, *The Strategic Bombing of Germany, 1940–1945*, 111.

7. Craven and Cate, *The Army Air Forces in World War II*, Vol. II, 151–52; Mullins, *An Escort of P-38s*, 45; Playfair, *The Mediterranean and Middle East*, Vol. IV, 235, 284; Rust, *The Twelfth Air Force Story in World War II*, 12; Shores, Ring, and Hess, *Fighters over Tunisia*, 145, 158–69; "Twelfth Air Force Official History through February 1943"; Pyle, *Here Is Your War*, 127–30; Gulley et al., *The Hour Has Come*, 74–76; "Counter Air-Counter Air Force Operations in the Mediterranean Theatre," File 650.03-2, Center for Air Force History.

8. Hair, *The Saga of 54 and More*, 69–72, 76–82; Shores, Ring, and Hess, *Fighters over Tunisia*, 177, 180–84, 190, 198, 200; Craven and Cate, *The Army Air Forces in World War II*, Vol. II, 144, 152; Gulley et al., *The Hour Has Come*, 81, 83; Blake and Stannaway, *"Adorimini,"* 30–32, 36–39. Craven and Cate, *The Army Air Forces in World War II*, Vol. II, 144, seems to understate U.S. fighter losses in this series of missions.

9. Playfair, *The Mediterranean and Middle East*, Vol. IV, 241; Craven and Cate, *The Army Air Forces in World War II*, Vol. II, 146–47; Tunisian Campaign, 319th Bomb Group Medium, Roll BO 240, Center for Air Force History; Operations Bulletin No. 2, May 31, 1943; Col. Anthony G. Hunter, "Counter-Shipping Missions, Tactics, and Formations," March 15, 1943, 1–2, Roll BO 229, Center for Air Force History; Report of Col. Stuart Towle; Corey, *Bombs on the Target*, 28–29. The AAF official history erroneously implies that sea sweeps began only in January, postdates the participation of the 319th Group, and wrongly identifies *Saturno* as a German ship.

10. Nesbit, *The Armed Rovers*, 125–26; Hinsley et al., *British Intelligence in the Second World War*, Vol. II, 573; Playfair, *The Mediterranean and Middle East*, Vol. IV, 245; Fioravanzo, *La Difesa Del Traffico con L'Africa Settentrionale*, 186–87; Oyster and Oyster, *The 319th in Action*, 30–31; Blake and Stannaway, *"Adorimini,"* 28–29; Hair, *The Saga of 54 and More*, 60–65; Group History, 310th Bomb Group.

11. Craven and Cate, *The Army Air Forces in World War II*, Vol. II, 147–48; Rust, *The Twelfth Air Force Story in World War II*, 13; Hair, *The Saga of 54 and More*, 66–68; Nesbit, *The Armed Rovers*, 126–27; Shores, Ring, and Hess, *Fighters over Tunisia*, 144, 159, 162, 165; Oyster and Oyster, *The 319th in Action*, 31; Blake and Stannaway, *"Adorimini,"* 29–30; Fioravanzo, *La Difesa Del Traffico con L'Africa Settentrionale*, 395; Mission Report, Operation No. 20, 21 January 1943, 319th Bomb Group, Roll BO 239.

12. Samuel Eliot Morison, *Coral Sea and Midway* (Boston: Little, Brown, 1949), 159, n. 38; James H. Belote and William M. Belote, *Titans of the Sea* (New York: Harper and Row, 1975), 48, 346–47; C. Vann Woodward, *Battle for Leyte Gulf* (New York: Ballantine, 1957), 55, 67; Harold Buell, *Dauntless Helldivers* (New York: Dell, 1992), 68–74.

13. Fioravanzo, *La Difesa Del Traffico con L'Africa Settentrionale*, 188; Hinsley et al., *British Intelligence in the Second World War*, Vol. II, 573; Freeman, *B-26 Marauder at War*, 36, 41–43; Mission Report, Operation Number 21, 22 January 1943, 319th Bomb Group, Roll BO 239; Oyster and Oyster, *The 319th in Action*, 31, 170. Play-

fair, *The Mediterranean and Middle East*, Vol. IV, 241, wrongly attributes the Ruhr's sinking to RAF and Fleet Air Arm planes.

14. Oyster and Oyster, *The 319th in Action*, 31, 171–73; Fioravanzo, *La Difesa Del Traffico con L'Africa Settentrionale*, 395; Mission Report, Operation Number 22, 23 January 1943, 319th Bomb Group, Roll BO 239; Shores, Ring, and Hess, *Fighters over Tunisia*, 170–71.

15. Nesbit, *The Armed Rovers*, 127–28; Playfair, *The Mediterranean and Middle East*, Vol. IV, 242; Fioravanzo, *La Difesa Del Traffico con L'Africa Settentrionale*, 189.

16. Hair, *The Saga of 54 and More*, 69–70; Corey, *Bombs on the Target*, 29; Fioravanzo, *La Difesa Del Traffico con L'Africa Settentrionale*, 396; Mission Report, Operation Number 23, 27 January 1943, 319th Bomb Group, Roll BO 239.

17. Mission Report, Operation Number 24, 28 January 1943, 319th Bomb Group, Roll BO 239; Fioravanzo, *La Difesa Del Traffico con L'Africa Settentrionale*, 190–91.

18. Corey, *Bombs on the Target*, 30; Oyster and Oyster, *The 319th in Action*, 32–33, 39, 168, 174; Rust, *The Twelfth Air Force Story in World War II*, 15; Mission Reports, Operation Number 26, 27, 28, and 29, 319th Bomb Group, Roll BO 239.

19. Fioravanzo, *La Difesa Del Traffico con L'Africa Settentrionale*, 198–99, 399; Playfair, *The Mediterranean and Middle East*, Vol. IV, 247; Nesbit, *The Armed Rovers*, 128; Craven and Cate, *The Army Air Forces in World War II*, Vol. II, 149; Hair, *The Saga of 54 and More*, 84–85.

20. Martin Blumenson, *Kasserine Pass* (Boston: Houghton Mifflin, 1966); Bennett, *Ultra and Mediterranean Strategy*, 196–209; Playfair, *The Mediterranean and Middle East*, Vol. IV, 287–305, 328–29; Howe, *Northwest Africa: Seizing the Initiative*, 319–480; Macksey, *Crucible of Power*, 145–71; Jackson, *Battle for North Africa*, 415–434; Harmon, *Combat Commander*, 111–15, 146.

21. Nesbit, *The Armed Rovers*, 131–32; Fioravanzo, *La Difesa Del Traffico con L'Africa Settentrionale*, 201–2; Playfair, *The Mediterranean and Middle East*, Vol. IV, 247; Craven and Cate, *The Army Air Forces in World War II*, Vol. II, 149; Shores, Ring, and Hess, *Fighters over Tunisia*, 214; Blake and Stannaway, *"Adorimini,"* 41–42; Hair, *The Saga of 54 and More*, 86; Hinsley et al., *British Intelligence in the Second World War*, Vol. II, 573–74; Group History, 310th Bomb Group.

    It is interesting to note the incredible muddle of claims about the *Thorsheimer* convoy. The 310th Bomb Group historians credited the attack with sinking a cruiser and damaging a freighter, as well as sinking the tanker. The AAF official history reports "damage" to a cruiser and the sinking of two small escorts, while it casts doubt on the idea that the British finished off *Thorsheimer*. The British history, in contrast, claims that the night attacks on February 20–21 had already damaged the tanker before the AAF struck.

22. Craven and Cate, *The Army Air Forces in World War II*, Vol. II, 149; Fioravanzo, *La Difesa Del Traffico con L'Africa Settentrionale*, 203–6, 401; Nesbit, *The Armed Rovers*, 132–34; Hair, *The Saga of 54 and More*, 86–88; Shores, Ring, and Hess, *Fighters over Tunisia*, 216, 218; Blake and Stannaway, *"Adorimini,"* 42–43.

23. Walter D. Edmonds, *They Fought with What They Had* (Boston: Little, Brown, 1951), 130.

24. Playfair, *The Mediterranean and Middle East*, Vol. IV, 248; Craven and Cate, *The Army Air Forces in World War II*, Vol. II, 183, 187–88; Shores, Ring, and Hess, *Fighters over Tunisia*, 220, 227; Fioravanzo, *La Difesa Del Traffico con L'Africa Settentrionale*, 204–5, 351; 301st Bombardment Group History, Roll BO 208, Center for Air Force History; Entries for February 25, 26, and 28, War Diary, 1st Fighter

Group; "Tactics and Techniques of Heavy Bombardment in Support of the Ground Forces in the North African Theatre," 3 May 1943, RG 331 AFHQ Microfilm RG-50H, National Archives; Command Informational Bulletin 5, July 1943, 4, File 142.034-3, Center for Air Force History; Operations Bulletin No. 2, Northwest African Air Forces, May 31, 1943, 1–2.

25. Playfair, *The Mediterranean and Middle East*, Vol. IV, 244; Mars, *British Submarines at War, 1939–1945*, 172–73; Simpson, *Periscope View*, 276–83; C. E. T. Warren and James Benson, *The Midget Raiders* (New York: Ballantine, 1968), 84–92.

26. Playfair, *The Mediterranean and Middle East*, Vol. IV, 242–43.

27. Patrol Report, HMS P212 (*Sahib*), RG 331 AFHQ Microfilm R-6-A, National Archives; Playfair, *The Mediterranean and Middle East*, Vol. IV, 243, 246; Fioravanzo, *La Difesa Del Traffico con L'Africa Settentrionale*, 184–87, 191–92, 333, 334, 335, 340, 342, 344, 346; Wingate, *The Fighting Tenth*, 266–78.

28. Fioravanzo, *La Difesa Del Traffico con L'Africa Settentrionale*, 191; Playfair, *The Mediterranean and Middle East*, Vol. IV, 247–48; Patrol Report, HMS P211 (*Safari*), RG 331 AFHQ Microfilm R-6-A, National Archives; Bryant, *Submarine Commander*, 199–204.

29. Fioravanzo, *La Difesa Del Traffico con L'Africa Settentrionale*, 192–94, 199, 201, 345, 349; Playfair, *The Mediterranean and Middle East*, Vol. IV, 247–48, 412; Wingate, *The Fighting Tenth*, 278–86; Patrol Report, HMS Turbulent, RG 331 AFHQ Microfilm R-6-A, National Archives.

30. *Eisenhower Papers*, Vol. II, 974.

31. Playfair, *The Mediterranean and Middle East*, Vol. IV, 247–50; Hinsley et al., *British Intelligence in the Second World War*, Vol. II, 574; Howe, *Northwest Africa: Seizing the Initiative*, 510; Fioravanzo, *La Difesa Del Traffico con L'Africa Settentrionale*, 438–41; Roskill, *The War at Sea*, Vol. II, 432.

CHAPTER 6

1. Jackson, *The Battle for North Africa*, 440–62; Howe, *Northwest Africa: Seizing the Initiative*, 508, 510–72, 592 n.38; Macksey, *Crucible of Power*, 186–224.

2. Mark, *Aerial Interdiction in Three Wars*, 37; Howe, *Northwest Africa: Seizing the Initiative*, 509–10.

3. Mark, *Aerial Interdiction in Three Wars*, 36–37; Howe, *Northwest Africa: Seizing the Initiative*, 510–14; Playfair, *The Mediterranean and Middle East*, Vol. IV, 247, 274–75, 407–9; Fioravanzo, *La Difesa Del Traffico con L'Africa Settentrionale*, 352–69.

4. Playfair, *The Mediterranean and Middle East*, Vol. IV, 411; Craven and Cate, *The Army Air Forces in World War II*, Vol. II, 185–87; Davis, *Carl Spaatz and the Air War in Europe*, 186–89; U.S. Army Air Force, *Ultra and the History of the United States Strategic Air Force*, 26; Hinsley et al., *British Intelligence in the Second World War*, Vol. II, 574, 576; R. H. Humphreys, "The Use of 'U' in the Mediterranean and Northwest African Theatres of War," 26.

5. Fioravanzo, *La Difesa Del Traffico con L'Africa Settentrionale*, 212–13; Playfair, *The Mediterranean and Middle East*, Vol. IV, 412; Craven and Cate, *The Army Air Forces in World War II*, Vol. II, 187; Gulley, *The Hour Has Come*, 91; Entries for March 2–10, 1943, War Diary, 97th Bomb Group; Entries for March 1–4, 1943, War Diary, 1st Fighter Group; Entries of March 4, 1943, War Diary, 301st Bomb Group, Roll BO 208, Center for Air Force History; Northwest African Air Forces

Daily Operational Summaries, March 4, 1943, RG 331 AFHQ Microfilm RG-48-F, National Archives. (Hereafter, this source will be listed as NAAF Opsums, with date.)

6. Fioravanzo, *La Difesa Del Traffico con L'Africa Settentrionale*, 213–14; Blake and Stannaway, *"Adorimini,"* 46; Shores, Ring, and Hess, *Fighters over Tunisia*, 241; Gulley, *The Hour Has Come*, 91; Hair, *The Saga of 54 and More*, 96–98; Group History, 310th Bomb Group; NAAF Daily Opsum, March 8, 1943.

7. Gulley, *The Hour Has Come*, 93; Fioravanzo, *La Difesa Del Traffico con L'Africa Settentrionale*, 216, 354; Group History, 310th Bomb Group; Shores, Ring, and Hess, *Fighters over Tunisia*, 243–44; Entries for March 8 and 10, 1943, War Diary, 97th Bomb Group; Mullins, *An Escort of P-38s*, 56; Entries for March 8 and 10, 1943, War Diary, 1st Fighter Group.

8. Craven and Cate, *The Army Air Forces in World War II*, Vol. II, 186–87; Hunter, "Counter-Shipping Missions, Tactics, and Formations"; Report of Col. Stuart Towle, 4; Interview with Col. Engler, Command Informational Bulletin 43–112, 5 July 1943, 4, File 142.034-5, Center for Air Force History; "Bombardment Tactics and Techniques Employed in Counter-Shipping Attacks," 5, NAAF Operations Bulletin in No. 2, File 650.01-2, Center for Air Force History.

9. Fioravanzo, *La Difesa Del Traffico con L'Africa Settentrionale*, 353; Mission Report, 11 March 1943, 17th Bomb Group, Roll BO 082, Center for Air Force History; Sea Search Mission Report, 12 March 1943, 381st Squadron, 310th Bomb Group, Roll BO 229, Center for Air Force History; NAAF Daily Opsums, March 11 and March 12, 1943; Shores, Ring, and Hess, *Fighters over Tunisia*, 245–46; Hair, *The Saga of 54 and More*, 99–101; O. K. Earl, ed., *The Thunderbird Goes to War* (Ann Arbor, Mich.: Braun-Brumfield, 1991), 45, 46, 47; Blake and Stannaway, *"Adorimini,"* 46–47.

10. Fioravanzo, *La Difesa Del Traffico con L'Africa Settentrionale*, 216–20; Nesbit, *The Armed Rovers*, 135–36; Shores, Ring, and Hess, *Fighters over Tunisia*, 250–51. Playfair, *The Mediterranean and Middle East*, Vol. IV, 411, erroneously reports that *Sterope* was sunk.

11. "A Simplified History of the 321st Bomb Group (M)," Roll BO 240, Center for Air Force History; Shores, Ring, and Hess, *Fighters over Tunisia*, 254; Rust, *The Twelfth Air Force Story in World War II*, 16; Fioravanzo, *La Difesa Del Traffico con L'Africa Settentrionale*, 404; War Diary, Entry of March 16, 1943, Sheet 6; War Diary, 301st Bomb Group, Roll BO 208, Center for Air Force History.

12. Nesbit, *The Armed Rovers*, 136–38; Blake and Stannaway, *"Adorimini,"* 48–50; Mission Report, 22 March 1943, 17th Bomb Group, Roll BO 082, Center for Air Force History; Mission Report, 20 March 1943, 82nd Fighter Group, Roll BO 168, Center for Air Force History; History, 321st Bombardment Group, (M) Roll BO 240; NAAF Daily Opsums, March 20, 22, 1943; Fioravanzo, *La Difesa Del Traffico con L'Africa Settentrionale*, 222–24; Rust, *The Twelfth Air Force Story in World War II*, 16; Shores, Ring, and Hess, *Fighters over Tunisia*, 257–58, as on some other occasions, provide different figures for the number of P-38s dispatched, and for losses and claims.

13. Impact, May 1943 (New York: James Parton, 1980), 22; Playfair, *The Mediterranean and Middle East*, Vol. IV, 411–12; NAAF Daily Opsums, March 22, 1943; Craven and Cate, *The Army Air Forces in World War II*, Vol. II, 188; Shores, Ring, and Hess, *Fighters over Tunisia*, 259.

14. NAAF Daily Opsums, March 31, 1943; Playfair, *The Mediterranean and Middle East*, Vol. IV, 392, 412–13, 423; Shores, Ring, and Hess, *Fighters over Tunisia*, 261–62, 276; Fioravanzo, *La Difesa Del Traffico con L'Africa Settentrionale*, 225–27, 360–61; Craven and Cate, *The Army Air Forces in World War II*, Vol. II, 188; Blake and Stannaway, "Adorimini," 50–51; Freeman, *B-26 Marauder at War*, 133.

15. Rust, *The Ninth Air Force in World War II*, 22, 26–30; Craven and Cate, *The Army Air Forces in World War II*, Vol. II, 171–72, 182–83; Dugan and Stewart, *Ploesti*, 47–48.

16. Craven and Cate, *The Army Air Forces in World War II*, Vol. II, 176, 181; Playfair, *The Mediterranean and Middle East*, Vol. IV, 238–29, 392–93; Hinsley et al., *British Intelligence in the Second World War*, Vol. II, 606; U.S. Army Air Force, *Ultra and the History of the United States Strategic Air Force*, 26; Olmsted, *Blue Skies*, 39–90; Shores, Ring, and Hess, *Fighters over Tunisia*, 385–87, 389, 395–96, 403–4; Air Ministry, The Rise and Fall of the German Air Force, 249–54; Tactical Notes on Operations in N.W. Africa by RAF Fighter Squadrons between December 1942 and March 1943, RG 331 AFHQ Microfilm R50-H, National Archives; Tactical Bulletin: Fighter Operations in the North African Campaign, RG 331 AFHQ Microfilm R50-H, National Archives; "Interview on Aspects of the Air Campaign in Africa," in Command Informational Intelligence Series 43-115, 5 July 1943, 3, 142.034-3, Center for Air Force History.

17. Howe, *Northwest Africa: Seizing the Initiative*, 682–83; Playfair, *The Mediterranean and Middle East*, Vol. IV, 410–11, 416–17; Roskill, *The War at Sea*, Vol. II, 432; Hinsley et al., *British Intelligence in the Second World War*, Vol. II, 607; Fioravanzo, *La Difesa Del Traffico con L'Africa Settentrionale*, 440–43.

18. NAAF Operations Bulletin No. 2, May 31, 1943, 6–7; Entry for April 4, War Diary, 1st Fighter Group; Report of Col. Stuart Towle, 8; 310th Bomb Group, History.

19. Craven and Cate, *The Army Air Forces in World War II*, Vol. II, 191–92; Playfair, *The Mediterranean and Middle East*, Vol. IV, 392, 413; U.S. Army Air Force, Ultra and the History of the United States Strategic Air Force, 31.

20. Dennis E. McClendon, *The Lady Be Good*, rev. ed. (Blue Ridge Summit, Pa.: Tab, 1987).

21. Craven and Cate, *The Army Air Forces in World War II*, Vol. II, 189; Playfair, The Mediterranean and Middle East, Vol. IV, 358, 415; Hinsley et al., *British Intelligence in the Second World War*, Vol. II, 608; Syrett, "Northwest Africa, 1942–1943," 250–51; Tactics Employed by the Northwest African Air Force Against Enemy Aerial Transport, 1 July 1943, 1–3, File 142.034-3, Center for Air Force History; "The Battle Story of Flax," 7–8, Operations Bulletin No. 1, A-3 Section, HQ Northwest African Air Forces, File 650.01-1, Center for Air Force History.

22. Shores, Ring, and Hess, *Fighters over Tunisia*, 289–92; Syrett, "Northwest Africa, 1942–1943," 251; Craven and Cate, *The Army Air Forces in World War II*, Vol. II, 189; "The Battle Story of Flax," 8–10; Mullins, An Escort of P-38s, 57; Tactics Employed by the Northwest African Air Force Against Enemy Aerial Transport, 3–5; Blake and Stannaway, *"Adorimini,"* 52–54; Group History, 310th Bomb Group; Entry for April 5, 1943, War Diary, 97th Bomb Group; Entry for April 5, 1943, War Diary, 301st Bomb Group; Entry for April 5, 1943, 1st Fighter Group; Playfair, *The Mediterranean and Middle East*, Vol. IV, 358 n.1, 393, 415.

23. Syrett, "Northwest Africa, 1942–1943," 251–52; Shores, Ring, and Hess, *Fighters over Tunisia*, 301-2, 304; Blake and Stannaway, *"Adorimini,"* 54–56; Christy and

Ethell, *P-38 Lightning at War*, 61; "The Battle Story of Flax," 8–10; Entries for April 10 and 11, 1943, War Diary, 1st Fighter Group.

24. Craven and Cate, *The Army Air Forces in World War II*, Vol. II, 190–91; Playfair, *The Mediterranean and Middle East*, Vol. IV, 416; Hinsley et al., *British Intelligence in the Second World War*, Vol. II, 608; Syrett, "Northwest Africa, 1942–1943," 252–53; Rust, *The Ninth Air Force in World War II*, 31–32; Thruelsen and Arnold, *Mediterranean Sweep*, 85–93; Shores, Ring, and Hess, *Fighters over Tunisia*, 315, 322–25, 340–42; James Brown, *Eagles Strike* (Cape Town: Purnell, 1974), 366–71 (Vol. 4 of the South African official history, South African Forces World War II); "The Battle Story of Flax," 10–11; Headquarters 57th Fighter Group, Operational and Intelligence Summary No. 96, Operations for April 18, 1943, Roll BO 153, Center for Air Force History. Playfair credits the U.S. 79th Fighter Group with participating in the April 22 fight, but U.S. sources do not support this. Shore reports much lower Allied as well as Axis losses in the Flax action of April 19 than official Allied sources.

25. Fioravanzo, *La Difesa Del Traffico con L'Africa Settentrionale*, 230–31; Rust, *The Twelfth Air Force Story in World War II*, 1, 9; Gulley, *The Hour Has Come*, 94; Hair, *The Saga of 54 and More*, 109–10; NAAF Daily Opsums, April 6, 1943; Entry for April 6, 1943, War Diary, 97th Bomb Group; Entry for April 6, 1943, War Diary, 301st Bomb Group.

26. Playfair, *The Mediterranean and Middle East*, Vol. IV, 393; F. K. von Plehwe, *End of an Alliance* (Oxford: Oxford University Press, 1971), 6–9; Deakin, *The Brutal Friendship*, 211–16, 262–78; Friedrich Ruge, *Der Seekrieg* (Annapolis, Md.: Naval Institute Press, 1957), 332–33.

27. Craven and Cate, *The Army Air Forces in World War II*, Vol. II, 184, 192, 194–95; Rust, *The Twelfth Air Force Story in World War II*, 19; Rust, *The Ninth Air Force in World War II*, 28, 30.

28. Rust, *The Twelfth Air Force Story in World War II*, 19; Entry for April 10, 1943, War Diary, 97th Bomb Group; Entry for April 10, 1943, War Diary, 301st Bomb Group; Entry for April 13, 1943, War Diary, 1st Fighter Group; "Bombardment Tactics and Techniques Employed in Counter-Shipping Attacks," 3; History, 310th Bomb Group; Playfair, *The Mediterranean and Middle East*, Vol. IV, 392, 413, 414; Martin Middlebrook and Chris Everitt, *The Bomber Command War Diaries* (New York: Penguin, 1990), 374, 379–80.

29. Playfair, *The Mediterranean and Middle East*, Vol. IV, 392, 413–14, 444, 456; Craven and Cate, *The Army Air Forces in World War II*, Vol. II, 184, 192, 195; Rust, *The Ninth Air Force in World War II*, 30; Gulley, *The Hour Has Come*, 94–95; Syrett, "Northwest Africa, 1942–1943," 256–58; "The Twelfth Air Force in the Tunisian Campaign," 36–39, 46.

30. Playfair, *The Mediterranean and Middle East*, Vol. IV, 412; Hezlet, *The Submarine and Seapower*, 153; Fioravanzo, *La Difesa Del Traffico con L'Africa Settentrionale*, 215–16; Wingate, *The Fighting Tenth*, 285–86; Mars, *The British Submarines at War, 1939–1945*, 175; Patrol Report, HMS *Trooper*, RG 331 AFHQ Microfilm R-6-A, National Archives.

    British sources attribute the destruction of *Thunderbolt* to the corvette *Cicogna*; the Italians credit it to *Libra*.

31. Fioravanzo, *La Difesa Del Traffico con L'Africa Settentrionale*, 220–25, 355–57; Patrol Report, HMS *Trooper*.

32. Wingate, *The Fighting Tenth*, 286–98; Playfair, *The Mediterranean and Middle East*, Vol. IV, 412.

33. Patrol Report, HMS *Saracen*, RG 331 AFHQ Microfilm R-6-A, National Archives; Patrol Report, HMS *Safari*, RG 331 AFHQ Microfilm R-6-A, National Archives; Bryant, Submarine Commander, 208–22; Playfair, *The Mediterranean and Middle East*, Vol. IV, 414.

34. Patrol Report, HMS *Unruly*, RG 331 AFHQ Microfilm R-6-A, National Archives; Playfair, *The Mediterranean and Middle East*, Vol. IV, 414; Wingate, *The Fighting Tenth*, 285–86; Roskill, *The War at Sea*, Vol. II, 432; Lipscomb, *The British Submarine*, 216–18.

35. Fioravanzo, *La Difesa Del Traffico con L'Africa Settentrionale*, 231–33, 362–64, 442–43; Nesbit, *The Armed Rovers*, 138; NAAF Daily Opsums, April 12, 1943; Entry for April 12, 1943, War Diary, 301st Bomb Group; Blake and Stannaway, *"Adorimini,"* 58.

36. Roskill, *The War at Sea*, Vol. II, 439–40; Playfair, *The Mediterranean and Middle East*, Vol. IV, 413, 414–15; Bragadin, *The Italian Navy in World War II*, 248; Fioravanzo, *La Difesa Del Traffico con L'Africa Settentrionale*, 233–37.

37. Fioravanzo, *La Difesa Del Traffico con L'Africa Settentrionale*, 232–45, 411; Nesbit, *The Armed Rovers*, 138–39; Playfair, *The Mediterranean and Middle East*, Vol. IV, 413–15; Gulley, *The Hour Has Come*, 95; Wingate, *The Fighting Tenth*, 286. The Italian official history mistakenly attributes the destruction of *Foggia* to a mine.

38. Jackson, *The Battle for North Africa*, 470–82; Shores, Ring, and Hess, *Fighters over Tunisia*, 352, 372, 375; Hinsley et al., *British Intelligence in the Second World War*, Vol. II, 606–13; U.S. Army Air Force, *Ultra and the History of the United States Strategic Air Force*, 26; Craven and Cate, *The Army Air Forces in World War II*, Vol. II, 201, 204; Howe, *Northwest Africa: Seizing the Initiative*, 663, 664, 667.

39. NAAF Operations Bulletin No. 2, May 31, 1943, 38–39; Olmsted, *Blue Skies*, 89; Pyle, *Here Is Your War*, 281; Alan Moorehead, *The March to Tunis* (New York: Harper and Row, 1965), 564–66; *New York Times*, May 10, 1943, 1.

40. NAAF Daily Opsums, April 29, May 6, 1943; Entries for April 26, 29, 1943, War Diary, 1st Fighter GrouItalian records, which rarely note losses of Siebels and landing craft but which seem to be meticulous in recording arrivals and departures, show no return voyages by such craft from Africa after April 29.

41. Fioravanzo, *La Difesa Del Traffico con L'Africa Settentrionale*, 241–50, 252–54; Playfair, *The Mediterranean and Middle East*, Vol. IV, 413–14, 422–23; Rust, *The Ninth Air Force in World War II*, 32; Ragner C. Lind, ed., *The Falcon: Combat History of the 79th Fighter Group* (Munich: Bruckmann, 1946), 27; Shores, Ring, and Hess, *Fighters over Tunisia*, 353–55, 357–59; Hinsley et al., *British Intelligence in the Second World War*, Vol. II, 612.

42. Roskill, *The War at Sea*, Vol. II, 432; Playfair, *The Mediterranean and Middle East*, Vol. IV, 416–18; Bragadin, *The Italian Navy in World War II*, 248–49; Fioravanzo, *La Difesa Del Traffico con L'Africa Settentrionale*, 444; Hezlet, *The Submarine and Seapower*, 224.

43. Howe, *Northwest Africa: Seizing the Initiative*, 666, 675; Playfair, *The Mediterranean and Middle East*, Vol. IV, 459–60; Murray, *Strategy for Defeat*, 159, 163.

Bibliography

UNPUBLISHED MATERIALS
Materials on the U.S. Twelfth and Ninth Air Forces and their component units are on microfilm at the Center for Air Force History in Washington, D.C. Through no fault of the excellent personnel of the Center, these records are not always easy to use. Especially in the early months of the North African campaign, they often were written under poor conditions on low-grade wartime paper and were very poorly microfilmed in the 1970s, with many repetitions, omissions, and unreadable frames. Many microfilmed items have no page numbers. Group histories, war diaries, mission reports, and occasionally other items of interest (e.g., Col. Hunter's report on "Counter-Shipping Missions, Tactics, and Formations," March 15, 1943, 1–2, Roll BO 229, Center for Air Force History) can be found on the numbered BO rolls. Much material on tactics, equipment, and higher command are in files 142.034-3, 142.034-5, 650.01-1, and 650.03-2. Material from higher headquarters and British sources, generally in much better shape, can be found at the National Archives in the Allied Force Headquarters files in Records Group 331, including the Daily Operational Summaries of the Northwest African Air Forces and patrol reports from British submarines. However, the distribution of the various records is not always clear. The Operations Bulletins of the Northwest African Air Forces are at the Center For Air Force History.

The manuscript collection of the National Archives in Washington, D.C., contains some valuable materials in printed form, notably: General Conrad Seibt, "Railroad, Sea, and Air Transport Situation for Supply of Africa through Italy (Jan.–May 1943)," Ms D-093, Historical Division, HQ U.S. Army, Europe (1947), Records Group 338 and SRH-037 Reports received by the U.S. War Department on the use of Ultra in the European theater, World War II: The Use of "U" in the Mediterranean and Northwest African Theatres of War, by Group Captain R. H. Humphreys, National Archives and Records Administration.

PUBLISHED WORKS
Air Ministry. *The Rise and Fall of the German Air Force*. New York: St. Martin's Press, 1983.
Barker, Ralph. *The Ship Busters*. London: Pan, 1959.
Beck, Alfred, et al. *The Corps of Engineers: The War against Germany*. Washington, D.C.: Center for Military History, 1985.
Belot, Raymond de. *The Struggle for the Mediterranean*. Princeton, N.J.: Princeton University Press, 1951.
Belote, James H., and Belote, William M. *Titans of the Sea*. New York: Harper and Row, 1975.

Bennett, Ralph. *Ultra and Mediterranean Strategy.* New York: William Morrow, 1989.

Blake, Steve, and John Stannaway. *"Adorimini": A History of the 82nd Fighter Group.* Boise, Idaho: 82nd Fighter Group History, 1992.

Blumenson, Martin. *Kasserine Pass.* Boston: Houghton Mifflin, 1966.

Bowman, Martin. *Wellington: The Geodetic Giant.* Washington, D.C.: Smithsonian Institution Press, 1990.

Boyne, Walter. *Clash of Wings.* New York: Simon and Schuster, 1994.

Bradley, Omar. *A Soldier's Story.* New York: Popular Library, 1970.

Bragadin, Marc Antonio. *The Italian Navy in World War II.* Annapolis, Md.: United States Naval Institute Press, 1957.

Breuer, William. *Geronimo.* New York: St. Martin's Press, 1988.

Brown, James. *Eagles Strike.* Cape Town: Purnell, 1974.

Bryant, Ben. *Submarine Commander.* New York: Ballantine, 1960.

Buell, Harold. *Dauntless Helldivers.* New York: Dell, 1992.

Caidin, Martin. *Flying Forts.* New York: Ballantine, 1969.

Caidin, Martin. *The Fork-Tailed Devil.* New York: Ballantine, 1971.

Calvocoressi, Peter. *Top Secret Ultra.* New York: Ballantine, 1981.

Cameron, Ian (Donald Payne). *Red Duster, White Ensign.* New York: Bantam, 1983.

Carell, Paul (Paul K. Schmidt). *Foxes of the Desert.* New York: Bantam, 1967.

Chandler, Alfred D. et al. *The Papers of Dwight David Eisenhower: The War Years.* Baltimore: Johns Hopkins University Press, 1970.

Christy, Joe, and Ethell, Jeffrey. *P-38 Lightning at War.* New York: Scribner's, 1979.

Churchill, Winston. *The Second World War,* Vol. IV. New York: Bantam, 1962.

Clark, Mark. *Calculated Risk.* New York: Harper, 1950.

Cooper, Matthew. *The German Air Force.* New York: Jane's, 1981.

Corey, Wilford G. *Bombs on the Target.* Privately published, 1946.

Craven, Wesley F., and Cate, James Lea. *The Army Air Forces in World War,* 7 vols. Chicago: University of Chicago Press, 1948–1958.

Davis, Richard G. *Carl Spaatz and the Air War in Europe.* Washington, D.C.: Smithsonian Institution Press, 1992.

Deakin, F. W. *The Brutal Friendship,* 2nd rev. ed. New York: Doubleday/Anchor, 1968.

Delves, Ken. *The Winged Bomb.* Leicester, U.K.: Midland Counties Publishers, 1985.

D'Este, Carlo. *Bitter Victory.* New York: Dutton, 1988.

Dugan, James, and Carroll Stewart. *Ploesti.* New York: Ballantine, 1973.

Dunn, Walter Scott. *Second Front Now 1943.* Tuscaloosa: University of Alabama Press, 1980.

Earl, O. K., ed. *The Thunderbird Goes to War.* Ann Arbor, Mich.: Braun-Brumfield, 1991.

Edmonds, Walter D. *They Fought with What They Had.* Boston: Little, Brown, 1951.

Eisenhower, Dwight D. *Crusade in Europe.* New York: Avon, 1968.

Ellis, John. *Brute Force.* New York: Viking, 1990.

Feis, Herbert. *Churchill, Roosevelt, and Stalin.* Princeton, N.J.: Princeton University Press, 1957.

Fioravanzo, Giuseppe. *La Difesa Del Traffico con L'Africa Settentrionale, dal 1 Ottobre 1942 alla Caduta Della Tunisia,* Vol. VIII, *La Marina Italiana Nella Seconda Guerra Mondiale.* Rome: Marina Militare, 1964.

Francis, Devon. *Flak Bait.* New York: Duell, Sloane, and Pearce, 1948.

Fraser, David. *Alan Brooke.* New York: Atheneum, 1982.

Freeman, Roger. *B-17 Fortress at War.* New York: Scribner's, 1979.

Freeman, Roger. *B-26 Marauder at War.* London: Arms and Armour Press, 1991.

Freeman, Roger. *The Mighty Eighth.* Garden City, N.Y.: Doubleday, 1970.

Glines, Carroll. *The Doolittle Raid.* New York: Orion Books, 1988.

Grigg, John. *1943: The Victory That Never Was.* New York: Hill and Wang, 1980.

Gulley, Thomas F., et al. *The Hour Has Come: The 97th Bomb Group in World War II.* Dallas: Taylor, 1993.

Hair, Charles. *The Saga of 54 and More.* Anaheim, Calif.: Robinson Typographics, 1987.

Hamel, Eric. *Aces Against Germany.* New York: Pocket Books, 1995.

Harmon, Ernest. *Combat Commander.* Englewood Cliffs, N.J.: Prentice Hall, 1970.

Havener, J. K. *The Martin B-26 Marauder.* Blue Ridge Summit, Pa.: Tab, 1988.

Hezlet, Arthur. *The Submarine and Seapower.* New York: Stein and Day, 1967.

Higgins, Trumbull. *Soft Underbelly.* New York: Macmillan, 1968.

Higgins, Trumbull. *Winston Churchill and the Second Front.* New York: Oxford University Press, 1957.

Hinsley, F. H. *British Intelligence in the Second World War,* abr. ed. New York: Cambridge University Press, 1993.

Hinsley, F. H. et. al. *British Intelligence in the Second World War.* 3 vols. New York: Cambridge University Press, 1979–1988.

Howe, George F. *Northwest Africa: Seizing the Initiative.* Washington, D.C.: Department of the Army, 1957.

Impact, Vol. I. New York: James Parton, 1980.

Jackson, W. G. F. *The Battle for North Africa.* New York: Mason Charter, 1975.

Jellison, Charles. *Besieged.* Hanover, N.H.: University Press of New England, 1984.

Jones, Lloyd. *US Bombers.* Fallbrook, Calif.: Aero, 1980.

Kesselring, Albert. *A Soldier's Record.* New York: William Morrow, 1954.

Lamb, Charles. *To War in a Stringbag.* New York: Bantam, 1980.

Levine, Alan J. *The Strategic Bombing of Germany, 1940–1945.* Westport, Conn.: Praeger, 1992.

Lewin, Ronald. *Rommel as Military Commander.* New York: Ballantine, 1970.

Lewin, Ronald. *Ultra Goes to War.* New York: Pocket Books, 1980.

Liddell-Hart, B. H., ed. *The Rommel Papers.* New York: Harcourt, Brace, 1953.

Liebling, A. J. *Mollie and Other War Pieces.* New York: Schocken Books, 1989.

Lind, Ragnar C., ed. *The Falcon: Combat History of the 79th Fighter Group.* Munich: Bruckmann, 1946.

Lipscomb, F. W. *The British Submarine.* London: Adam and Charles, 1954.

Lloyd, Hugh. *Briefed to Attack.* London: Hodder and Stoughton, 1949.

Macintyre, Donald. *The Battle for the Mediterranean.* New York: Norton, 1965.

Macksey, Kenneth. *Crucible of Power.* London: Hutchinson, 1969.

Mark, Eduard. *Aerial Interdiction in Three Wars.* Washington, D.C.: Center for Air Force History, 1994.

Mars, Alistair. *British Submarines at War, 1939–1945.* Annapolis, Md.: Naval Institute Press, 1971.

Matloff, Maurice, and Edwin Snell. *Strategic Planning for Coalition Warfare, 1941–1942.* Washington, D.C.: Department of the Army, 1953.

McClendon, Dennis E. *The Lady Be Good,* rev. ed. Blue Ridge Summit, Pa.: Tab, 1987.

Mellenthin, F. W. von. *Panzer Battles.* New York: Ballantine, 1971.

Middlebrook, Martin, and Everitt, Chris. *The Bomber Command War Diaries.* New York: Penguin, 1990.

Moorehead, Alan. *The March to Tunis.* New York: Harper and Row, 1965.

Morison, Samuel Eliot. *Coral Sea and Midway—Volume IV of History of United States Naval Operations in World War II*. Boston: Little, Brown, 1949.

Morison, Samuel Eliot. *Operations in North African Waters—Volume II of History of United States Naval Operations in World War II*, rev. ed. Boston: Little, Brown, 1961.

Morison, Samuel Eliot. *Sicily, Salerno, Anzio—Volume IX of History of United States Naval Operations in World War II*. Boston: Little, Brown, 1954.

Mowrey, George E. *Landing Craft and the War Production Board*, WPB Special Study No. 11, rev. ed. Washington, D.C., 1946.

Mullins, John. *An Escort of P-38s*. St. Paul, Minn.: Phalanx, 1995.

Murray, Williamson. *Strategy for Defeat*. Maxwell Air Force Base, Ala.: Airpower Research Institute, 1983.

Nesbit, Roy. *The Armed Rovers*. Shrewsbury, U.K.: Airlife, 1995.

Olmsted, Bill. *Blue Skies*. Toronto: Stoddart, 1987.

Overy, R. J. *The Air War*. New York: Stein and Day, 1981.

Oyster, Harold, and Oyster, Esther M. *The 319th in Action*. Privately published, 1987.

Paxton, Robert O. *Vichy France*. New York: Norton, 1974.

Phillips, C. E. Lucas. *Alamein*. Boston: Little Brown, 1962.

Playfair, I. S. O. *The Mediterranean and Middle East*, Vol. IV. London: Her Majesty's Stationery Office, 1966.

Plehwe, F. K. von. *End of an Alliance*. Oxford: Oxford University Press, 1971.

Poolman, Kenneth. *Night Strike from Malta*. London: Jane's, 1980.

Pyle, Ernie. *Here Is Your War*. Cleveland: World, 1945.

Raff, Edson D. *We Jumped to Fight*. New York: Eagle, 1944.

Roskill, S. W. *The War at Sea*, 3 vols. London: Her Majesty's Stationery Office, 1954–1961.

Ruge, Friedrich. *Der Seekrieg*. Annapolis, Md.: Naval Institute Press, 1957.

Rust, Kenn C. *The Ninth Air Force in World War II*. 2nd ed. Fallbrook, Calif.: Aero, 1970.

Rust, Kenn C. *The Twelfth Air Force Story in World War II*. Temple City, Calif.: Historical Air Album, 1975.

Sadkovich, James J. *The Italian Navy in World War II*. Westport, Conn.: Greenwood Press, 1994.

Sainsbury, Keith. *The North African Landings*. Newark: University of Delaware Press, 1979.

Shores, Christopher, Hans Ring, and William N. Hess. *Fighters over Tunisia*. London: Neville Spearman, 1975.

Simpson, George W. *Periscope View*. London: Macmillan, 1972.

Smith, Peter C. *Operation Pedestal*, 2nd rev. ed. London: William Kimber, 1987.

Smith, Peter C. *The Story of the Torpedo Bomber*. London: Almark, 1974.

Thruelsen, Richard, and Elliot Arnold. *Mediterranean Sweep*. New York: Duell, Sloan, and Pearce, 1944.

Tibbets, Paul. *Mission Hiroshima*. New York: Stein and Day, 1985.

U.S. Army Air Force. *Ultra and the History of the United States Strategic Air Force in Europe vs. the German Air Force*. Frederick, Md.: University Publications of America, 1980.

Van Creveld, Martin. *Supplying War*. London: Cambridge University Press, 1977.

Wagner, Ray. *American Combat Planes*, 3rd ed. Garden City, N.Y.: Doubleday, 1982.

Warren, C. E. T., and James Benson. *The Midget Raiders*. New York: Ballantine, 1968.

Wedemeyer, Albert. *Wedemeyer Reports*. New York: Henry Holt, 1958.

Weigley, Russell. *Eisenhower's Lieutenants.* Bloomington: Indiana University Press, 1981.

Welchman, Gordon. *Hut Six Ultra.* New York: McGraw-Hill, 1982.

Wingate, John. *The Fighting Tenth.* London: Leo Cooper, 1991.

Woodward, C. Vann. *Battle for Leyte Gulf.* New York: Ballantine, 1957.

Zemke, Hubert, and Roger Freeman. *Zemke's Wolfpack.* New York: Pocket Books, 1991.

ARTICLES

Driscoll, Col. John. "Impact of Weapons Technology on Air Warfare, 1941–1945." *Air Power Historian,* January 1959, 28–38.

Mitcham, Samuel, Jr. "Arnim." In *Hitler's Generals,* ed. Correlli Barnett. New York: Weidenfeld, 1989, 335–56.

Sherlock, John. "Pacific Marauder." *American Aviation Historical Society Journal,* Fall 1966, 190–96.

Sun, Jack. "Fighter Armament of World War II." *Aerospace Historian,* Summer 1981, 74–81.

Syrett, David. "Northwest Africa, 1942–1943." In *Case Studies in the Achievement of Air Superiority,* ed. Benjamin Franklin Cooling. Washington, D.C.: Center for Air Force History, 1994, 223–69.

Index

Page numbers in italics indicate illustrations.

Stackpole Military History Series

Real battles. Real soldiers. Real stories.

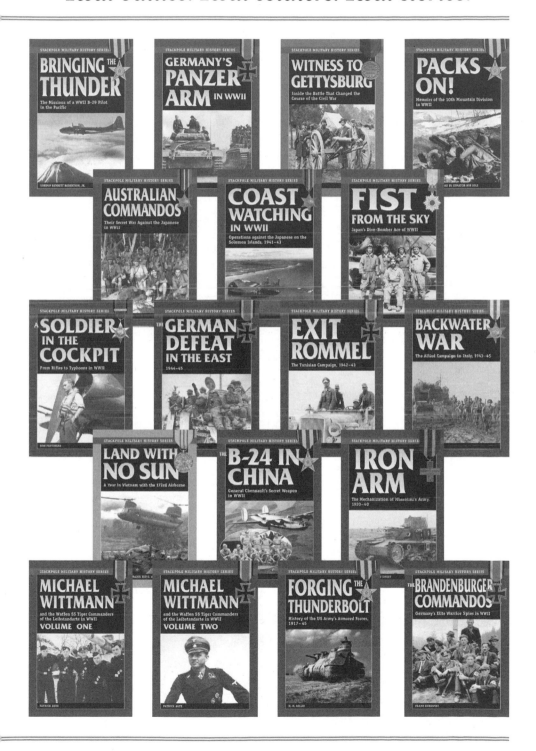

Stackpole Military History Series

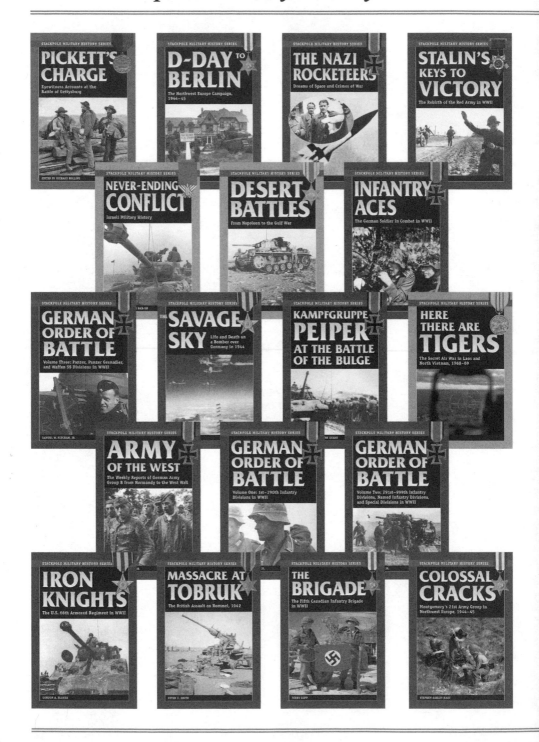

Real battles. Real soldiers. Real stories.

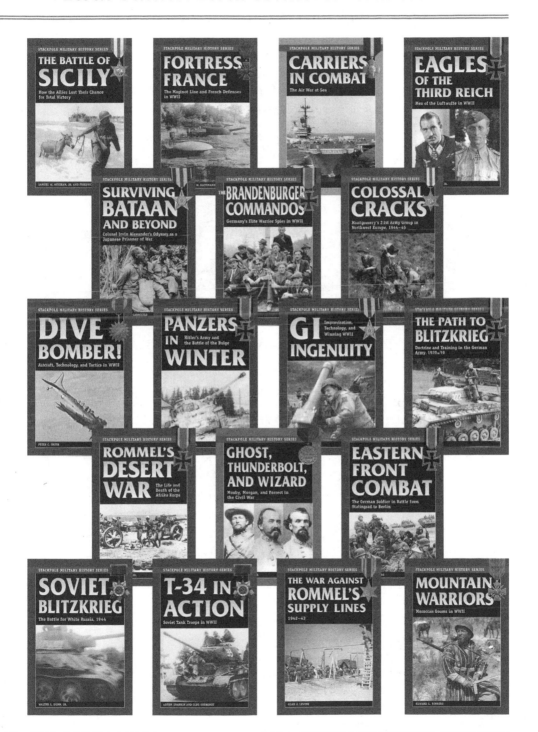

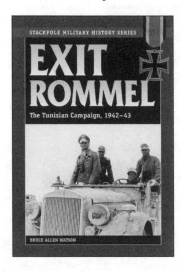

Stackpole Military History Series

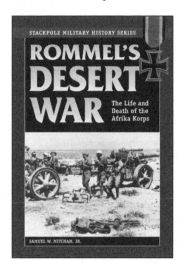

ROMMEL'S DESERT WAR
THE LIFE AND DEATH OF THE AFRIKA KORPS
Samuel W. Mitcham, Jr.

In a series of battles marked by daring raids and quick armored thrusts, Erwin Rommel and his Afrika Korps waged one of World War II's toughest campaigns in the North African desert in 1942. In June the Desert Fox recaptured Tobruk, a triumph that earned him a field marshal's baton and seemed to put all of North Africa within his grasp. By fall, however, after setbacks at Alam Halfa and the battles of El Alamein, the Afrika Korps teetered on the brink of destruction.

$16.95 • Paperback • 6 x 9 • 272 pages • 19 b/w photos, 13 maps

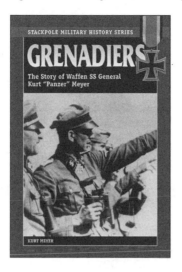

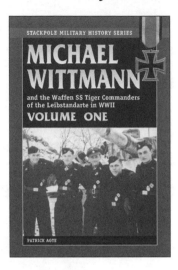

Stackpole Military History Series

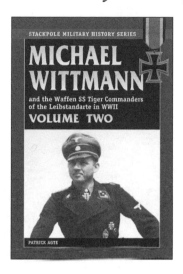

MICHAEL WITTMANN AND THE WAFFEN SS TIGER COMMANDERS OF THE LEIBSTANDARTE IN WORLD WAR II
VOLUME TWO
Patrick Agte

Barely two months after leaving the Eastern Front,
Michael Wittmann and the Leibstandarte found themselves in
Normandy facing the Allied invasion in June 1944. A week after D-Day,
Wittmann achieved his greatest success, single-handedly destroying
more than a dozen British tanks and preventing an enemy
breakthrough near Villers Bocage. He was killed several months later
while leading a Tiger battalion against an Allied assault. The
Leibstandarte went on to fight at the Battle of the Bulge and in
Hungary and Austria before surrendering in May 1945.

$19.95 • Paperback • 6 x 9 • 400 pages • 287 photos • 15 maps • 7 charts

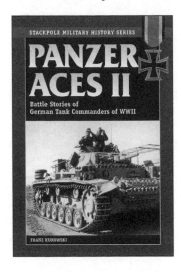